Cambridge IGCSE® & O Level
Complete Chemistry Workbook

Fourth Edition

Roger Norris

OXFORD
UNIVERSITY PRESS

Great Clarendon Street, Oxford, OX2 6DP, United Kingdom

Oxford University Press is a department of the University of Oxford. It furthers the University's objective of excellence in research, scholarship, and education by publishing worldwide. Oxford is a registered trade mark of Oxford University Press in the UK and in certain other countries

© Oxford University Press 2022

The moral rights of the authors have been asserted

First published in 2022

All rights reserved. No part of this publication may be reproduced, stored in a retrieval system, or transmitted, in any form or by any means, without the prior permission in writing of Oxford University Press, or as expressly permitted by law, by licence or under terms agreed with the appropriate reprographics rights organization. Enquiries concerning reproduction outside the scope of the above should be sent to the Rights Department, Oxford University Press, at the address above.

You must not circulate this work in any other form and you must impose this same condition on any acquirer

British Library Cataloguing in Publication Data
Data available

978-1-38-203840-9

3 5 7 9 10 8 6 4 2

Paper used in the production of this book is a natural, recyclable product made from wood grown in sustainable forests. The manufacturing process conforms to the environmental regulations of the country of origin.

Printed in China by Shanghai Offset Printing Products Ltd

Acknowledgements

®IGCSE is the registered trademark of Cambridge International Examinations.

The publishers would like to thank the following for permissions to use their photographs:

Cover image: Sputnik/Science Photo Library

All artwork by Aptara, Q2A Media & Oxford University Press.

Although we have made every effort to trace and contact all copyright holders before publication this has not been possible in all cases. If notified, the publisher will rectify any errors or omissions at the earliest opportunity.

Links to third party websites are provided by Oxford in good faith and for information only. Oxford disclaims any responsibility for the materials contained in any third party website referenced in this work.

Introduction

This workbook is designed to accompany the *Cambridge IGCSE & O Level Complete Chemistry Fourth Edition* student book. It is designed to help you develop the skills you need in order to help you do well in your IGCSE Chemistry examination. Each page of questions provides additional questions related to the assessment objectives of the latest Cambridge IGCSE and O Level syllabuses.

This revised edition matches the content order and units of the student book.

The questions focus on the areas you need to know about for your exam:
- Knowledge (memory work) and understanding (applying your knowledge to answer questions about familiar or unfamiliar situations or substances).
- Handling information from data, tables, and graphs.
- Solving problems (including chemical equations and chemical calculations).
- Experimental skills and investigations.

The first 19 Units correspond with the units in the student book and include a range of question types that you will come across in your chemistry examinations:
- Choosing words to complete sentences: you are usually given a list of words to choose from. This will help you learn and remember key facts.
- Putting statements in the correct order or selecting the correct statement from a list.
- Testing your ability to understand chemical formulae and to construct equations.
- Undertaking chemical calculations involving reacting masses, concentration, empirical and molecular formulae, and percentage yield.
- Some questions ask you to interpret data from diagrams, graphs, and tables. Others ask you to interpret the results of investigations that may be unfamiliar.
- Some pages include questions involving extended answers. These will help you organise your arguments and understand the depth of answer that is needed.

Other important features of this workbook that should help you succeed in chemistry include:
- Each unit has an extension box. The questions in these boxes are designed to challenge you. Many of them will develop your chemistry skills further. Some go beyond IGCSE and are there to stimulate your interest in chemistry. Many ask you to find relevant material from books or the internet.
- A unit on practical aspects of chemistry including devising and evaluating experiments, apparatus, materials, and tests for ions and gases.
- A unit on mathematics for chemistry. This includes practice in writing formulae, rearranging expressions, working through calculations, and drawing graphs.
- A unit with revision tips, which we hope will be helpful. This unit also explains how to analyse what a question is asking about, including the use of command words.
- A selection of IGCSE-style questions of the type that are set in the theory papers will help you to see connections between different parts of the syllabus.
- A unit with a selection of project ideas, describing experiments and analysis. Some of these could be done at home.
- Full answers to all the questions, including the extension questions.
- A glossary to help you understand the meaning of important chemical terms.

We hope that the range of differing exercises in this workbook will help you develop your skills in and understanding of chemistry and help you succeed in this subject.

Contents

1 States of matter

1.1	Everything is made of particles	2
1.2	Solids, liquids, and gases	3
1.3	The particles in solids, liquids, and gases	4
1.4	Heating and cooling curves	5
1.5	A closer look at gases	6

2 Atoms and elements

2.1	Meet the elements	7
2.2	More about atoms	8
2.3	How electrons are arranged	9
2.4	Isotopes and A_r	10

3 Atoms combining

3.1	Compounds, mixtures, and chemical change	11
3.2	Why do atoms form bonds?	12
3.3	The ionic bond	13
3.4	More about ions	14
3.5	The covalent bond	15
3.6	Covalent compounds	16
3.7	Comparing ionic and covalent compounds	17
3.8	Giant covalent structures	18
3.9	The bonding in metals	19

4 Reacting masses and chemical equations

4.1	The names and formulae of compounds	20
4.2	Equations for chemical reactions	21
4.3	The masses of atoms, molecules, and ions	22
4.4	Calculations about mass and percentage	23

5 Using moles

5.1	The mole	24
5.2	Calculations from equations	25
5.3	Reactions involving gases	26
5.4	The concentration of a solution	27
5.5	Finding the empirical formula	28
5.6	From empirical to final formula	29
5.7	Finding % yield and % purity	30

6 Redox reactions

6.1	Oxidation and reduction	31
6.2	Redox and electron transfer	32
6.3	Redox and oxidation numbers	33
6.4	Oxidising and reducing agents	34

7 Electricity and chemical change

7.1	Conductors and non-conductors	35
7.2	The principles of electrolysis	36
7.3	The reactions at the electrodes	37
7.4	Electroplating	38

8 Energy changes in reactions

8.1	Energy changes in reactions	39
8.2	A closer look at energy changes	40
8.3	Calculating enthalpy changes	41
8.4	The hydrogen-oxygen fuel cell	42

9 The rate of reaction

9.1	Introducing reaction rates	43
9.2	Measuring the rate of a reaction	44
9.3	Changing the rate (part I)	45
9.4	Changing the rate (part II)	46
9.5	Explaining rate changes	47
9.6	Catalysts	48

10 Reversible reactions and equilibrium

10.1	Reversible reactions	49
10.2	Shifting the equilibrium	50
10.3	The Haber process	51
10.4	The Contact process	52

11 Acids, bases, and salts

11.1	Acids and bases	53
11.2	A closer look at acids and alkalis	54
11.3	The reactions of acids and bases	55
11.4	A closer look at neutralisation	56
11.5	Oxides	57
11.6	Making salts (part I)	58
11.7	Making salts (part II)	59
11.8	Finding concentration by titration	60

12 The Periodic Table

12.1	The Periodic Table: an overview	61
12.2	Group I: the alkali metals	62
12.3	Group VII: the halogens	63
12.4	More about the trends	64
12.5	The transition elements	65

13 The behaviour of metals

13.1	Comparing metals and non-metals	66
13.2	Comparing metals for reactivity	67
13.3	Metals in competition	68
13.4	The reactivity series	69
13.5	The rusting of iron	70

Contents

14 Extracting and using metals
14.1	Metal ores and metal extraction	71
14.2	Extracting iron	72
14.3	Extracting aluminium	73
14.4	Making use of metals	74
14.5	Alloys	75

15 Chemistry of the environment
15.1	Our environment and us	76
15.2	What is in river water?	77
15.3	Our water supply	78
15.4	Fertilisers	79
15.5	Air, the gas mixture we live in	80
15.6	Air pollution from fossil fuels	81
15.7	Two greenhouse gases	82
15.8	Tackling climate change	83

16 Organic chemistry
16.1	Petroleum: a fossil fuel	84
16.2	Refining petroleum	85
16.3	Four families of organic compounds	86
16.4	The alkanes	87
16.5	Cracking alkanes	88
16.6	The alkenes	89
16.7	The alcohols	90
16.8	The carboxylic acids	91

17 Polymers
17.1	Introducing polymers	92
17.2	Addition polymerisation	93
17.3	Condensation polymerisation	94
17.4	Plastics	95
17.5	The plastics problem	96
17.6	Tackling the plastics problem	97
17.7	Proteins	98

18 Separation and purification
18.1	Making a substance in the lab	99
18.2	Solutions and solubility	100
18.3	Separating a solid from a liquid	101
18.4	Separating by distillation	102
18.5	Paper chromatography (part I)	103
18.6	Paper chromatography (part II)	104
18.7	Checking purity	105

19 Experiments and tests in the lab
19.1	The scientific method and you	106
19.2	Writing up an experiment	107
19.3	Preparing and testing gases	108
19.4	Testing for cations	109
19.5	Testing for anions	110

20 Mathematics for chemistry
20.1	Counting atoms and using brackets	111
20.2	Rearranging expressions	112
20.3	Large numbers, small numbers, and percentages	113
20.4	Volumes and areas	114
20.5	Working through calculations	115
20.6	Drawing graphs (1)	116
20.7	Drawing graphs (2)	117
20.8	Drawing graphs (3)	118

21 Revision
21.1	Using command words (1)	119
21.2	Using command words (2)	120
21.3	Helping you revise	121
21.4	Active revision	122
21.5	Mind mapping	123
21.6	Making mind maps	124

22 Exam-style questions
125

23 Project ideas
23.1	Comparing the hardness of different samples of water	135
23.2	Comparing the energy released when burning different foods	136
23.3	The effect of temperature on solubility	137
23.4	Finding the percentage by mass of carbon in different carbonates	138

Glossary	139
Answers	142
Data sheet: The periodic table of the elements	165

States of matter

1.1 Everything is made of particles

1. A student placed a crystal of a blue dye at the bottom of a beaker of water. After 5 minutes, the crystal disappeared. After 1 day, the solution was blue throughout.

   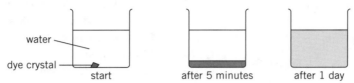

   a. Suggest how you could use a thin glass tube to place the crystal at the bottom of the beaker of water.

   ....

   .... [2]

   b. State the name of the process occurring when:

   i. the dye changes from a solid to a solution. ......*dissolve*.. [1]

   ii. the colour spreads throughout the water. ......*diffusion*.. [1]

   c. Use ideas about moving particles to explain the results shown in the diagram.

   ....

   ....

   .... [3]

   d. Draw lines to link the names of the particles on the left with the correct definitions on the right.

atom	— a particle with a positive or negative charge
ion	— two or more atoms joined (bonded) together
molecule	— the smallest neutral particle that can take part in a chemical change

   [1]

> **Extension**
>
> 2. a. Which are larger, dust particles or the particles of oxygen and nitrogen in the air? Explain how you know this. [2]
>
>   b. Explain, in terms of moving particles, why dust particles in still air appear to move about in an irregular way. [3]
>
>   c. The diagrams show four substances A, B, C, and D. Classify these as single atoms, molecules, or ions. [4]
>
>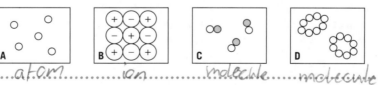
>
>   A ......*atom*...... B ......*ion*...... C ......*molecule*...... D ......*molecule*......

States of matter — 1.2 Solids, liquids, and gases

1. Describe the general properties of liquids and gases in terms of (i) their volume and (ii) how they spread out.

   liquids (i) .... (ii) .... [2]

   gases (i) .... (ii) .... [2]

2. Statements **A**, **B**, **C**, and **D** are about the properties of solids liquids or gases. For each statement deduce the correct state of matter: solid, liquid, or gas.

   A It takes the shape of its container and has a surface. ....

   B It spreads everywhere throughout the container. ....

   C It has a definite shape. ....

   D It can be poured onto a flat surface, where it spreads out completely. .... [4]

3. Complete the diagram by writing the names of the changes of state A, B, C, and D.

   solid ⇄ (A/C) liquid ⇄ (B/D) gas

   [4]

4. The table shows the melting points and boiling points of three substances.

Substance	Melting point / °C	Boiling point / °C
ethanol	−117	79
methane	−182	−164
naphthalene	81	218

   a. Which substance has the lowest melting point? .... [1]

   b. Which substance is a solid at room temperature? Explain your answer.

   .... [2]

   c. Which substance is a liquid at room temperature? Explain your answer.

   ....

   .... [2]

Extension

5. a. Iodine melts at 114 °C and boils at 184 °C. Explain why iodine seems to change directly from a solid to a gas when you heat a crystal of iodine in a boiling tube. [2]

   b. Suggest how you could show that iodine does form a liquid at room pressure. [2]

States of matter
1.3 The particles in solids, liquids, and gases

1. a. Use the correct words from the list to complete the sentences.

    apart   attraction   fixed   highest   inside   irregular   lattice   lowest
    repulsion   rotate   strong   surface   together   vibrate   weak

    The particles in a solid are arranged in a .... pattern (..............). The forces of ....
    between the particles are .... enough to keep them .... and so the particles
    only .... When a liquid evaporates, the particles with the .... energy leave
    the .... of the liquid first. [8]

    b. Box A shows the arrangement of 7 particles in a gas. Complete the boxes B and C to show the arrangement of 16 particles in a solid and 16 particles in a liquid.

    A (gas)   B (solid)   C (liquid)   [4]

    c. Complete these sentences correctly by writing the words *gas*, *liquid*, or *solid* in the spaces provided.

    The forces of attraction between the particles in a .... are stronger than those between ....
    particles but weaker than those between the particles in a .... Particles in a .... only
    vibrate. Particles in a .... move more slowly than those in a .... [6]

    d. Describe the difference between boiling and evaporation.

    ....
    .... [2]

    e. For each of the changes **i** to **iv** state whether energy is absorbed or released.

    i. Bromine melts ....

    ii. Water freezes ....

    iii. Gaseous sulfur changes to solid sulfur ....

    iv. Ethanol boils .... [4]

    Extension

    f. Arsenic changes directly from solid to gas at 613 °C. Describe what happens to the particles of arsenic in terms of their arrangement, separation, and motion during this change of state. [3]

    g. Silicon melts at 1410 °C. Phosphorus melts at 44 °C. Explain the difference in these melting points by referring to forces between the particles and energy. [4]

States of matter

1.4 Heating and cooling curves

1. Complete the following sentences about a cooling curve using words from the list.

   constant   decreases   freezes   kinetic   released   temperature

   When a liquid above room temperature cools, the .... energy of the particles .... The

   ………………….. of the liquid falls. At the melting point, the temperature stays .... for a time. This is because

   thermal energy (heat) is being ………………………… when a liquid .... [6]

2. The diagram shows a heating curve for substance T.

   What is the physical state or states of T at the following points?

   A .... [1]

   B .... [1]

   C .... [1]

   D .... [1]

   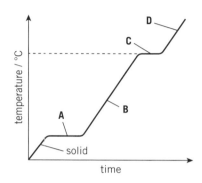

3. When a solid is heated, the temperature increases at first and then remains constant for a short time before increasing again. Explain why the temperature increases, then remains constant.

   ....

   ....

   ....

   .... [4]

4. Draw a cooling curve to show how the temperature changes when steam at 120 °C is cooled slowly until ice is formed at −10 °C. On your curve show the melting and boiling points of water.

[4]

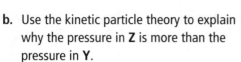

States of matter — 1.5 A closer look at gases

1. Box **Y** shows particles of gas in a container with a plunger.

   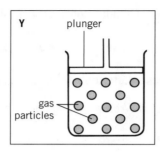
   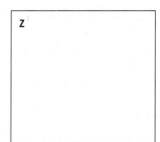

   a. Draw a diagram in box **Z** to show what happens when the gas is compressed. [1]

   b. Use the kinetic particle theory to explain why the pressure in **Z** is more than the pressure in **Y**.

   ....

   ....

   .... [3]

   c. What happens to the pressure when the temperature decreases at constant volume?

   .... [1]

2. The table shows how the volume of a gas changes with temperature and pressure.

Pressure / atm	Volume of gas at different temperatures / cm³			
	20 °C	40 °C	80 °C	160 °C
1	60	64	72	88
2	30	32	36	44
4	15	16	18	22

   a. Describe exactly how the volume varies with pressure when the temperature is constant.

   .... [2]

   b. Describe how the volume varies with temperature when the pressure is constant.

   .... [1]

3. A diffusion experiment is set up as shown.

   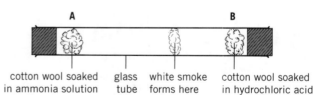

   a. Ammonia solution forms ammonia gas. Hydrochloric acid forms hydrogen chloride gas. Explain why the white solid forms and why it is closer to **B** than **A**.

   ....

   ....

   .... [3]

Extension

   b. Use books or the internet to find other gases that could replace hydrochloric acid in this experiment. [2]

   c. Methylamine reacts with hydrochloric acid in a similar way to ammonia. The relative molecular mass of hydrochloric acid is 36.5. The relative molecular mass of methylamine is 31. How does the position of the white ring change when methylamine is used? Explain your answer. [3]

Atoms and elements — 2.1 Meet the elements

1. Complete these sentences about atoms and element using words from the list.

    broken   chemical   down   element   smallest

    Atoms are the .... particles of matter which can take part in a .... change.

    Atoms cannot be .... by chemical means. An ....

    contains only one type of atom. [5]

2. The diagram shows part of the Periodic Table. Not all elements have been included.

						H							
Li										B	C	N	O
Na	Mg									Al			
K	Ca				Fe	Co	Ni	Cu					
Rb											Sn		

    Answer these questions using **only** the elements shown in the table.

    a. Give the name of one element in Group IV. .... [1]

    b. Give the name of an element in Period 5. .... [1]

    c. Give the name of one transition element. .... [1]

    d. Which element is in Period 3 and Group II? .... [1]

    e. On the Periodic Table above, shade in the boxes of the non-metallic elements. [2]

    f. Which two groups of elements are not shown? .... and .... [2]

3. The diagram shows six different substances. Each circle represents an atom.

    Classify these as single elements, single compounds, or mixtures.

    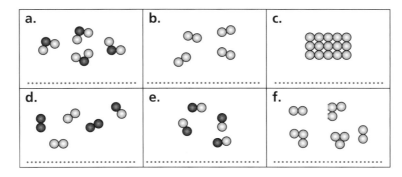

    [6]

Extension

4. Use textbooks or the internet to make a list of the differences of between a compound of iron and sulfur (iron sulfide) and a mixture of iron and sulfur. [3]

7

Atoms and elements — 2.2 More about atoms

1. Complete these sentences about atoms using words from the list.

   arranged   chemical   electrons   levels   neutrons   nucleus   shells   smallest

   Atoms are the .... particles of matter which can take part in a .... change. Each atom consists of a .... made up of protons and .... Outside the nucleus are the .... These are .... in electron .... or energy .... [8]

2. a. Give the sign of the charge (if any) on:

   i. an electron ....   ii. a neutron ....   iii. a proton .... [3]

   b. A proton has a relative mass of 1.

   i. Suggest the meaning of the term relative mass.

   .... [1]

   ii. State the relative mass of one electron. .... [1]

3. a. Define proton number. .... [1]

   b. State another name for proton number. .... [1]

   c. State the relationship between proton number and the order of the elements in the Periodic Table.

   .... [1]

4. Deduce the number of electrons, protons and neutrons in the following atoms. Use the information in the Periodic Table to help you.

   a. An atom of iron, which has a mass number of 58. [3]

   b. An atom of hydrogen, which has a mass number of 1. [3]

   c. An atom of bromine, which has a mass number of 81. [3]

   d. An atom of krypton, which has a mass number of 84. [3]

5. An atom of lithium has 4 neutrons.

   Draw and label a diagram of this lithium atom to show the position of each subatomic Draw each particle as a small circle (○) with the correct charge inside the circle.

   [6]

6. Deduce the mass number of an atom having 62 protons and 87 neutrons.

   .... [1]

Atoms and elements — 2.3 How electrons are arranged

1. Complete these sentences about electrons using words from the list.

   configuration   electron   group   one   outer   period   seven   two

   The arrangement of the electrons in shells is called the electron .... An atom of fluorine has nine electrons, ... in the first shell and .... in the second shell. Atoms of elements in the same .... have the same number of electrons in their .... shell. As we move across a ...., each atom has .... more .... in its outer shell than the element before it. [8]

2. Complete the table to show the electron configuration of the atoms shown.

Element	Number of electrons in an atom	Electron arrangement
nitrogen		
oxygen		
fluorine		
neon		
sodium		
argon		
calcium		

   [8]

3. Draw the electron configuration of these atoms. Show all the electron shells. Draw the electrons in pairs where possible.

aluminium	carbon	chlorine	helium
magnesium	neon	phosphorus	potassium

   [8]

4. Explain, in terms of electronic configuration, why atoms of neon are unreactive.

   ....

   .... [3]

Atoms and elements — 2.4 Isotopes and A_r

1. Complete the definition of isotopes using words from the list.

   atoms   compound   electrons   element   mass   molecules   neutrons   protons

   Isotopes are .... of the same .... with the same number of .... but different numbers of .... [4]

2. Three isotopes of hydrogen are

   ^1_1H ^2_1H ^3_1H

   a. Deduce the proton number of hydrogen. .... [1]

   b. What is unusual about the isotope ^1_1H compared with other isotopes?

   .... [1]

3. Deduce the number of protons, neutrons, and electrons in each of these atoms or ions.

Atom or ion	Number of protons	Number of neutrons	Number of electrons
$^{35}_{17}Cl$			
$^{136}_{58}Ce$			
$^{23}_{11}Na^+$			
$^{31}_{15}P^{3-}$			

   [12]

4. In the space on the right give the symbol for an isotope of lanthanum, La, which has 57 protons and 82 neutrons. [1]

5. Deduce the relative atomic mass of a sample of rhenium, Re, which contains two isotopes:

   $^{185}_{75}Re$ (abundance = 37.1%) and $^{187}_{75}Re$ (abundance = 62.9%).

   Give your answer to four significant figures.

   [3]

Extension

6. Define relative atomic mass using the following words in your definition:

   average   carbon-12   element   isotopes   mass   one-twelfth

   [3]

Atoms combining   3.1 Compounds, mixtures, and chemical change

1. Underline the changes that are physical changes.

   burning magnesium in air   separating iron from sulfur using a magnet

   rusting of iron   melting zinc

   distilling plant oils from a mixture of plant oils and water   [3]

2. Complete the table to show the difference between a compound and a mixture using words from the list. Some words may be used more than once.

   any   average   combined   definite   different   elements   physical   present   separated

Compound	Mixture
The .... cannot be .... by .... means.	The substances in it can be .... by .... means.
The properties are .... from those of the .... which went to make it.	The properties are the .... of the substances in it.
The elements are .... in a .... proportion by mass.	The substances can be .... in .... proportion by mass.

   [6]

3. In different chemical reactions, energy can be given out or taken in.

   a. Give one observation that shows that energy is given out during a reaction.

   .... [1]

   b. Give one observation that shows that energy is taken in during a reaction.

   .... [1]

   c. Give one example of a physical change where energy is absorbed.

   .... [1]

   d. Give one example of a physical change where energy is released.

   .... [1]

4. Write chemical formulae for the following compounds.

   a. CH_4 b. C_2H_6 c. H_2S d. NH_3 (structural diagrams shown)

   [4]

5. Write word equations for these reactions.

   a. Tin(II) oxide reacting with hydrochloric acid to produce tin(II) chloride and water.

   .... [1]

   b. Calcium carbonate being heated to make calcium oxide and carbon dioxide.

   .... [1]

   c. Copper reacting with hot concentrated sulfuric acid to produce copper(II) sulfate, water and sulfur dioxide.

   .... [1]

11

Atoms combining   **3.2 Why do atoms form bonds?**

1. Read the following passage then answer the question which follows.

   Chlorine is a green gas which dissolves in water to from a slightly acidic solution. Sodium is a silvery metal which reacts violently with water. When sodium reacts with chlorine, heat is given out and a white powder (sodium chloride) is formed. Sodium chloride dissolves in water and forms a solution which is not acidic.

   What information in the passage tells you that sodium chloride is a compound and not a mixture?

   ....

   ....

   .... [3]

2. Complete these sentences about ionic compounds.

   a. An ion is a .... particle. [1]

   b. Ions have unequal numbers of .... and .... [2]

3. Put a ring around the electron arrangements which are stable ions or atoms.

   2,8   2,5   2,8,8   2,8,8,2   2   2,8,3   2,8,18,8   [4]

4. Complete the diagrams below to show the electrons arrangement of the stable ions.

   Include brackets and charges.

   a.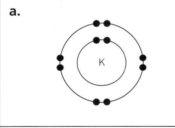
   b.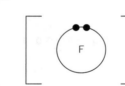
   c.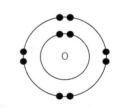
   d.
   e.
   f.

   [6]

Extension

5. a. Use books or formulae to find the charges on the stable ions of the following transition elements: vanadium, iron, cobalt, and copper. [2]

   b. What do you notice about the charges on these ions? [2]

Atoms combining — 3.3 The ionic bond

1. Complete the passage about ionic structures using words from the list.

   alternate   atoms   bonds   giant   ions   irregular   lattice
   molecular   negative   positive   regular   strong   weak

   A sodium chloride .... is a .... arrangement of .... sodium ions and .... chloride ions which .... with each other. The ions are held together by .... ionic .... This structure is called a .... ionic structure. [8]

2. Link the phrases on the left with the phrases on the right to make four correct sentences.

Ionic compounds are formed	.... it loses one or more electrons.
Ionic compounds have no	.... it gains one or more electrons.
When a metal atom forms an ion	.... overall charge.
When a non-metal atom forms an ion	.... by the reaction of metals with non-metals.

   [2]

3. a. Complete the ionic structure of magnesium sulfide. Show all the electrons as dots.

    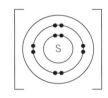

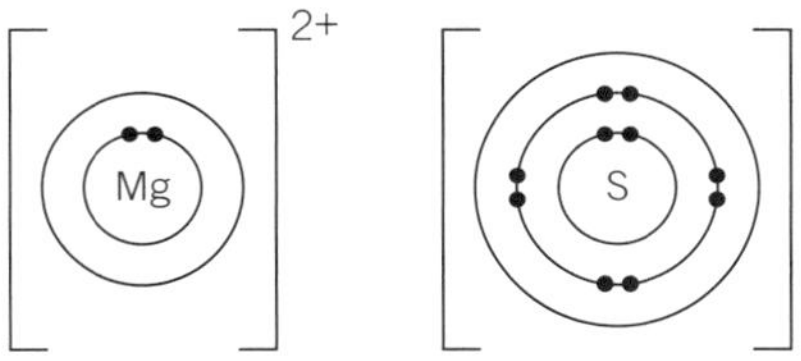

   [3]

   b. Draw ionic diagrams for lithium chloride and magnesium fluoride in a similar way as in part a.

lithium chloride	magnesium fluoride
Li Cl	F Mg F
[3]	[4]

   c. The nitride ion is N^{3-}. Draw an ionic diagram for calcium nitride. [4]

   Extension

Atoms combining — 3.4 More about ions

1. a. Work out the formulae of compounds **A** to **H** using the list of ions below.

   Al^{3+} Br^- Ca^{2+} Cl^- Fe^{3+} H^+ K^+ Mg^{2+} N^{3-} Na^+ O^{2-} S^{2-}

   A magnesium bromide ....   **B** sodium oxide ....

   C hydrogen chloride ....   **D** aluminium chloride ....

   E potassium nitride ....   **F** calcium sulfide ....

   G aluminium sulfide ....   **H** iron(III) oxide ....   [8]

   b. Work out the formulae of compounds **I** to **P**. Use the list of compound ions below to help you.

   CO_3^{2-} HCO_3^- NH_4^+ NO_3^- OH^- SO_4^{2-}

   I magnesium nitrate ....   [1]

   J potassium sulfate ....   [1]

   K ammonium nitrate ....   [1]

   L ammonium sulfate ....   [1]

   M calcium hydroxide ....   [1]

   N sodium hydrogen carbonate ....   [1]

   O aluminium nitrate ....   [1]

   P lithium carbonate ....   [1]

2. Name compounds **O** to **V**.

   Q MgI_2 ....   [1]

   R $Sr(OH)_2$ ....   [1]

   S $FeSO_4$ ....   [1]

   T $Zn(NO_3)_2$ ....   [1]

   U $(NH_4)_2CO_3$ ....   [1]

   V $Ca(HCO_3)_2$ ....   [1]

Extension

3. Use the list of ions below to work out the formulae for compounds **a.** to **e.**

   manganate(VII) MnO_4^- peroxide O_2^{2-} phosphate PO_4^{3-} sulfite SO_3^{2-}

   a. potassium manganate(VII)   **b.** sodium peroxide   **c.** calcium phosphate

   d. calcium sulfite   **e.** sodium phosphate   [5]

Atoms combining — 3.5 The covalent bond

1. Complete the passage about covalent bonding using words from the list.

   configuration   donated   electrons   hydrogen   noble
   number   pair   protons   shared

   A covalent bond is formed when a .... of .... is .... between two atoms leading to the .... gas electronic .... [5]

2. a. Define the term *molecule*.

   .... [1]

   b. Draw a circle around the molecules which are diatomic.

   CO Cl_2 N_2 N_2O_4 O_2 O_3 P_4 S_8 [2]

3. a. Draw diagrams to show the electron configuration for each of these diatomic molecules. Show only the outer shell electrons.

i. hydrogen	ii. bromine
iii. oxygen	iv. nitrogen

   [4]

   b. i. How many electrons are there around each atom in part **a**?

   .... [1]

   ii. What is the significance of this number of electrons for the hydrogen, oxygen, or nitrogen molecules?

   ....

   .... [3]

Extension

4. Some metals can form compounds with chlorine or hydrogen which are simple covalent molecules. Use books or the internet to find simple covalent compounds of three different metals. [3]

Atoms combining — 3.6 Covalent compounds

1. a. Draw dot-and-cross diagrams to show the electron configuration (electron arrangement) of each of these covalent molecules. Show only the outer shell electrons.

hydrogen bromide, HBr	water, H_2O
ammonia, NH_3	hydrogen sulfide, H_2S
methane, CH_4	phosphorus trichloride, PCl_3
carbon dioxide, CO_2	ethene, C_2H_4

   [8]

   b. Which of these molecules have non-bonded pairs of electrons (lone pairs of electrons)?

   .... [2]

Extension

2. Draw dot-and-cross diagrams to show the electron configuration of each of these covalent molecules. Show only the outer shell electrons.

   a. methanol, CH_3OH b. ethyne, C_2H_2 c. hydrazine, N_2H_4 d. ethanol, C_2H_5OH [4]

Atoms combining
3.7 Comparing ionic and covalent compounds

1. The table gives some properties of some simple covalent molecules and ionic compounds.
   Complete the table by writing either 'covalent' or 'ionic' in the last column.

Compound	Melting point / °C	Solubility in water	Electrical conductivity when molten	Covalent or ionic?
magnesium oxide	2852	soluble	conducts	
carbon tetrachloride	−23	insoluble	does not conduct	
potassium bromide	734	soluble	conducts	
carbon disulfide	−111	insoluble	does not conduct	
octane	−57	insoluble	does not conduct	

[2]

2. Link the properties **A** to **G** on the left with the correct reasons **1** to **7** on the right.

A Simple covalent molecules have low melting points…	**1** … because there are no ions or electrons present to conduct.
B Ionic compounds have high melting points …	**2** … because the molecules cannot form strong enough intermolecular forces with water molecules.
C Simple covalent molecules do not conduct electricity …	**3** … because they can form relatively strong bonds with the water molecules.
D Some simple molecules do not dissolve in water …	**4** … because the forces of attraction between the molecules are low.
E Ionic compounds conduct electricity when molten …	**5** … because they can form relatively strong intermolecular forces with solvent molecules.
F Many ionic compounds dissolve in water…	**6** … because the ions are free to move.
G Some molecular compounds dissolve in organic solvents …	**7** … because there are strong forces of attraction between all the ions.

[3]

3. Draw a circle around the formulae of the substances which will dissolve in organic solvents.

   $Ca^{2+}O^{2-}$ CS_2 I_2 Na^+Cl^- S_8 [1]

4. Explain why ionic compounds do not conduct electricity when solid.

   .... [2]

Extension

5. a. The simple covalent molecules CH_3OH, C_2H_5OH, and $C_6H_{12}O_6$ dissolve in water.

   The simple covalent molecules CH_4, C_6H_{14}, and CH_3Cl do not dissolve in water.

   What feature of the molecules seems to make them soluble in water? [1]

   b. Use books or the internet to find three other examples of simple covalent molecules which are soluble in water. [3]

Atoms combining

3.8 Giant covalent structures

1. Some physical properties, **A** to **F** are shown below.

   A conducts electricity   **B** does not conduct electricity   **C** hard

   D high melting point   **E** low melting point   **F** soft

   Write the letters of the properties which refer to:

   diamond .... [1]

   graphite .... [1]

   silicon dioxide .... [1]

2. Link the observations **A** to **E** on the left with the explanations **1** to **5** on the right.

A Giant covalent structures have a high melting point …	**1** … because the delocalised electrons are free to move along the layers.
B Graphite conducts electricity …	**2** … because the weak forces between the layers can easily be overcome.
C Diamond does not conduct electricity …	**3** … because the carbon atoms are packed closer to each other on average.
D Graphite is soft …	**4** … because it takes a lot of energy to break the large number of strong bonds.
E Diamond is denser than graphite …	**5** … because all its electrons are involved in covalent bonding.

   [2]

3. **a.** Complete these sentences by adding the correct number.

   i. Each atom in diamond forms .... covalent bonds with other atoms. [1]

   ii. Each atom in graphite forms .... covalent bonds with other atoms. [1]

   iii. Each silicon atom in silicon dioxide forms .... covalent bonds with oxygen atoms but each oxygen atom forms .... covalent bonds with silicon atoms. [2]

   b. Describe the arrangement of the atoms in:

   diamond .... graphite .... [2]

Extension

4. Which two of diamond, graphite, and silicon dioxide are allotropes? Explain your answer.

   .... [1]

5. There are two forms of the compound boron nitride, BN. One of these forms is similar to graphite.

   a. In this form of boron nitride, the atoms alternate. Draw the structure of this form of boron nitride. [3]

   b. Explain why boron nitride can be used as a lubricant. [2]

Atoms combining — 3.9 The bonding in metals

1. a. Complete the diagram below to show the structure of a metal. Label your diagram.

   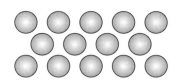

   [4]

   b. Use the information in your diagram to explain:

   i. why metals conduct electricity.

   .... [2]

   ii. why metals are ductile.

   ....
   ....
   .... [3]

   iii. why metals such as nickel have high melting points.

   ....
   .... [2]

2. The bar chart shows the melting point of six successive elements **A** to **F** in the Periodic Table.

   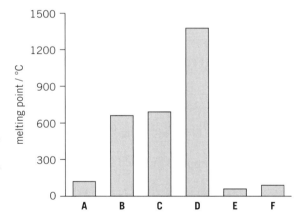

   a. One of these elements is a giant covalent structure.

   Which one? .... [1]

   b. Which elements are metals?

   Give a reason for your answer.

   ....
   ....
   .... [2]

   c. Which elements are non-metals?

   Give a reason for your answer.

   ....
   .... [2]

Extension

3. Bronze is a mixture of copper and tin. Tin atoms are larger than copper atoms. Use your knowledge the structure of metals to explain why bronze is less malleable than either copper or tin alone. [2]

19

Reacting masses and chemical equations
4.1 The names and formulae of compounds

1. Complete these sentences about the formulae of compounds using words from the list.

   atoms   bonded   hydrogen   ionic   molecular   nitrogen   ratio

   The formula for giant covalent and .... compounds is the .... of .... or ions in the compound. The formula of a simple molecule shows exactly how many atoms are .... together in each molecule. For example, ammonia has one .... and three .... atoms so its .... formula is NH_3. [7]

2. a. Complete the table to show the combining powers (valencies) of the elements shown.

		H							
Li				B	C	N	O	F	Ne
Na	Mg			Al			S	Cl	
K	Ca	transition elements	Zn					Br	

   [10]

   b. Which atoms in the table lose electrons when they form ions?
   .... [1]

   c. Which atoms in the table gain electrons when they form ions?
   .... [1]

   d. Name two atoms in the table which share electrons when they form compounds.
   .... [1]

   e. Write the formulae of the following compounds by balancing the valencies.

   i. A compound of H and S ....   ii. A compound of B and O ....

   iii. A compound of C and S ....   iv. A compound of C and Br ....

   v. A compound of Ca and N ....   vi. A compound of Al and O ....

   vii. The simplest compound of C and H .... [7]

3. Work out the combining powers (valencies) of the elements in these compounds:

   a. O in hydrogen peroxide, H_2O_2
   b. Fe in Fe_2O_3
   c. C in carbon monoxide, CO
   d. Cu in Cu_2O
   e. Pb in $PbCl_4$
   f. H in magnesium hydride, MgH_2 [6]

Extension

Reacting masses and chemical equations

4.2 Equations for chemical reactions

1. Write chemical equations for these 'model' reactions.

   a. $O=O$ and $\begin{array}{c} H-H \\ H-H \end{array}$ gives $\begin{array}{c} H-O-H \\ H-O-H \end{array}$

   .... [2]

   b. C and C + O=O gives C≡O and C≡O

   .... [2]

2. Complete these examples to show the stages in writing equations.

   a.
                      H_2 + Cl_2 → HCl

   atoms   ..... × H + ... × Cl   ..... × H ..... × Cl [1]

   balance H_2 + Cl_2 → .....HCl [1]

   b.   Mg + O_2 → MgO

   atoms   ..... × Mg + ... × O   ..... × Mg ..... × O [1]

   balance O   ..... × Mg + ... × O → ..... MgO [1]

   balance Mg   ..... Mg + O_2 → ..... MgO [1]

3. Balance these equations.

   a. K + Br_2 → KBr

   .... [1]

   b. Al + O_2 → Al_2O_3

   .... [1]

   c. Na + O_2 → Na_2O

   .... [1]

   d. N_2 + H_2 → NH_3

   .... [1]

   e. Rb + H_2O → RbOH + H_2

   .... [1]

   f. I_2O_5 + CO → I_2 + CO_2 [1]

   g. MgO + HNO_3 → $Mg(NO_3)_2$ + H_2O [1]

   h. $Ca(OH)_2$ + HCl → $CaCl_2$ + H_2O [1]

   i. PbO + NH_3 → Pb + N_2 + H_2O [1]

Extension

Reacting masses and chemical equations
4.3 The masses of atoms, molecules, and ions

1. Complete these sentences about relative masses of particles using words from the list.

   A_r average   carbon-12   isotopes   formula   molecular M_r sum   twelfth

   Relative atomic mass (symbol ....) is the .... mass of naturally occurring .... of an element compared to one- .... of the mass of an atom of .... The relative .... mass (symbol ....) is the .... of the relative atomic masses of the atoms in a molecule. For ionic substances, we use the term relative .... mass. [9]

2. a. Complete the table to calculate the relative molecular mass or relative formula mass of the compounds shown.

Compound	Number of each atom	A_r of atom	M_r calculation
phosphorus trichloride PCl_3	P = Cl =	P = 31 Cl = 35.5	1 × 31 + 3 × ...... _____ M_r = ...
magnesium hydroxide $Mg(OH)_2$		Mg = 24 O = 16 H = 1	 + _____ M_r = ...
ethanol C_2H_5OH		C = 12 O = 16 H = 1	 + _____ M_r = ...
ammonium sulfate $(NH_4)_2SO_4$		N = 14 H = 1 S = 32 O = 16	 + _____ M_r = ...
glucose $C_6H_{12}O_6$		C = 12 H = 1 O = 16	 + _____ M_r = ...

   [10]

   b. Calculate the relative molecular/formula mass of these compounds.

      i. $Al_2(SO_4)_3$ .... [1]

      ii. $Co(NO_3)_2$ .... [1]

      iii. $Cr(CO)_6$ .... [1]

   c. Calculate the relative formula mass of these compounds.

      i. $Sr(NO_3)_2 \cdot 4H_2O$ ii. $Fe(ClO_4)_2 \cdot 6H_2O$ iii. $Ba(BrO_3)_2$ iv. $Mn(NO_3)_2 \cdot 6H_2O$ [4]

Extension

Reacting masses and chemical equations

4.4 Calculations about mass and percentage

1. Complete the following by using values of M_r to calculate the masses of reactants and products.

   a. i. $\qquad 2H_2 \quad + \quad O_2 \quad \rightarrow \quad 2H_2O$

   $\qquad\qquad 2 \times \ldots\ldots \quad + \quad 1 \times \ldots\ldots \quad \rightarrow \quad 2 \times \ldots\ldots$ [1]

   $\qquad\qquad \ldots\ldots\ g \quad + \quad \ldots\ldots\ g \quad \rightarrow \quad \ldots\ldots\ g$ [1]

   ii. $\qquad 2Al \quad + \quad 3Cl_2 \quad \rightarrow \quad 2AlCl_3$

   $\qquad\qquad 2 \times \ldots\ldots \quad + \quad 3 \times \ldots\ldots \quad \rightarrow \quad 2 \times \ldots\ldots$ [1]

   $\qquad\qquad \ldots\ldots\ g \quad + \quad \ldots\ldots\ g \quad \rightarrow \quad \ldots\ldots\ g$ [1]

   b. Use simple proportion to do these calculations about the reacting masses.

   When 48 g of magnesium is burnt completely in oxygen, 80 g of magnesium oxide is formed.

   $\qquad\qquad 2\ Mg \quad + \quad O_2 \quad \rightarrow \quad 2\ MgO$

   $\qquad\qquad 48\ g \qquad\qquad\qquad\qquad\quad 80\ g$

   i. Complete the calculation to show the mass of magnesium oxide formed when 12 g of magnesium is burnt.

   $\dfrac{\ldots\ldots}{\ldots\ldots} \times 80 = \ldots\ldots\ g$ [2]

   ii. What mass of magnesium is needed to form 8 g of magnesium oxide?

   .... [1]

   iii. What mass of magnesium oxide is formed when 168 g of magnesium is burnt?

   .... [1]

2. a. Complete the calculation to show the percentage by mass of carbon in ethane, C_2H_6.

   $\dfrac{2 \times \ldots\ldots}{(\ldots \times 12) + (\ldots \times 1)} \times 100 = \ldots\ldots\ \%$ [2]

   b. Calculate the percentage by mass of nitrogen in ammonia, NH_3. Show your working.

   ....

   ....

   .... % [2]

   c. Calculate the percentage by mass of sodium in sodium phosphate, Na_3PO_4. Show your working.

   ....

   ....

   .... % [2]

3. A chemist made 30.00 g of aluminium chloride. Chemical analysis showed that it contained 29.25 g of pure aluminium chloride. Calculate the % purity of the aluminium chloride.

   .... % [1]

Using moles

5.1 The mole

1. Link the words **A** to **D** on the left with the correct descriptions **1** to **4** on the right.

A Avogadro constant	1 The average mass of the isotopes of an element compared with $\frac{1}{12}$ th of the mass of an atom of carbon-12.
B molar mass	2 The number of atoms, ions, or molecules in a mole of atoms, ions, or molecules.
C mole	3 The mass of a mole of substance in grams.
D relative atomic mass	4 The amount of substance that has the Avogadro number of particles.

   [2]

2. Complete the table using the A_r values below.

   C = 12, Ca = 40, H = 1, O = 16, P = 31, S = 32, Na = 23, Cl = 35.5

Element or compound	Formula mass, M_r	Mass taken / g	Number of moles
O_2	32	4	
NaCl		11.7	
$CaSO_4$		27.2	
P_2O_5			0.4
CO_2			0.1
P_4		86.8	
CH_4			24.0

   [13]

3. Calculate the number of molecules of ethene, C_2H_4, in 560 g of ethene by following the steps below.

   a. Relative molecular mass of ethene = ... [1]

   b. Moles of ethene = ... [1]

   c. Number of molecules of ethene (Avogadro constant = 6.02×10^{23}) =

      .... [1]

4. 0.2 moles of aluminium has a mass of 5.4 g.

   Calculate the relative atomic mass of aluminium.

   [2]

Using moles

5.2 Calculations from equations

1. Complete these equations to show the reacting masses.

   a. i. $\quad$ 2Mg $\quad+\quad$ O_2 $\quad\rightarrow\quad$ 2MgO

   $\quad\quad\quad$ 2 × .... $\quad+\quad$ 1 × .... $\quad\rightarrow\quad$ 2 × .... [1]

   $\quad\quad\quad$ .... g $\quad+\quad$ .... g $\quad\rightarrow\quad$ .... g [1]

   ii. $\quad$ 4PH_3 $\quad\rightarrow\quad$ P_4 $\quad+\quad$ 6H_2

   $\quad\quad\quad$ 4 × .... $\quad\rightarrow\quad$ 4 × .... $\quad+\quad$ 6 × .... [1]

   $\quad\quad\quad$ .... g $\quad\rightarrow\quad$ .... g $\quad+\quad$ .... g [1]

   iii. $\quad$ CS_2 $\quad+\quad$ 3Cl_2 $\quad\rightarrow\quad$ CCl_4 $\quad+\quad$ S_2C_2

   $\quad\quad\quad$ 1 × .... $\quad+\quad$ 3 × .... $\quad\rightarrow\quad$ 1 × .... $\quad+\quad$ 1 × .... [1]

   $\quad\quad\quad$ .... g $\quad+\quad$ .... g $\quad\rightarrow\quad$ .... g $\quad+\quad$ .... g [1]

   b. Use the number of moles shown in the equation below to answer the questions which follow.

   $\quad\quad\quad\quad\quad$ $I_2O_5 + 5CO \rightarrow I_2 + 5CO_2$

   $\quad\quad$ M_r values $\quad\quad$ 334 $\quad$ 140 $\quad\quad$ 254 $\quad$ 220

   i. How many moles of CO react with 1 mole of I_2O_5? .... [1]

   ii. How many moles of CO_2 are formed from 1 mole of CO? .... [1]

   iii. How many moles of I_2 are formed using 10 moles of CO? .... [1]

   iv. What mass of CO_2 is formed using 24.84 g of I_2O_5 and excess CO?

   .... [2]

   v. What mass of I_2 is formed using 21 g of CO and excess I_2O_5?

   .... [2]

2. 168 g of iron reacts excess oxygen to form 232 g of an oxide of iron.

   $\quad\quad\quad\quad\quad$ iron $\quad+\quad$ oxygen $\quad\rightarrow\quad$ iron oxide

   a. Calculate the mass of oxygen in the iron oxide. .... [1]

   b. Calculate the moles of oxygen in the oxide. .... [1]

   c. Calculate the moles of iron in the iron oxide. .... [1]

   d. Calculate the ratio of the iron to oxygen to give the formula of this oxide of iron.

   ratio .... formula .... [2]

Extension

3. Calculate the mass of CCl_4 formed from 2 moles of Cl_2 in the presence of excess CS_2. Use the equation in **1.a.iii.** [2]

Using moles

5.3 Reactions involving gases

1. Complete these relationships:

   a. 1 dm³ = ... cm³ [1]

   b. One mole of gas at r.t.p. occupies .... dm³. [1]

   c. Volume of gas at r.t.p. in dm³ = ... × .... [1]

   d. Moles of gas at r.t.p. = ... [1]

   ....

2. Complete the table to show the mass, moles, or volume of different gases.

Gas	M_r of gas	Mass of gas / g	Moles of gas / mol	Volume of gas / dm³
ammonia	17	8.5		
oxygen	32			48
carbon dioxide	44	3.08		
hydrogen chloride		292	8	
ethane	30			3

   [10]

3. Nitrogen(I) oxide, N_2O, decomposes when heated to form two other gases. The graph shows how the volume of gas (corrected to r.t.p.) changes during the decomposition.

   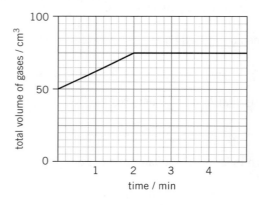

   a. Deduce the volume of nitrogen(I) oxide at the start of the experiment. .... [1]

   b. Deduce the volume of gases present at the end of the experiment. .... [1]

   c. Deduce the ratio volume of gas at start : volume of gases at the end. .... [1]

   d. Use this ratio to complete the balanced equation for this reaction.

   $$\ldots\ldots N_2O(g) \rightarrow \ldots.. N_2(g) + O_2(g)$$ [1]

4. Propane burns in excess oxygen to form carbon dioxide and water.

   $$C_3H_8(g) + 5O_2(g) \rightarrow 3CO_2(g) + 4H_2O(g)$$

   Calculate the volume of $CO_2(g)$ formed when 8.8 g of propanol is completely burnt. [3]

Extension

Using moles

5.4 The concentration of a solution

1. Complete these relationships.

   a. concentration in mol/dm³ = = $\dfrac{\text{amount of solute in ....}}{\text{.................. in ....}}$ [3]

   b. amount of solute (moles) = [1]

   c. volume (dm³) = [1]

2. a. Change these values into cm³.

   i. 0.2 dm³ .... [1]   ii. 0.04 dm³ .... [1]

   iii. 3.5 dm³ .... [1]   iv. 0.008 dm³ .... [1]

   b. Change these values into dm³.

   i. 25 cm³ .... [1]   ii. 750 cm³ .... [1]

   iii. 4000 cm³ .... [1]   iv. 156 cm³ .... [1]

3. Complete the table to show the missing values in the table.

Solute	M_r of solute	Mass of solute / g	Volume of solution/ cm³ or dm³	Concentration of solution in mol/dm³
sodium hydroxide	40	8	250 cm³	
silver nitrate	170		200 cm³	0.5
copper(II) sulfate	160	40		0.125
potassium sulfate	174	3.48	750 cm³	
ammonium chloride	53.5		5.0 dm³	0.8
sulfuric acid	98	4.9		2.0

[6]

4. The solubility of copper(II) fluoride, CuF_2, in water is 4.54×10^{-3} mol/dm³.
   0.15 g of copper(II) fluoride was added to 200 cm³ of water and stirred until no more dissolved.
   Calculate the mass of copper(II) fluoride remaining.
   A_r values: Cu = 64, F = 19 [4]

Using moles
5.5 Finding the empirical formula

1. Complete the following calculations to find the empirical formulae.

   a. A compound of lead and chlorine contains 20.7 g of lead and 14.2 g of chlorine.
      A_r values: Pb = 207, Cl = 35.5

      moles of Pb = ... mol   moles of Cl = ... mol   [1]

      Divide by   Pb   Cl   ....
      lowest number
      of moles   ....   [1]

      Result of division = ...   = ...

      Simplest ratio .... So empirical formula is ....   [2]

   b. A compound of carbon and hydrogen contains 85.7% of carbon and 14.3% of hydrogen by mass.
      A_r values: C = 12, H = 1

      mole % of C = ... mol   mole % of H = ... mol   [1]

      Divide by   C   ....   H   ....
      lowest number
      of moles   ....   [1]

      Result of division = ...   = ...

      Simplest ratio .... So empirical formula is ....   [2]

   c. Deduce the empirical formula of a compound containing 87.5% nitrogen and 12.5% hydrogen.
      A_r values: H = 1, N = 14

      Empirical formula .... [3]

2. Aluminium burns in a stream of chlorine to form aluminium chloride.

   a. Suggest how you could use this apparatus to find the empirical formula of aluminium chloride.   [8]

   b. What safety precautions are needed when carrying out this experiment?   [3]

Using moles
5.6 From empirical to final formula

1. Complete these sentences about empirical and molecular formulae using words from the list.

   actual   atoms   compound   empirical   ionic   molecular   molecules   simplest

   The molecular formula of a .... shows the .... number of ....
   that combine. The empirical formula shows the .... ratio of atoms which combine.
   The formula of an .... compound is the same as its .... formula. [6]

2. Write the empirical formula of the following compounds whose molecular formula has been given.

   a. hydrogen peroxide, H_2O_2 Empirical formula .... [1]

   b. cyclohexane, C_6H_{12} Empirical formula .... [1]

   c. dinitrogen tetroxide, N_2O_4 Empirical formula .... [1]

   d. antimony(III) oxide, Sb_4O_6 Empirical formula .... [1]

   e. butane, C_4H_{10} Empirical formula .... [1]

   f. phosphorus(V) oxide, P_4O_{10} Empirical formula .... [1]

   g. sodium sulfate, Na_2SO_4 Empirical formula .... [1]

3. Complete the table to deduce the empirical formula mass and molecular formulae of compounds **A** to **D**.
   A_r values: C = 12, Cl = 35.5, H = 1, O = 16, P = 31, S = 32

Empirical formula	Empirical formula mass / g	Relative molecular mass, M_r / g	Molecular formula
A P_2O_3		220	
B SCl		135	
C CH_2O		60	
D CCl_2		332	

   [8]

4. 360 g of a compound of carbon, hydrogen, and oxygen only, contains 144 g of carbon and 24 g of hydrogen. The compound has a relative molecular mass of 180.
   Deduce the empirical and molecular formulae of this compound. [5]

Using moles

5.7 Finding % yield and % purity

1. 18 g of limestone was reacted with excess dilute hydrochloric acid. 3840 cm³ of carbon dioxide was formed at r.t.p. Work through the calculation to find the percentage purity of an impure sample of limestone, calcium carbonate, $CaCO_3$.
Give your answer to two significant figures. A_r values: C = 12, Ca = 40, O = 16

$$CaCO_3(s) + 2HCl(aq) \rightarrow CaCl_2(aq) + CO_2(g) + H_2O(l)$$

   a. Molar mass of calcium carbonate = ... g/mol [1]

   b. Volume of CO_2 in dm³ = ... dm³ [1]

   c. Moles of CO_2 = ... = ... mol [1]

   ....

   d. Moles of $CaCO_3$ in impure limestone = ... mol [1]

   e. Mass of $CaCO_3$ in impure limestone = ... g [1]

   f. Percentage purity = ... × .... = ...% [1]

   ....

2. Methyl benzoate can be prepared by reacting methanol with benzoic acid.

$$\underset{\text{methanol}}{CH_3OH} + \underset{\text{benzoic acid}}{C_6H_5CO_2H} \rightarrow \underset{\text{methyl benzoate}}{C_6H_5CO_2CH_3} + H_2O$$

When 24.4 g of benzoic acid is reacted with excess methanol, 25.84 g of methyl benzoate is produced. Work through the calculation to find the percentage yield of methyl benzoate. A_r values: C = 12, H = 1, O = 16

   a. Molar mass of benzoic acid = ... g/mol [1]

   b. Moles of benzoic acid = ... mol [1]

   c. Moles of methyl benzoate expected (if 100 % yield) = ... mol [1]

   d. Molar mass of methyl benzoate = ... g/mol [1]

   e. Mass of methyl benzoate expected (if 100 % yield) = ... g [1]

   f. Percentage yield = ... × .... = ...% [1]

   ....

3. A student reacts 5.4 g of aluminium with excess oxygen.

$$4Al + 3O_2 \rightarrow 2Al_2O_3$$

The mass of aluminium oxide produced is 8.67 g. Calculate the percentage yield.
A_r values: Al = 27, O = 16 [4]

Extension

30

Redox reactions
6.1 Oxidation and reduction

1. Complete these sentences abut oxidation and reduction using words from the list.

   gain   heat   loss   oxidation   reactants   redox   reduction

   Reactions which involve both oxidation and .... are called .... reactions.

   Oxidation is the .... of oxygen and reduction is the .... of oxygen.

   Combustion involves the .... of a substance in which .... is given out

   and one or more of the .... is a gas. [7]

2. Draw arrows to show which of the elements or compounds have undergone oxidation and which have undergone reduction. An example is given below.

   Example:

   $$CuO(s) + H_2(g) \longrightarrow Cu(s) + H_2O(l)$$
   (oxidation arrow from CuO to H₂O; reduction arrow from H₂ to Cu)

   a. $2H_2(g) + O_2(g) \rightarrow 2H_2O(l)$ [2]

   b. $PbO(s) + H_2(g) \rightarrow Pb(s) + H_2O(l)$ [2]

   c. $Fe_2O_3(s) + 3C(g) \rightarrow 2Fe(s) + 3CO(g)$ [2]

   d. $C(s) + H_2O(g) \rightarrow CO + H_2(g)$ [2]

   e. $ZnO(s) + C(s) \rightarrow CO(g) + Zn(s)$ [2]

   f. $3Fe(s) + 4H_2O(g) \rightarrow Fe_3O_4(s) + 4H_2(g)$ [2]

Extension

3. Which substances in these equations undergo oxidation and which undergo reduction.

   a. $CH_4 + 3O_2 \rightarrow 2CO_2 + 2H_2O$ [2]

   b. $CS_2 + 2H_2 \rightarrow 2H_2S + C$ (Hint: oxygen and sulfur are in the same group.) [2]

Redox reactions

6.2 Redox and electron transfer

1. Complete these half equations. Balance the charges by adding electrons.
   State whether oxidation or reduction has taken place.

   a. $Ca \rightarrow Ca^{2+} + ...$ Oxidation or reduction? .... [2]

   b. $Cl_2 + ... \rightarrow ....Cl^-$ Oxidation or reduction? .... [2]

   c. $Al^{3+} + ... \rightarrow ....$ Oxidation or reduction? .... [2]

   d. $Fe^{2+} \rightarrow Fe^{3+} + ...$ Oxidation or reduction? .... [2]

   e. $O_2 + ... \rightarrow ....O^{2-}$ Oxidation or reduction? .... [2]

   f. $Pb^{4+} + 2e^- \rightarrow ....$ Oxidation or reduction? .... [2]

   g. $.....Br^- \rightarrow .... + ...$ Oxidation or reduction? .... [2]

2. Write down the formulae of the ions present in each of these compounds.

   a. NaOH   .... and .... [1]   b. $MgCl_2$ .... and .... [1]

   c. $Ba(NO_3)_2$ .... and .... [1]   d. $CuSO_4$ .... and .... [1]

   e. Al_2O_3 .... and .... [1]   f. $Fe(OH)_2$ .... and .... [1]

3. Write ionic equations for these reactions. In each case, cancel the spectator ions.

   The first one has been partly done for you. Where a solid or liquid is formed do not separate into ions.

   a. $CuCl_2(aq) + 2NaOH(aq) \rightarrow Cu(OH)_2(s) + 2NaCl(aq)$

   ions   .... + ... $2Na^+ + 2OH^-$ $2Na^+ + 2..........$ [2]

   cancel   .... + ~~..........~~   ~~$2Na^+ + 2OH^-$~~   ~~$2Na^+ + 2..........$~~   [1]

   equation $Cu^{2+}(aq) + ...(aq) \rightarrow ....(s)$ [1]

   b. $BaCl_2(aq) + MgSO_4(aq) \rightarrow BaSO_4(s) + MgSO_4(aq)$

   ions   .... + ... + ... + ...   [2]

   cancel   .... + ... + ... + ...   [1]

   equation   .... [1]

Extension

4. Write ionic equations for these reactions.

   a. $Pb(NO_3)_2(aq) + 2KCl(aq) \rightarrow PbCl_2(s) + 2KNO_3(aq)$ [2]

   b. $Cl_2(aq) + 2KI(aq) \rightarrow I_2(s) + 2KCl(aq)$ [2]

Redox reactions — 6.3 Redox and oxidation numbers

1. Complete these sentences about oxidation number (oxidation state) using words from the list.

   atoms   compound   electrons   shared   zero

   Oxidation number tells us how many .... each atom of an element has gained, lost, or

   .... when forming a .... The oxidation number of .... of

   an uncombined element is .... [5]

2. Use the oxidation numbers in the list to deduce the oxidation states of the atoms or ions which are underlined.

   Group I ions and hydrogen in compounds: +1
   Group II ions in compounds: +2
   Most Group III atoms or ions in compounds: +3
   Oxygen atoms or ions in compounds: –2 (except in peroxides where it is –1)
   Group VII atoms or ions in compounds: –1

   a. $\underline{Fe}O$ .... [1]   b. $\underline{Mn}O_2$ .... [1]   c. $Na_2\underline{S}$ .... [1]

   d. $\underline{Fe}Cl_3$ .... [1]   e. $H_2\underline{O}_2$ .... [1]   f. $\underline{Ge}Cl_4$ .... [1]

   g. $\underline{B}_2O_3$ .... [1]   h. $\underline{Cu}_2O$ .... [1]   i. $\underline{S}O_3$ .... [1]

3. Write the oxidation numbers in the spaces underneath the underlined elements and suggest whether the underlined atoms or ions have undergone oxidation or reduction in each of the following equations.

   a. $4\underline{Fe} + 3O_2 \rightarrow 2\underline{Fe}_2O_3$

   ....   Oxidation or reduction? .... [2]

   b. $\underline{C} + O_2 \rightarrow \underline{C}O_2$

   ....   Oxidation or reduction? .... [2]

   c. $\underline{Pb}O + H_2 \rightarrow \underline{Pb} + H_2O$

   ....   Oxidation or reduction? .... [2]

   d. $\underline{Cl}_2 + 2KBr \rightarrow Br_2 + 2K\underline{Cl}$

   ....   Oxidation or reduction? .... [2]

   e. $2\underline{P} + 3Cl_2 \rightarrow 2\underline{P}Cl_3$

   ....   Oxidation or reduction? .... [2]

Extension

4. Deduce the oxidation numbers of the underlined atoms.

   a. $K\underline{Mn}O_4$ b. $Mg\underline{S}O_4$ c. $\underline{N}O_2^-$ d. $\underline{S}O_3^{2-}$ e. $\underline{P}_2O_5$ [5]

Redox reactions

6.4 Oxidising and reducing agents

1. The phrases below are about oxidising and reducing agents.
   Link the beginnings **A** to **D** on the left with the endings **1** to **4** on the right.

A An oxidising agent ...	1 ... increases during a redox reaction.
B The oxidation state of an oxidising agent ...	2 ... gets oxidised during a redox reaction.
C A reducing agent ...	3 ... gets reduced during a redox reaction.
D The oxidation state of a reducing agent ...	4 ... decreases during a redox reaction.

   [2]

2. The boxes show phrases describing the use of potassium manganate(VII) and potassium iodide in redox reactions.
   Make these phrases into two sentences describing the use of these two reagents.

... an oxidising agent ...	... to red-brown ...
... in the presence of a reducing agent.	... which turns from colourless ...
... in the presence of an oxidising agent.	... which turns from purple ...
... to colourless ...	... a reducing agent ...

   Acidified potassium manganate(VII) is ....

   ....

   .... [2]

   Acidified potassium iodide is ....

   ....

   .... [2]

3. Identify the oxidising and reducing agents in these equations.
   Underline the reducing agent and draw a circle around the oxidising agent.

   a. $2Mg + O_2 \rightarrow 2MgO$ [1]

   b. $PbO + H_2 \rightarrow Pb + H_2O$ [1]

   c. $2I^- + Cl_2 \rightarrow I_2 + 2Cl^-$ [1]

   d. $H_2O_2 + 2I^- \rightarrow I_2 + 2H_2O$ [1]

   Extension

   e. $3CuO + 2NH_3 \rightarrow 3Cu + N_2 + 3H_2O$ [1]

   f. $Zn + Cu^{2+} \rightarrow Zn^{2+} + Cu$ [1]

Electricity and chemical change

7.1 Conductors and non-conductors

1. a. i. Label the diagram to show the apparatus used to show whether or not a solid conducts electricity. [2]

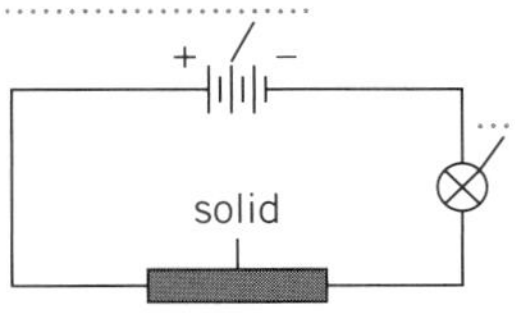

   ....

   solid

   ii. On the diagram above, draw an arrow to show the direction of flow of the electrons. [1]

2. Define the terms:

   Electrolyte .... [1]

   Electrolysis ....

   .... [2]

   Insulator .... [1]

3. Link the phrases **A** to **D** on the left with the phrases **1** to **4** on the right.

A Molten sodium chloride conducts electricity …	1 … because there are free electrons which move when a voltage is applied.
B Metals conduct electricity …	2 … because the ions are not free to move.
C Sulfur does not conduct electricity …	3 … because the ions are free to move.
D Solid sodium chloride does not conduct electricity …	4 … because none of the electrons is free to move.

   [2]

4. Aluminium with a steel core is used in high voltage power cables.

   a. Give two properties of aluminium that are related to this use.

   .... [1]

   b. Give two properties of steel that are related to this use.

   .... [2]

> **Extension**
>
> 5. Use textbooks or the internet to find some substances that have delocalised electrons and why the presence of delocalised electrons is not always associated with electrical conduction. [4]

35

Electricity and chemical change

7.2 The principles of electrolysis

1. Complete the diagram of an electrolysis cell by labelling the anode, the cathode, the electrolyte, and the direction of current flow in the external circuit.

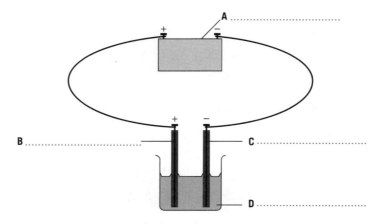

[4]

2. Complete these sentences about metal reactivity using words from the list.

   hydrogen   ions   less   more   silver   sodium   water

   More reactive elements such as .... are .... likely to form ions than .... reactive elements such as .... If a metal is more reactive than ...., its .... stay in solution and hydrogen arising from hydrogen ions in .... bubbles off. [7]

3. Complete the table to show the electrode products and observations at the anode when various substances are electrolysed using graphite electrodes.

Electrolyte	Cathode (−) product	Anode (+) product	Observations at the anode
Concentrated KCl(aq)			
ZnBr(l)			
Dilute H_2SO_4(aq)			
Dilute NaCl(aq)			
Concentrated HCl(aq)			
Dilute $AgNO_3$(aq)			

[18]

Extension

4. What substances are formed at the anode and cathode when the following solutions are electrolysed? Give reasons for your answers.

   a. concentrated aqueous sodium bromide [4]

   b. moderately concentrated sodium chloride [4]

Electricity and chemical change

7.3 The reactions at the electrodes

1. On the diagrams below, show
   - The movement of ions during electrolysis by drawing arrows.
   - What happens to the ions in terms of electron loss or gain to or from the electrodes (show this by curly arrows and e⁻).

   a. molten zinc bromide

   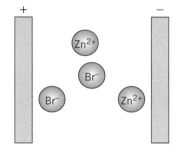

   b. dilute sulfuric acid

   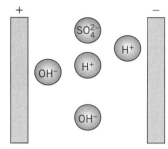

   c. concentrated hydrochloric acid

   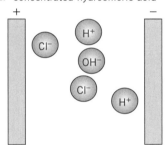

   d. aqueous copper(II) sulfate

   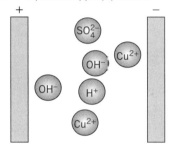

   [8]

2. a. Complete these sentences using words from the list.

   anode   cathode   gain   lose   negative   positive

   i. When .... ions .... electrons, reduction occurs. [2]

   ii. When .... ions .... electrons, oxidation occurs. [2]

   iii. Reduction takes place at the .... and oxidation at the .... [1]

   b. Complete these half equations for the reaction at the electrodes.

   i. $Zn^{2+} + ...\rightarrow Zn$ [1]

   ii. $........Cl^- \rightarrow .... + ...$ [2]

   iii. $........H^+ + ... \rightarrow ....$ [2]

   iv. $Al^{3+} + ... \rightarrow ....$ [1]

3. Write half equations for these reactions at a graphite electrode.

   a. The conversion of hydroxide ions to oxygen and water. [2]

   b. The conversion of oxide ions to oxygen molecules. [2]

Electricity and chemical change
7.4 Electroplating

1. Copper(II) sulfate can be electrolysed using graphite electrodes or copper electrodes. Complete the table to show what happens at each electrode and to the electrolyte.

What happens ...	Using graphite electrodes	Using copper electrodes
to the mass of the electrodes.	anode: cathode:	anode: cathode:
to the appearance of the electrodes during electrolysis.	anode: cathode:	anode: cathode:
to the electrolyte. (Give any observations.)		

   [10]

2. A nickel jug can be electroplated with silver. Look at the diagram on the right and then answer the questions.

   a. On the diagram label the anode, **A**, the cathode, **C**, and the electrolyte, **E**. [2]

   b. Describe what happens to the cathode as the electroplating proceeds.

   ....

   ....

   ....

   ....

   .... [2]

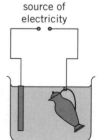

source of electricity

Extension

3. Write ionic equations for the reactions at

   a. the anode, when aqueous copper(II) sulfate is electrolysed using graphite electrodes [2]

   b. the cathode when an object is electroplated with nickel. (You will have to find out the usual charge on nickel ions to answer this question.) [2]

Energy changes in reactions

8.1 Energy changes in reactions

1. Describe these changes as either exothermic or endothermic.

   a. The decomposition of copper(II) carbonate by heating .... [1]

   b. Burning paraffin .... [1]

   c. Your tongue gets cold when you put sherbet on it .... [1]

   d. The temperature of the solution rises when concentrated hydrochloric acid is diluted.

   .... [1]

2. a. Complete these reaction pathway (energy level) diagrams for an exothermic and an endothermic reaction. Include

   • the words 'reactants' and 'products'

   • an arrow in each diagram in the correct position.

   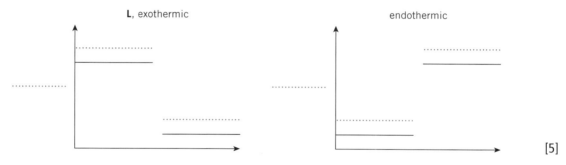
   [5]

   b. Explain how energy level diagram **L** represents an exothermic reaction.

   .... [1]

3. Complete these sentences using words from the list.

   energy   enthalpy   increase   surroundings   temperature   thermal

   An exothermic reaction transfers .... energy to the .... This leads to an

   .... in the .... of the surroundings. The transfer of thermal ....

   during a reaction is called the .... change. [6]

Extension

4. Propane burns in excess oxygen.

   $C_3H_8(g) + 5O_2(g) \rightarrow 3CO_2(g) + 4H_2O(l)$ Energy change = –2219 kJ/mol propane

   a. Calculate the enthalpy change when 8.8 g of propane is burnt. [2]

   b. Calculate the enthalpy change when 4.8 dm³ of carbon dioxide is produced. [3]

5. Use textbooks or the internet to define (a) activation energy and (b) enthalpy change. Write down the symbols and units for these terms. [6]

39

Energy changes in reactions

8.2 A closer look at energy changes

1. Link the words **A** to **D** on the left with the descriptions **1** to **4** on the right.

A activation energy	1 The thermal energy change in a chemical reaction.
B enthalpy change	2 The general progress of a reaction from reactants to products.
C reaction pathway	3 The energy that is involved in heating or cooling.
D thermal energy	4 The minimum energy needed for colliding particles to react.

   [2]

2. Draw a labelled reaction pathway diagram, including activation energy, for an endothermic reaction. Include the following:

   - The axes suitably labelled.
   - The words 'reactant' and 'products'.
   - The activation energy as an arrow.
   - The enthalpy change as an arrow.

   [5]

3. State two differences between the reaction pathway diagram for an exothermic reaction and an endothermic reaction.

   ....

   .... [2]

Extension

4. Calcium carbonate can be converted to calcium oxide and carbon dioxide.

   $$CaCO_3(s) \rightarrow CaO(s) + CO_2(g) \qquad \text{Energy change, } \Delta H = +178 \text{ kJ}$$

   What type of enthalpy change is taking place during this reaction and how does the information above show this? [3]

Energy changes in reactions
8.3 Calculating enthalpy changes

1. Order these phrases to describe the relationship between bond breaking and bond making in exothermic and endothermic reactions. Then write them out in the correct order in the spaces below. Most phrases may be used more than once.

... in forming new bonds ...		... than the energy absorbed ...
... is greater ...		... in the reactants.
... in breaking the bonds ...		... the energy released ...
... in the products ...		... is less ...

   In an exothermic reaction ....

   .... [1]

   In an endothermic reaction ....

   .... [1]

2. Complete the table to calculate the energy change when methane reacts with excess oxygen to form carbon dioxide and water.

   $$H-\underset{\underset{H}{|}}{\overset{\overset{H}{|}}{C}}-H \; + \; 2\,O{=}O \; \rightarrow \; O{=}C{=}O \; + \; 2\,H-O-H$$

   Bond energies in kJ / mol : C–H 413, O=O 498, C=O 805, O–H 464

Bonds broken (endothermic +) / kJ	Bonds formed (exothermic –) / kJ
4 × (C–H) = 4 × 413 = ...	
... × (O=O) = ... = ...	
Total	

   Overall energy change = (+ ....) + (– ....) = ... kJ   [5]

Extension

3. Calculate the energy change of the reaction shown using the bond energies above and H–H = 436 kJ/mol.

   $$2H_2(g) \; + \; O_2(g) \; \rightarrow \; 2H_2O(g)$$ [5]

4. The bond energy of the C=O bond in CO_2 is 805 kJ/mol. The bond energy of the C=O bond in propanone CH_3COCH_3 is 749 kJ/mol. Suggest why they are different. [2]

Energy changes in reactions

8.4 The hydrogen-oxygen fuel cell

1. Complete these sentences about fuel cells using words from the list.

   alkali   electrons   external   negative   oxygen   platinum   porous   reactions

   A fuel cell consists of two .... electrodes coated with .... The electrolyte is either an acid or an .... Hydrogen and .... are bubbled through the porous electrodes where the .... take place. When connected to an .... circuit, ... flow from the .... electrode to the positive electrode. [8]

2. The diagram shows a hydrogen oxygen fuel cell.

   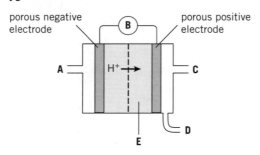

   a. Give the name of the instrument labelled **B**. .... [1]

   b. The product of the reaction in the fuel cell is water. Which letter **A**, **C**, **D**, or **E** shows where water is collected?

   .... [1]

   c. Which letter **A**, **C**, **D**, or **E** shows where hydrogen enters the cell? .... [1]

3. Complete these half equations for the reactions taking place in the fuel cell.

   a. ....H_2 + ...OH^- → ....H_2O + ... [2]

   b. .... + ... H_2O + ... → .... OH^- [2]

4. Give two advantages and two disadvantages of using fuels cells instead of petrol to power a car.

   Advantage 1 ....

   Advantage 2 ....

   Disadvantage 1 ....

   Disadvantage 2 ....

Extension

5. A copper rod and a magnesium rod are put into suitable electrolytes. When the rods are connected, a voltage is produced. Use textbooks or the internet to find out why a voltage is produced. [4]

The rate of reaction

9.1 Introducing reaction rates

1. Complete these sentences about methods for following the course of a reaction using words from the list.

   decreases   products   quickly   rate   second   time   used   volume

   To find the rate of reaction we can either measure how .... the reactants are

   .... up or how quickly the .... are formed. To calculate the

   .... of reaction we need to find out how some measurement changes with

   .... For example, the .... of gas given off per ....

   or how the mass of the reaction mixture ....with time. [8]

2. Put these in order of increasing rate of reaction.

   A immediate precipitation   B rusting   C paint drying   D magnesium burning in air

   .... [1]

3. The diagrams show the reaction of 50% nitric acid with copper.

   (at the start: colourless nitric acid, copper powder)
   (after 5 minutes: blue solution, bubbles of colourless gas)
   (after 20 minutes)

   a. Give three pieces of information from the diagram that show a chemical reaction is occurring.

   ....
   ....
   .... [3]

   b. Suggest three different ways by which you could measure the rate of this reaction.

   1 ....

   2 ....

   3 .... [3]

> **Extension**
>
> 4. Suggest why the course of this reaction can be followed by measuring electrical conductivity.
>
> $$H_2O_2(aq) + 2I^-(aq) + 2H^+(aq) \rightarrow 2H_2O(l) + I_2(ac)$$
>
>   .... [2]

The rate of reaction
9.2 Measuring the rate of a reaction

1. The decomposition of hydrogen peroxide is speeded up by catalysts.

   $$2H_2O_2(aq) \rightarrow 2H_2O(l) + O_2(g)$$

   A student investigated how the rate of reaction changes when two different catalysts are used. The results using catalyst **A** are shown below.

   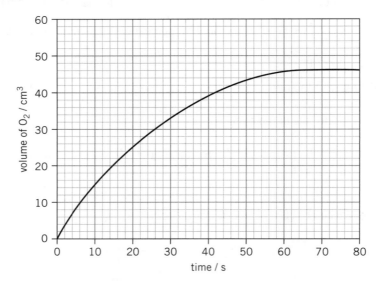

   a. At what time is the reaction just complete? .... [1]

   b. What volume of gas has been released when the reaction is just complete?

   .... [1]

   c. What volume of gas has been produced in the first 30 seconds of the reaction?

   .... [1]

   d. Calculate the average rate of reaction in the first 30 seconds of the reaction. Draw lines on the graph to show how you did this.

   .... [2]

   e. The reaction was repeated using catalyst **B**. The results are shown in the table.

Time / s	0	4	10	20	30	40	50	60	70	80
Volume / cm³	0	16	27	38	43	45	45.5	46	46	46

   Plot a graph of these results on the same grid as for catalyst **A** above. Draw the curve of best fit through the points. [2]

> **Extension**
>
> 2. Measurement of change in gas volume or mass with time can be used to calculate rate of reaction. Use textbooks or the internet to find out about other methods of following the course of a reaction and why they work. [6]

The rate of reaction
9.3 Changing the rate (part I)

1. A student investigated how increasing the temperature affects the rate of the reaction of magnesium with 1.0 mol/dm³ hydrochloric acid. The student measured the volume of hydrogen given off in 1 minute at seven different temperatures. The table shows the results.

Temperature / °C	20	30	41	45	50	55	60
Volume of H_2 / cm³	10	20	44	56	80	110	160

   a. Plot a graph of these results on the grid below. Draw the best curve through the points.

   [5]

   b. Describe the shape of the graph of rate of reaction against temperature.

   .... [2]

2. Magnesium reacts with dilute hydrochloric acid. The rates of reaction can be compared by measuring how the volume of hydrogen gas volume of hydrogen gas produced changes with time.

   The experiment was done three times using different concentrations of hydrochloric acid. The results are shown.

   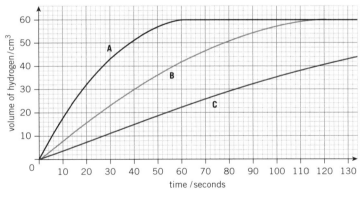

   a. Which line represented the most concentrated hydrochloric acid? .... [1]

   b. Calculate the average rate of reaction over the first 60 seconds for line **B**.

   .... [1]

   Extension

   c. For line **A**, deduce the rates of reaction at 20 s and 40 s by calculating the value of each gradient.
   See Unit 21.8 for details of how to do this. [4]

45

The rate of reaction
9.4 Changing the rate (part II)

1. Look at the cube of marble (calcium carbonate) labelled **A** in the diagram.

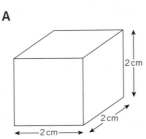
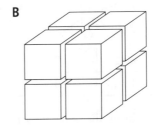

   a. i. Calculate the surface area of cube **A** (see Unit 21.4 if you are not sure how to do this).
   .... [1]

   ii. Now imagine that this cube is cut into 8 separate cubes (**B** in the diagram above). Calculate the total surface area of these 8 cubes. Show your working.

   ....
   .... [2]

   iii. Which set of cubes **A** or **B** has the greatest number of calcium and carbonate ions exposed for reaction with hydrochloric acid? .... [1]

   b. 4 g of large marble chips was reacted with excess dilute hydrochloric acid.

   $$CaCO_3(s) + 2HCl(aq) \rightarrow CaCl_2(aq) + CO_2(g) + H_2O(l)$$

   The experiment was repeated with 4 g of medium-sized marble chips then with 4 g of small marble chips. All other conditions remained the same.

   On the axes below draw a sketch graph to show how the volume of carbon dioxide released changes with time using large, **L**, medium, **M**, and small, **S**, marble chips. Label your lines **L**, **M** and **S**.

   [2]

2. Hydrogen reacts with chlorine to produce hydrogen chloride. The reactants and product are all gases. The reaction is carried out in a container of volume 1 dm^3.
   Describe and explain the effect on the reaction rate when:

   a. the same gas mixture is put into a container of 2 dm^3 at the same temperature.
   .... [2]

   b. the pressure of the same gas mixture is increased at the same temperature.
   .... [2]

3. Explain why there is a danger of explosions in saw-mills, where wood is cut up.
   .... [4]

The rate of reaction

9.5 Explaining rate changes

1. Complete these sentences about the collision theory of rates of reaction using words from the list.

   bonds   collide   energy   faster   frequency   increases   kinetic   rate   successful

   In order to react, particles must .... with each other. The collisions must have

   enough .... to break .... to allow a reaction to happen.

   Increasing the concentration of a reactant .... the .... of collisions and

   increases the .... of reaction. Increasing temperature makes particles move

   .... and increases the ....energy of the particles so that there are

   more .... collisions. [9]

2. Use the particle diagrams below to answer the following questions about the reaction.

   $Mg(s) + 2HCl(aq) \rightarrow MgCl_2(aq) + H_2O(l)$

   a. Complete the diagram on the right to show the particles of acid and water in a concentrated solution of acid.

   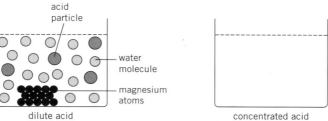

   dilute acid   concentrated acid [3]

   b. Complete the diagram on the right to show the relative number of acid, magnesium, and water particles when the reaction is nearly complete.

   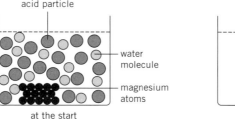 

   at the start   near the end [3]

3. Use the collision theory to explain why 1 g of magnesium powder reacts more rapidly than 1 g of magnesium ribbon with 1 mol/dm³ hydrochloric acid.

   ....

   ....

   .... [3]

Extension

4. Use books or the internet to find out how solid inorganic catalysts work. [4]

47

The rate of reaction   9.6 Catalysts

1. Catalysts speed up the decomposition of hydrogen peroxide.

$$2H_2O_2(aq) \rightarrow 2H_2O(l) + O_2(g)$$

A simple way of comparing the effect of catalysts is to add two drops of washing-up liquid to the solution under test and then measure the height of the foam produced.

The results of adding different substances to the same concentration of hydrogen peroxide are shown in the diagram.

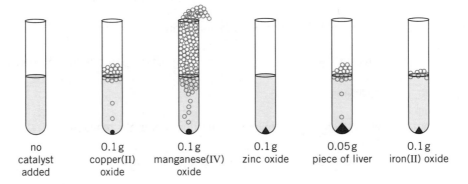

no catalyst added | 0.1 g copper(II) oxide | 0.1 g manganese(IV) oxide | 0.1 g zinc oxide | 0.05 g piece of liver | 0.1 g iron(II) oxide

a. Suggest why a foam was formed without shaking the tubes.

.... [2]

b. Which substance is the best catalyst for the reaction? .... [1]

c. Use the information in the diagram to explain why the piece of liver is a better catalyst than copper(II) oxide.

.... [2]

d. i. Liver contains biological catalysts. What is the general name given to a biological catalyst?

.... [1]

ii. What could you do to the piece of liver to make it a more efficient catalyst in this reaction? Explain your answer.

.... [2]

e. Suggest a more accurate method for comparing the rates of this catalysis.

.... [3]

Extension

2. Use books or the internet to explain

   a. how enzymes catalyse chemical reactions in living organisms

   b. the general conditions needed for enzyme catalysis. [7]

Reversible reactions and equilibrium

10.1 Reversible reactions

1. Hydrated and anhydrous cobalt(II) chloride can be converted to one another.

$$CoCl_2 \cdot 6H_2O \rightleftharpoons CoCl_2 + 6H_2O$$
pink hydrated — blue anhydrous

   a. What is the meaning of the symbol $\rightleftharpoons$? .... [1]

   b. What is observed when water is added to anhydrous cobalt(II) chloride?

   .... [1]

   c. How could you change pink cobalt(II) chloride to blue cobalt(II) chloride?

   .... [1]

   d. Explain the meaning of these terms:

   i. water of crystallisation ....

   .... [1]

   ii. anhydrous .... [1]

2. Complete these sentences:

   a. In a .... system, no substances escape from the reaction mixture. [1]

   b. At equilibrium, the rate of the .... reaction is equal to the .... of

   the .... reaction. [2]

3. When a mixture of hydrogen and iodine is heated, an equilibrium mixture with hydrogen iodide is formed.

$$H_2(g) + I_2(g) \rightleftharpoons 2HI(g)$$

   In the box on the right, draw the molecules in this equilibrium mixture which contains more product than reactants.

   Use · to represent a molecule of I_2

   Use o to represent a molecule of H_2

   Use □ to represent a molecule of HI [3]

Extension

4. a. For the reaction shown in question 3, draw a sketch graph to show how the concentration of HI changes with time, starting with a mixture of only H_2 and I_2. [3]

   b. On the same sketch graph, draw a line to show how the concentration of HI changes with time, starting with pure HI. [3]

Reversible reactions and equilibrium

10.2 Shifting the equilibrium

1. Sulfur dioxide reacts with oxygen to form an equilibrium mixture with sulfur trioxide.

   $$2SO_2(g) + O_2(g) \rightleftharpoons 2SO_3(g) \quad \text{energy released}$$

   Complete the following sentences about this reaction.

   a. When oxygen is removed the position of equilibrium shifts to the .... [1]

   b. If the temperature is increased the position of equilibrium shifts so that the

      concentration of $2SO_3(g)$ .... [1]

   c. Decreasing the pressure shifts the position of equilibrium to the .... because there are

      .... moles of gas molecules in the equation on the .... [3]

   d. Adding a catalyst .... [1]

2. In which direction does the position of equilibrium shift when the pressure on each of these reactions is increased?

   a. $CO(g) + 2H_2(g) \rightleftharpoons CH_3OH(g)$ .... [1]

   b. $CaCO_3(s) \rightleftharpoons CaO(s) + CO_2(g)$ .... [1]

   c. $4HCl(g) + O_2(g) \rightleftharpoons 2H_2O(g) + 2Cl_2(g)$ .... [1]

   d. $2HCl(g) \rightleftharpoons H_2(g) + Cl_2(g)$ .... [1]

3. When bismuth trichloride, $BiCl_3$ is added to water the following reaction occurs:

   $$BiCl_3(aq) + H_2O(l) \rightleftharpoons BiClO(s) + 2HCl(aq)$$
   $$\text{colourless solution} \qquad\qquad \text{white precipitate}$$

   a. What would you see when concentrated HCl is added to the mixture?

      .... [1]

   b. What would you see when a large volume of water was added to the reaction mixture?

      .... [1]

   c. Explain why increasing pressure has no effect on this reaction.

      .... [1]

> **Extension**
>
> 4. Use textbooks or the internet to find out the best conditions for the synthesis of sulfur trioxide (question 1). Why are these conditions used? [8]

Reversible reactions and equilibrium

10.3 The Haber process

1. Ammonia is manufactured by the Haber process. Complete these sentences about this process using words from the list.

   compressed   converter   hydrogen   iron   natural   oxygen   steam

   The hydrogen is made by reacting .... gas with .... The nitrogen comes from the air after .... has been removed by reaction with .... The nitrogen and hydrogen are .... and pumped into a .... where they react at 450 °C in the presence of a catalyst of .... [7]

2. Complete the equation for the synthesis of ammonia.

   $N_2(g)$ + ...(g) $\rightleftharpoons$ ....(g) [2]

3. The graph below shows the effect of temperature and pressure on the percentage yield of ammonia.

   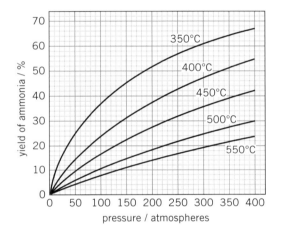

   a. Describe the effect of pressure on the percentage yield.

   .... [1]

   b. How does the data in the graph show that the reaction is exothermic?

   .... [1]

   c. What is the percentage yield of ammonia at 200 atmospheres and 350 °C?

   .... [1]

   d. State one advantage and one disadvantage of using a low temperature in the reaction.

   ....

   .... [2]

4. Draw and label a reaction pathway diagram for ammonia synthesis showing the overall energy change and the activation energy of the catalysed and uncatalysed reaction. [6]

Reversible reactions and equilibrium
10.4 The Contact process

1. In the Contact process, sulfur dioxide is converted to sulfur trioxide in the presence of vanadium(V) oxide.

$$2SO_2(g) + O_2(g) \rightleftharpoons 2SO_3(g)$$

   a. What is the purpose of the vanadium(V) oxide?

   .... [1]

   b. The graph below shows the percentage conversion of SO_2 to SO_3 at different temperatures. The pressure was just above atmospheric pressure.

   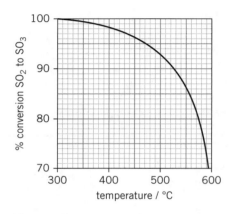

   i. Describe in detail the effect of temperature on the percentage conversion of SO_2 to SO_3.

   ....

   .... [2]

   ii. Deduce the percentage conversion of SO_2 to SO_3 at 500 °C.

   .... [1]

   iii. How does the data in the graph show that the reaction is exothermic?

   .... [1]

   c. i. Predict the effect of increasing the pressure on this reaction. Explain your answer.

   .... [1]

   .... [2]

   ii. Explain why the reaction does not need to be carried out at high pressure.

   .... [1]

Extension

2. a. Construct a balanced equation for the reaction of concentrated sulfuric with carbon to form sulfur dioxide, carbon dioxide, and water. [2]

   b. Construct a balanced equation for the oxidation of hydrogen sulfide by concentrated sulfuric acid to form sulfur dioxide, sulfur, and water. [2]

Acids, bases, and salts 11.1 Acids and bases

1. a. State the colours of these indicators in acidic or alkaline solution.

    i. Litmus in alkaline solution .... [1]

    ii. Methyl orange in alkaline solution .... [1]

    iii. Thymolphthalein in alkaline solution .... [1]

    iv. Methyl orange in acidic solution .... [1]

    v. Litmus in acidic solution .... [1]

   b. Describe how to use litmus paper to find out if a liquid is acidic or alkaline.

      ....

      .... [3]

2. a. Link these acids and alkalis by choosing the correct formula from the list.

    $Ca(OH)_2$ CH_3COOH H_2CO_3 HNO_3 H_3PO_4 H_2SO_4 $NaOH$ NH_3

    i. ammonia .... [1]   ii. ethanoic acid .... [1]

    iii. carbonic acid .... [1]   iv. sulfuric acid .... [1]

    v. calcium hydroxide .... [1]   vi. phosphoric acid .... [1]

    vii. nitric acid .... [1]   viii. sodium hydroxide .... [1]

   b. What group of atoms is found in all alkalis?

      .... [1]

   c. Sulfuric acid is a dibasic acid and phosphoric acid is a tribasic acid.

      Look at the formulae of these acids to suggest a link between the words dibasic and tribasic and hydrogen atoms in these molecules.

      .... [2]

3. Many acids and alkalis are corrosive. What dos the word *corrosive* mean?

   .... [1]

4. Complete these sentences about bases using words from the list.

   alkali   copper   dissolve   hydroxides   insoluble   oxides   soluble

   Bases are .... and hydroxides of metals. Most bases are ....

   in water. An example is .... (II) oxide. A soluble base is called an ....

   All Group I .... are alkalis because they .... easily in water. Calcium

   hydroxide is slightly .... in water and forms an alkaline solution. [7]

Extension

5. Use the internet to find out the hazards associated with concentrated and dilute sodium hydroxide, hydrochloric acid, sulfuric acid, and ammonia. [8]

Acids, bases, and salts

11.2 A closer look at acids and alkalis

1. a. Link the colours of these indicators to the following pH values.

   pH 3   pH 7   pH 11

   i.   Litmus is blue at .... [1]

   ii. Methyl orange is red at .... [1]

   iii. Universal indicator is green at .... [1]

   iv. Thymolphthalein is blue at .... [1]

   v.   Methyl orange is yellow at .... [1]

   b. Describe how to use universal indicator paper to find the pH of a solution.

   ....

   .... [3]

   c. Link the phrases **A** to **E** on the left with the pH values **1** to **5** on the right.

A highly acidic		1 pH 6
B neutral		2 pH 8
C highly alkaline		3 pH 1
D weakly acidic		4 pH 14
E weakly alkaline		5 pH 7

   [3]

2. Complete these sentences about strong and weak acids using words from the list.

   all   anions   equilibrium   hydrogen   ionised   molecules   water   partially

   Aqueous solutions of acids contain .... ions. In strong acids ....
   the acid .... are dissociated (...................................) to form hydrogen ions and
   .... When weak acids are dissolved in .... they become
   .... dissociated. We can write this as an .... ,
   for example, $CH_3COOH \rightleftharpoons CH_3COO^- + H^+$.   [8]

3. Ammonia reacts with water: $NH_3(g) + H_2O(l) \rightleftharpoons NH_4^+(aq) + OH^-(aq)$
   How does this equation show that aqueous ammonia is an alkali?

   .... [1]

Extension

4. Use the internet to find the solubilities of barium, calcium, and magnesium hydroxides. Suggest why there is a trend in the pH values of saturated solutions of these hydroxides. [4]

Acids, bases, and salts — 11.3 The reactions of acid and bases

1. Complete these word equations for the general reactions of acids.

   a. acid + metal → .... + ... [2]

   b. acid + metal oxide → .... + ... [2]

   c. acid + metal carbonate → .... + ... + ... [3]

   d. acid + metal hydroxide → .... + ... [2]

2. Complete these word equations.

   a. sodium hydroxide + nitric acid → .... [1]

   b. zinc oxide + hydrochloric acid → .... [1]

   c. iron + sulfuric acid → .... [1]

   d. sulfuric acid + lead carbonate → .... [1]

   e. barium hydroxide + nitric acid → .... [1]

   f. hydrochloric acid + tin oxide → .... [1]

3. Complete the balanced chemical equations for these reactions.

   a. $Zn + H_2SO_4 \rightarrow$ .... [1]

   b. $MgO + \ldots HNO_3 \rightarrow$ .... [2]

   c. $CuCO_3 + \ldots HCl \rightarrow$ .... [2]

   d. $\ldots NaOH + H_2SO_4 \rightarrow$ .... [2]

   e. $Na_2CO_3 + \ldots HCl \rightarrow$ .... [2]

   f. $Ca + \ldots HCl \rightarrow$ .... [2]

   g. $Ca(OH)_2 + \ldots HNO_3 \rightarrow$ .... [2]

4. What is the general name given to reactions **b**, **d**, and **g** in question 3?

   .... [1]

5. Complete the equation below for the reaction of an alkali with an ammonium salt.

   $$Ca(OH)_2 + \ldots NH_4Cl \rightarrow CaCl_2 + \ldots H_2O + \ldots$$ [2]

Extension

6. Farmers add ammonium sulfate to the soil to increase the growth of crop plants. Explain why adding calcium hydroxide to the soil at the same time as ammonium sulfate is not a good idea. [3]

Acids, bases, and salts — **11.4 A closer look at neutralisation**

1. Complete these simple definitions of an acid and a base.

   a. An acid reacts with a .... to form a .... and .... [3]

   b. A base reacts with an .... to form a .... and .... [3]

2. A more general definition of an acid is a proton donor.

   a. What is a proton? .... [1]

   b. Explain why a hydrogen ion can be described as a proton.

   ....

   .... [2]

   c. Define a base using the word proton.

   .... [1]

3. The equation below shows the ions present in the reactants and products of a neutralisation reaction.

   $$H^+(aq) + NO_3^-(aq) + Na^+(aq) + OH^-(aq) \rightarrow NO_3^-(aq) + Na^+(aq) + H_2O(l)$$

   a. Cancel out the spectator ions in this equation. [1]

   b. Write the ionic equation for this reaction.

   .... [1]

   c. Explain, in terms of ions, why this is a neutralisation reaction.

   .... [1]

4. Identify which are the acids and which are the bases in these equations in terms of the transfer of protons. The first one has been done for you.

   proton donated

   $2\overset{\frown}{HCl} + MgO \rightarrow MgCl_2 + H_2O$

   a. $NH_3 + H_2O \rightleftharpoons NH_4^+ + OH^-$ [1]

   b. $H_2S + H_2O \rightleftharpoons HS^- + H_3O^+$ [1]

Extension

5. Identify which are the acids and which are the bases in these equations.

   a. $HCOOH + HClO_2 \rightleftharpoons HCOOH^+ + ClO_2^-$ [2]

   b. $NH_4^+ + H_2O \rightleftharpoons H_3O^+ + NH_3$ [2]

Acids, bases, and salts — 11.5 Oxides

1. Complete these sentences about oxides using words from the list.

   acidic   acids   alkaline   alkalis   basic   left   Periodic   right

   Oxides of many metals on the .... of the .... Table react with water. These are called .... oxides. Some of these oxides react with .... to form .... solutions. Oxides of many non-metals on the .... of the Periodic Table reacts with .... These oxides are called acidic oxides. Many of these oxides react with water to form .... solutions. [8]

2. Complete these equations to show the reactions of some oxides with either acids or bases.

   a. MgO + ...HCl → .... + ... [2]

   b. SO_2 + ...$NaOH$ → Na_2SO_3 + ... [2]

   c. CuO + H_2SO_4 → .... + ... [1]

   d. CO_2 + ...$NaOH$ → Na_2CO_3 + ... [2]

   e. ZnO + ...HNO_3 → .... + ... [2]

   f. CaO + H_2SO_4 → .... + ... [1]

3. Complete these equations to show the reactions of some oxides with water to form acids or alkalis.

   a. SO_2 + H_2O → .... [1]

   b. CO_2 + H_2O → .... [1]

   c. CaO + H_2O → .... [1]

   d. P_4O_6 + ... H_2O → .... H_3PO_3 [1]

   e. Na_2O + H_2O → .... [1]

4. Some oxides react with both acids and alkalis. What is the name given to these oxides?

   .... [1]

Extension

5. Complete the equations for these reactions of zinc and aluminium oxides.

   a. .... + ... KOH → K_2ZnO_2 + ... [2]

   b. Al_2O_3 + ... HCl → .... + ... [2]

   c. Al_2O_3 + ... → $NaAlO_2$ + ... [2]

Acids, bases, and salts — 11.6 Making salts (part I)

1. Zinc sulfate can be made by first warming sulfuric acid with excess zinc.

   a. How is a solution of zinc sulfate obtained from the reaction mixture?

   .... [1]

   b. The solution of zinc sulfate is crystallised. Describe how you could obtain pure dry crystals of zinc sulfate from a mixture of the crystals and remaining solution.

   ....

   ....

   .... [3]

2. Crystals of copper(II) sulfate can be made by warming excess copper(II) oxide with sulfuric acid. Put the following stages in the correct order.

   A Allow the solution to cool and deposit crystals.
   B Pour the filtrate into an evaporating basin.
   C Wash and dry the crystals.
   D Filter the mixture to remove excess copper(II) oxide.
   E Warm the filtrate until the solution is very concentrated.
   F Filter off the crystals.

   The order is .... [2]

3. The diagram shows the stages in making a soluble salt (sodium chloride) by neutralising an alkali (sodium hydroxide) with an acid (hydrochloric acid). The first three stages are shown in the diagram.

   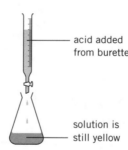
   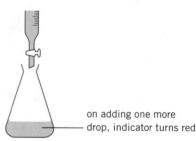

   Describe the next three stages of the procedure to get colourless crystals of sodium chloride.

   ....

   ....

   .... [3]

Extension

4. Use textbooks or the internet to help you answer these questions.

   a. Why should you not heat copper(II) nitrate too strongly when drying the crystals? [2]

   b. Why can you not use the titration method when preparing crystals of zinc sulfate? [2]

Acids, bases, and salts — 11.7 Making salts (part II)

1. Complete these sentences about solubility using words from the list.

   | ammonium | carbonates | compounds | hydroxides | nitrates | precipitate | solutions |

   Salts such as ...., sodium salts and .... salts are soluble in water.

   Many .... and .... are insoluble except those from Group I. An

   insoluble substance formed when two .... of soluble .... are mixed

   is called a .... [7]

2. Crystals of lead iodide can be made from solutions of lead nitrate and potassium iodide. Put the following stages in the correct order.

   A Filter the mixture.
   B Make up aqueous solutions of lead nitrate and potassium iodide.
   C Dry the residue of lead iodide in a warm oven.
   D Rinse the residue on the filter paper with distilled water.
   E Mix the solutions. A yellow precipitate forms.

   The order is .... [2]

3. State the meaning of these terms.

   Hydrated salt .... [1]

   Anhydrous salt .... [1]

   Water of crystallisation ....

   .... [1]

4. a. The equation below shows the ions present in the reactants and products of a precipitation reaction.

   $$Ag^+(aq) + NO_3^-(aq) + K^+(aq) + Br^-(aq) \rightarrow AgBr(s) + NO_3^-(aq) + K^+(aq)$$

   i. Cancel out the spectator ions in this equation. [1]

   ii. Write the ionic equation for this reaction.

       .... [1]

   b. Write ionic equations for these precipitation reactions.

   i. $BaCl_2(aq) + K_2SO_4(aq) \rightarrow BaSO_4(s) + 2KCl(aq)$

       .... [2]

   ii. $Pb(NO_3)_2(aq) + 2KCl(aq) \rightarrow PbCl_2(s) + 2KNO_3(aq)$

       .... [3]

   Extension

   iii. The reaction between iron(III) chloride and barium hydroxide. [3]

   iv. The reaction between sodium carbonate and magnesium iodide. [2]

Acids, bases, and salts — 11.8 Finding concentration by titration

1. Describe how you would prepare 250 cm³ of a standard solution of concentration 1.0 mol/dm³ sodium hydroxide.

   ....

   ....

   ....

   .... [4]

2. The table below shows the results of a titration experiment. The titration was repeated several times

	Rough titre	2nd titre	3rd titre	4th titre	5th titre
Final burette reading / cm³	33.00	33.30	32.10	32.90	34.65
Initial burette reading / cm³	0.05	1.20	0.10	0.05	02.50
Titre / cm³					

   a. Complete the last row in the table. [2]

   b. Which titres would you take to average? Explain why.

   ....

   .... [2]

3. Work through this calculation to find the concentration of a solution of sodium hydroxide when 25.0 cm³ of a solution of sodium hydroxide is exactly neutralised by 12.2 cm³ of sulfuric acid of concentration 0.100 mol/dm³.

   a. moles of acid = ... × $\frac{...........}{1000}$ = ... mol H_2SO_4 [1]

   b. The equation for the reaction is: $2NaOH + H_2SO_4 \rightarrow Na_2SO_4 + 2H_2O$

   i. How many moles of NaOH react with 1 mole of H_2SO_4? .... [1]

   ii. How many moles of NaOH are needed to react with the amount (in mol) of H_2SO_4 you calculated in part **a**?

   .... [1]

   c. Calculate the concentration of NaOH in 25 cm³ of the sodium hydroxide solution.

   [2]

Extension

4. 25.0 cm³ of a 0.05 mol/dm³ solution of barium hydroxide, $Ba(OH)_2$ was titrated with hydrochloric acid. It took 15.5 cm³ of hydrochloric acid to neutralise the barium hydroxide.
   Calculate the concentration of the hydrochloric acid. [4]

The Periodic Table — 12.1 The Periodic Table: an overview

1. a. A 'cell' of the Periodic table is shown below.

   48
   Cd
   112

   i. What does 48 represent .... [1]

   ii. What does 112 represent .... [1]

   b. Complete these sentences about the Periodic Table.

   i. The elements in the Periodic Table are arranged in order of increasing

      .... [1]

   ii. The groups are numbered .... to .... [1]

   iii. The period number tells you the number of ....
        in an atom. [1]

   iv. The outer shell electrons in an atom are called .... [1]

2. Explain why Group VIII elements are unreactive.

   ....
   .... [2]

3. Describe the position of metals and non-metals in the Periodic Table both across a period and down a group.

   ....
   ....
   ....
   .... [4]

4. Both hydrogen and Group I elements have one electron in their outer shell.

   Why is hydrogen not placed in Group I in the Periodic Table?

   ....
   .... [2]

Extension

5. Use textbooks or the internet to describe:

   a. how the structure of the Group V elements changes down the group in terms of being metals
      or non-metals [4]

   b. how the type of oxides formed by Group V elements changes down the group. [4]

The Periodic Table
12.2 Group I: the alkali metals

1. The table shows some properties of some Group I metals.

Group I metal	Density in g/cm³	Melting point / °C	Metallic radius / nm	Observations when the metal reacts with water
lithium	0.53	181	0.157	Moves over the surface very slowly Fizzes gently Does not melt or go into a ball Does not burst into flame
sodium	0.97	98	0.191	....
potassium	0.86		0.235	Moves over surface very rapidly Fizzes very rapidly Melts and goes into a ball then bursts into flame Slight 'pop' when reaction near the end
rubidium	1.53	39		....

   a. Complete the table by writing in

      i. The observations in the last column for sodium and rubidium. [6]

      ii. A prediction for the melting point of potassium and the metallic radius of rubidium. [2]

   b. Caesium is below rubidium in the Periodic Table. Predict a value for the density of caesium.

      .... [1]

2. Explain what happens in terms of electron transfer when sodium reacts with chlorine.

   ....
   ....
   .... [4]

Extension

3. Use textbooks or the internet to find out why it is easier to remove the outer electron from a potassium atom than it is to remove the outer electron from a sodium atom. [5]

62

The Periodic Table

12.3 Group VII: the halogens

1. The table shows some properties of fluorine, chlorine, bromine and iodine.

Halogen	Melting point / °C	Boiling point / °C	State at −40 °C	Colour	Atomic radius / nm
fluorine	−220	−188			
chlorine	−101	−35			
bromine	−7	59			
iodine	114	184			

   a. What is the trend in the melting points of the halogens?

   .... [1]

   b. Use the values of the melting and boiling points in the table to deduce the state of the halogens at −40 °C. Write your answers in the table. [4]

   c. Complete the fifth column to show the colours of the halogens at room temperature. [4]

   d. Draw an arrow in the sixth column to show the trend in atomic radius (smaller → larger). [1]

2. a. Complete these sentences about the displacement reactions of halogens using words from the list.

   bromine   chlorine   colourless   halide   halogen   less   more   orange

   When aqueous .... is added to a .... solution of potassium

   bromide, the solution turns .... because .... has been displaced.

   This is because a .... reactive .... displaces a ....

   reactive halogen from an aqueous solution of its .... [8]

   b. What would you observe when an aqueous solution of bromine is added to an aqueous solution of potassium iodide. Explain these observations.

   ....

   ....

   .... [4]

Extension

3. Write ionic equations for:

   a. the reaction of aqueous chlorine with aqueous magnesium iodide [2]

   b. the reaction of aqueous bromine with aqueous potassium astatide, KAt. [2]

The Periodic Table
12.4 More about the trends

1. The table shows some information about some of the elements in Period 3.

Element	Na	Mg	Al	Si	P	S	Cl
Electronic structure	2,8,1						
Melting point / °C	98	649	660	1410	590	119	−101
Formula of typical compounds	NaCl, Na$_2$O	MgCl$_2$, MgO	AlCl$_3$	SiCl$_4$, SiH$_4$	PCl$_3$, PH$_3$	H$_2$S	HCl
			....	....	....		
Valency in compound	1	2	3	4	3	2	1

   a. Complete the second line of the table to show the electronic structures. [1]

   b. Complete the fourth line of the table to show the formulae of the three oxides. [3]

   c. i. Describe how the melting points of the elements change across the period.

   .... [2]

   ii. What type of structures are Na, Mg, and Al?

   .... [2]

   iii. Explain in terms of structure and bonding why Si has the highest melting point in this period.

   ....
   .... [2]

   iv. Explain in terms of structure and bonding why the melting points P, S, and Cl are relatively low.

   ....
   .... [2]

2. Phosphorus also forms a chloride with the formula, PCl$_5$.

   a. Deduce the valency of the phosphorus in this compound. .... [1]

   b. Deduce the formula of the oxide of phosphorus which has the same valency as the phosphorus in PCl$_5$.

   .... [1]

Extension

3. Explain why the reactivity of the metals decreases from sodium to aluminium. [3]

The Periodic Table

12.5 The transition elements

1. The boxes below show the properties of five non-transition elements and of five transition elements. The boxes are muddled up. (M = metal)

A Melting point 1890 °C	B Forms a chloride of formula MCl_2 only
C Forms chlorides which are pink and green	D Density 7.87 g/cm³
E Forms chloride of type MCl_2, MCl_3, and MCl_4	F Forms a colourless chloride
G A compound of M is a good catalyst	H Melting point 725 °C
I Density 0.97 g/cm³	J Compounds of M show no catalytic activity

   a. Which letters represent the properties of transition elements?

   .... [3]

   b. Write the formulae of the transition element ions in the following compounds.

   i. Ag_2O .... ii. $CuSO_4$ .... [1]

   iii. $Cr(NO_3)_3$ .... iv. $Fe_2(SO_4)_3$ .... [1]

   c. Give two other typical properties of transition elements which are not mentioned above.

   .... [2]

2. The bar charts show the melting point and densities of some metals in Period 3.

   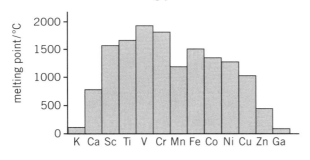
   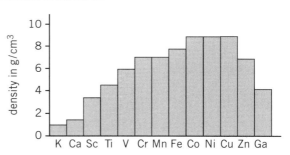

   a. What information in the bar charts suggests that calcium is not a transition element?

   .... [2]

   b. What is the pattern in the density of the metals across Period 3?

   .... [2]

Extension

3. Zinc is in the central block of the Periodic Table. Use textbooks and the internet to find out about the properties of zinc which suggest that it not a transition element.

   [4]

The behaviour of metals
13.1 Comparing metals and non-metals

1. a. The list below gives some properties of metals and non-metals. Underline the properties which are characteristic of **ALL** metals.

   brittle   conducts electricity   ductile   dull   high melting point
   high density   insulator   malleable   shiny   strong   [4]

   b. The table give some properties of diamond (carbon), sodium, and sulfur.

Diamond (carbon)	Sodium	Sulfur
melts above 3550 °C	melts at 98 °C	melts at 119 °C
does not conduct electricity	conducts electricity	does not conduct electricity
conducts heat quite well	conducts heat	does not conduct heat
shatters when hit	malleable	shatters when hit

   i. Give one way in which diamond behaves as a typical non-metal.
   .... [1]

   ii. Give one way in which diamond does not behave as a typical non-metal.
   .... [1]

   iii. Give one way in which sodium behaves as a typical metal.
   .... [1]

   iv. Give one way in which sodium does not behave as a typical metal.
   .... [1]

   v. Explain why sulfur is a typical non-metal.
   .... [1]

2. The table shows some properties of three metals.

Metal	Density in g/cm³	Melting point / °C	Electrical conductivity in Ω⁻¹m⁻¹	Relative strength
aluminium	2.70	660	0.41	7
copper	8.92	1038	0.54	13
iron	7.86	1535	0.11	21

   a. Which metal is best for making the body of an aircraft? Explain your answer.
   .... [2]

   b. Which metal is best for making a car body? Explain your answer.
   .... [2]

   c. Which metal is best for making electrical wiring? Explain your answer.
   .... [2]

3. Germanium, arsenic, and silicon are metalloids. Use books or the internet to write about the position of metalloids in the Periodic Table and their properties.   [6]

The behaviour of metals — 13.2 Comparing metals for reactivity

1. a. Complete these equations for the reactions of metals with water or steam.

   i. .... Na(s) + ... H_2O(l) → .... + ... [3]

   ii. .... Fe(s) + ... → Fe_3O_4(s) + ... [3]

   b. Complete these sentences about the reaction of metals with water.

   The products formed by metals which react with ....water, are a metal

   .... and .... The hydroxides are alkaline and so turn ....litmus

   .... The products formed by metals which only react with steam are a metal

   .... and .... Copper does not react with water because it is

   ....reactive than .... and cannot take the .... away from the

   hydrogen in the water. [10]

2. Some observations for the reaction of metals with water are given in the table.

Metal	Observations
barium	
calcium	Gives off bubbles rapidly with cold water, disappears quite quickly
lead	
magnesium	Gives a few bubbles with hot water, disappears slowly
zinc	Reacts when heated to red-heat with steam

   a. Put calcium, magnesium, and zinc, in order of their reactivity. Put the most reactive first.

   .... [1]

   b. Barium is more reactive than calcium and lead is less reactive than zinc.

   Write the observations for barium and lead in the table above. [3]

3. Put these metals in order of their reactivity using the information below.

Metal	Concentration of HCl(aq) in mol/dm³	Observations
iron	0.5	Slow bubbling
lead	6.0	Slow bubbling
lithium	0.5	Rapid stream of bubbles
magnesium	0.5	Steady stream of bubbles

   least reactive .... most reactive [1]

4. Write an ionic equation for the reaction of magnesium with hydrochloric acid.

   Split this equation into two half equations, one showing oxidation and the other reduction. [4]

The behaviour of metals — 13.3 Metals in competition

1. The diagram shows different metals placed in solutions of metal salts.

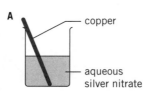
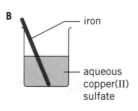
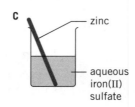
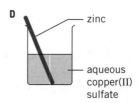

A: copper in aqueous silver nitrate
B: iron in aqueous copper(II) sulfate
C: zinc in aqueous iron(II) sulfate
D: zinc in aqueous copper(II) sulfate

Some of the results are shown in the table.

Experiment	Colour at the start	Colour after 20 minutes
A	metal: brown / solution: colourless	metal: silver-grey surface / solution: blue
B	metal: silvery grey / solution:	metal: .... / solution: ....
C	metal: grey / solution: light green	metal: .... / solution: colourless
D	metal: .... / solution:	metal: .... / solution: ....

[8]

a. Complete the table to show the colour changes.

b. Use the results to list the metals in order of their reactivity.

least reactive .... most reactive [1]

c. Explain why there would be no colour change when a copper rod is placed in aqueous zinc sulfate.

.... [1]

2. Identify the reducing agent and the oxidising agent in each of these equations.

a. $Fe(s) + CuO(s) \rightarrow FeO(s) + Cu(s)$

reducing agent .... oxidising agent .... [1]

b. $Fe_2O_3(s) + 3Mg(s) \rightarrow 2Fe(s) + 3MgO(s)$

reducing agent .... oxidising agent .... [1]

Extension

3. Split these equations into two half equations and identify the reducing agent.

a. $Zn(s) + CuSO_4(aq) \rightarrow ZnSO_4(aq) + Cu(s)$ [3]

b. $Mg(s) + Pb(NO_3)_2(aq) \rightarrow Pb(s) + Mg(NO_3)_2(aq)$ [3]

The behaviour of metals — 13.4 The reactivity series

1. Complete these sentences about the reactivity series using words from the list.

   carbon   electrons   exothermic   heated   less   more   positive   reduce   remove

   A ………………… reactive metal will ………………… the oxide of a ………………… reactive metal. This reaction is ………………… . The more reactive metal loses ………………… and forms ………………… ions more easily. Other reducing agents such as ………………… or hydrogen will ………………… oxygen from the oxide of a less reactive metal when ………………… . [9]

2. Part of the reactivity series is shown on the left but some of the metals are missing.

   a. Complete the table in the correct order of reactivity using the list of metals on the right

potassium	aluminium
…………………	
calcium	copper
…………………	
…………………	gold
carbon	
zinc	iron
…………………	
hydrogen	magnesium
…………………	
silver	sodium
…………………	

   [3]

   b. Which of these metals are extracted by electrolysis of their oxides and not by reduction with carbon? Explain your answer.

   ……
   …… [2]

3. Complete these equations for the reduction of some metal oxides to metals.

   a. Fe_2O_3 + …….CO → ………….. + …….CO_2 [2]

   b. ZnO + CO → ………….. + …………..   [1]

   c. ……..CuO + C → …….Cu + CO_2 [1]

4. Name the reducing agent in question 3.

   …… [1]

5. Explain why aluminium does not corrode easily although it is high in the reactivity series.

   ……
   …… [2]

The behaviour of metals — 13.5 The rusting of iron

1. a. State the name of two substances that are needed for iron to rust.

   .... and .... [2]

   b. The simplified formula of rust is $Fe_2O_3 \cdot 2H_2O$.

   Give the name of the compound $Fe_2O_3 \cdot 2H_2O$ .... [2]

2. a. Bicycle chains are oiled to prevent them rusting. Explain how oil prevents the chain from rusting.

   .... [2]

   b. Explain why oiling a bicycle chain will not prevent rusting completely.

   .... [2]

3. Complete these sentences about rusting using words from the list.

   corrodes   electrons   ions   iron   more   rusting   sacrificial   solution

   Blocks of zinc can be placed on the hull of a ship to stop it .... Zinc is ....

   reactive than .... so it loses .... and forms .... more

   easily than iron. The zinc ions go into .... and so the zinc .... instead of

   the iron. This is called .... protection. [8]

4. Suggest reasons for the following:

   a. The iron in a ship's hull rusts quicker than the same sort of iron on a bridge far from the sea.

   .... [2]

   b. An iron object in the desert rusts very slowly.

   .... [1]

5. Explain two ways in which galvanising with zinc prevents rusting.

   ....

   ....

   .... [4]

Extension

6. Blocks of magnesium can be placed on ships' hulls to prevent rusting. Explain using ideas about electron transfer why magnesium protects the hull from rusting. [4]

Extracting and using metals

14.1 Metal ores and metal extraction

1. The table shows the order of some metals in the reactivity series. It also shows the position of carbon.

Metal	Reactivity	Extracted by	Energy needed to extract the metal	Cost of extraction
lithium				
calcium				
cerium				
aluminium				
carbon				
zinc				
lead				
copper				
silver				
gold				

   a. Draw an arrow in the table to show the reactivity of the metals (least reactive → most reactive). [1]

   b. Complete the third column of the table to show which metals are extracted by heating their oxides with carbon and which are extracted by electrolysis. [2]

   c. i. In the fourth and fifth columns draw arrows to show the amount of energy needed to extract the metal (less energy → more energy) and the cost of extraction (lower cost → higher cost) [2]

      ii. Explain why there might be exceptions in the order in part c.i.

      .... [1]

   d. Which elements in the table can be found 'native' (not combined in compounds)?

      .... [1]

   e. Which elements could be extracted by reaction of their oxides with hydrogen?

      .... [1]

2. Manganese is extracted by reduction of manganese oxide with hot aluminium.
   Write a word equation for this reaction.

   .... [1]

3. Complete these equations for the reduction of some metal oxides.

   a. SnO_2 + ...C → .... + ... [2]

   b. ....NiO + CO + H_2 → .... + ... + H_2O [2]

   c. PbO + CO → .... + ... [2]

Extension

4. Write balanced equations for

   a. the reduction of chromium(III) oxide to chromium using aluminium [2]

   b. the reduction of iron(III) oxide with carbon monoxide to form iron. [2]

Extracting and using metals

14.2 Extracting iron

1. The diagram shows a blast furnace for the extraction of iron.

   On the diagram draw arrows and the following letters to show:

   A → where air is blown into the furnace

   B → where the iron ore is added to the furnace

   C → where the molten iron is removed

   D → where the slag is removed

   E → where waste gases exit the furnace [5]

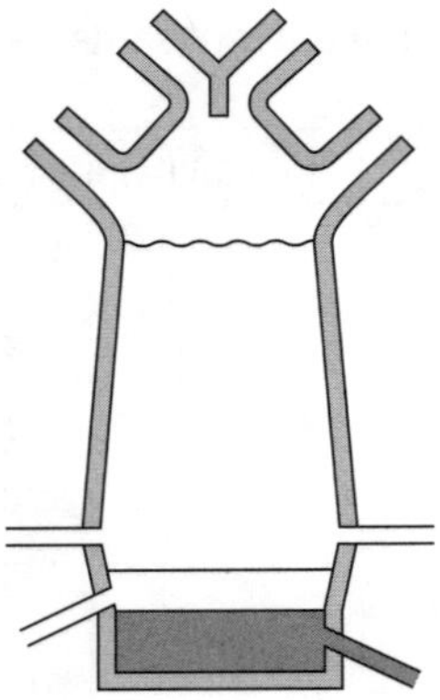

2. Iron(III) oxide is reduced in the furnace by carbon monoxide.

   What are the two stages in the formation of this carbon monoxide?

   ....

   .... [2]

3. The following phrases are about the purpose of the limestone added to the furnace but they are muddled up. Put these phrases in the correct order and then write them out in the correct order in the space below.

At the high temperatures in the furnace …	… silicon dioxide (sand) …	… which is an impurity in the ore.
The calcium oxide reacts with …	… and floats on top of the molten iron.	… to form calcium oxide.
… the limestone undergoes thermal decomposition …	… which runs down the furnace …	The calcium silicate formed is a slag …

   ....

   ....

   ....

   .... [3]

4. Complete this equation for the reduction of iron oxide to iron.

   $Fe_2O_3(s)$ + ... CO → .... + ... [2]

5. Use textbooks or the internet to find out three ways to make pure iron. [3]

Extracting and using metals

14.3 Extracting aluminium

1. The diagram shows an electrolysis cell used to extract aluminium from aluminium oxide.

   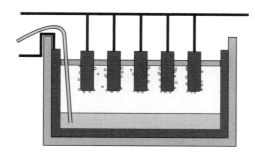

   On the diagram above, label the electrolyte as **E**, the cathode as **C**, the anode as **A**, and the molten aluminium as **M**. [4]

2. Complete these sentences about the electrolyte using words from the list. Not all the words are used.

calcite	cryolite	dissolved	energy	evaporated	high
low	melts	pressure	temperature	950	1500

   Aluminium oxide .... at a very high temperature. It would require too much

   .... to keep the aluminium oxide molten at this .... So the aluminium

   oxide is .... in molten .... and calcium fluoride. This lowers the

   operating temperature to about .... °C. The temperature is kept relatively

   .... by keeping the percentage of aluminium oxide in the mixture at 5%. [7]

3. a. Complete these equations for the reactions at the anode and cathode.

   i. Al^{3+} + ... → .... [2]

   ii. .... O^{2-} → .... + ... [2]

   b. Construct the overall equation for this electrolysis.

   .... [2]

4. Explain why the carbon anodes have to be renewed from time to time.

   ....

   .... [2]

Extension

5. The actual reaction at the cathode may involve two moles of Al_2O_3 splitting into an Al^{3+} ion and one other ion. The other ion then decomposes into Al_2O_3 and oxygen.

   Write equations for these reactions. [3]

Extracting and using metals

14.4 Making use of metals

1. Link the start of sentences **A** to **D** on the left with the endings **1** to **4** on the right.

   All the sentences are about the recycling of metals.

A Recycling reduces the amount of dust …	**1** … so there are fewer problems with disposal of unwanted materials.
B Recycling reduces the amount of carbon dioxide produced …	**2** … so that land can be used for other purposes such as agriculture.
C Recycling reduces the amount of waste …	**3** … from both mining and extracting the metal using carbon.
D Recycling reduces the need for mining ores …	**4** … caused by mining the ore.

   [2]

2. Complete the table about the uses and properties of different metals. (For tungsten and brass, think about the use and suggest properties which might be related to the use.)

Metal	Use	Properties that make it suitable for the use
aluminium	food containers	1. .... [1] 2. .... [1]
aluminium	overhead electrical cables	1. .... [1] 2. .... [1]
copper	electrical wiring	1. .... [1] 2. .... [1]
stainless steel	1. .... [1] 2. .... [1]	.... [1]
tungsten steel	for drilling other metals	1. .... [1] 2. .... [1]
brass	door handles	1. .... [1] 2. .... [1]

Extracting and using metals

14.5 Alloys

1. Link the metals **A** to **D** on the left with the phrases **1** to **4** on the right.

A aluminium aircraft alloy	1 a mixture of Cu and Zn
B brass	2 a mixture of Fe, C, and other elements
C chromium and nickel	3 these are found in stainless steel
D stainless steel	4 contains Al, Cu, and Mg

   [2]

2. Which one of the diagrams **A** to **D** best represents an alloy. .... [1]

   A   B   C   D

3. Complete the sentences about alloys using words from the list.

   alloyed   difference   force   harder   layers   mixtures   regular   prevents

   Alloys are .... of metals or mixtures of metals with non-metals. Alloys are often

   .... and stronger than pure metals. When a metal is .... with another

   metal, the .... in the size of the metal atoms makes the arrangement of the ....

   in the lattice less .... This .... the layers from sliding over each other as

   easily when a .... is applied. [8]

4. Complete the table about the uses and properties of different metals and alloys.

Alloy	Use	Properties which makes it suitable for the use
aluminium alloy	aircraft body	1. .... [1] 2. .... [1]
stainless steel	cutlery	1. .... [1] 2. .... [1]

5. Suggest why an alloy of tin and lead has lower melting point than either pure tin or pure lead.

   ....

   .... [2]

Chemistry of the environment

15.1 Our environment and us

1. Complete each of these paragraphs about air, water and soil using words from each list.

   a. digestive   gases   global   methane   oxygen   particulates   respiration   warming

   Air is a mixture of .... We need air in order to survive. We need the .... in the air for .... (the oxidation of food in the body). Polluted air may contain .... and harmful gases. Bacteria in the .... system of animals such as cows and sheep produce .... gas. Methane is a greenhouse gas which is responsible for increased .... [8]

   b. bacteria   body   chemicals   drinking   foods   pollutants   solvent

   About 50% of our .... is made up of water. Water acts as a .... for some of the .... in our body. It is also needed to transport digested .... and waste in the bloodstream. Our .... water must be free of harmful chemical .... and harmful .... [7]

   c. concentration   growth   harvested   lost   minerals   oxygen   rivers   soluble

   Crop plants need .... from the soil for healthy growth. Farmers put fertilisers on their fields to increase crop .... and to replace minerals that are .... from the soil when the crops are .... Many fertilisers are .... in water and can drain off the fields into .... and lakes when the ground is very wet. An increased .... of fertilisers in rivers and lakes causes a complex process called eutrophication to take place. This removes dissolved .... from the water and so aquatic life dies. [8]

2. Link the words **A** to **F** on the left with the phrases **1** to **6** on the right.

A	carbon dioxide	1 bacteria in their gut produce methane
B	farm animals	2 when dissolved, gets into rivers and indirectly causes death of water organisms
C	fertilisers	3 tiny particles which can cause cancer
D	particulates	4 contains harmful bacteria which can poison you if it gets into untreated water
E	toxic metals	5 gas responsible for increased global warming
F	sewage	6 present in factory waste and can poison you if they get into your body

[3]

Chemistry of the environment

15.2 What is in river water?

1. Link the words **A** to **F** on the left to their meanings **1** to **6** on the right.

A	deoxygenation	1	bacteria, viruses, and microscopic animals
B	heavy metals	2	removal of oxygen, especially from water or other liquids
C	microbes	3	elements such as mercury, lead, and copper which are poisonous
D	phosphates	4	waste solid and liquids produced by humans
E	sewage	5	poisonous
F	toxic	6	compounds found in most fertilisers which containing phosphorus

   [3]

2. Complete these sentences about plastic pollution in water using words from the list.

   fish   liver   microplastics   rivers   small   trap

   Plastics can get into the oceans from ships, coastal towns, and by transport in ……………………… from inland. Plastic fishing nets can ……………………… or kill ……………………… and other sea creatures. Very small particle of plastics called ……………………… have been found in drinking water. These particles are so ……………………… that they can get into our bloodstream and then to organs such as the ……………………… and kidneys, where they may cause harm.

   [6]

3. Link the start of these sentences about water pollutants **A** to **D** to their effects **1** to **4**.

A	Heavy metals …	1	… are generally unreactive but can harm aquatic life.
B	Nitrates …	2	… contains harmful microbes which cause disease.
C	Plastics …	3	… cause the deoxygenation of water by the process of eutrophication.
D	Sewage …	4	… such as mercury are toxic.

   [2]

Chemistry of the environment

15.3 Our water supply

1. Complete these sentences about water treatment using words from the list.

   | bacteria | branches | filter | harmful | insoluble | plant | settle | smells |

   In a water treatment ...., large objects such as plant .... are first trapped by metal screens. Other solid particles are then left to .... to the bottom of the tank. The water is then passed through a .... made of sand or gravel. This removes small .... particles. Carbon is added to remove bad .... Chlorine is then added to the water to kill .... which may be .... to health. [8]

2. Water from natural sources contains oxygen and mineral salts. State the beneficial effects of these substances.

   Oxygen ....

   Mineral salts .... [2]

3. The table shows the concentration in mg / dm³ of some ions present in water from three different sources.

Ion	Seawater	Rainwater	River water
Na^+	10 000	9	11
Ca^{2+}	900	2	1
K^+	1 000	1	4
SiO_3^{2-}	500	0.5	7
Cl^-	17 000	16	12
HCO_3^-	700	3	2
NO_3^-	trace	0.01	3

   a. Which positive ion in seawater in the table is present at the lowest concentration?

   .... [1]

   b. What are the major differences between rainwater and river water in terms of the concentration of the ions present?

   ....
   ....
   .... [3]

   c. Calculate the mass of chloride ions in 200 cm³ of the river water.

   Mass = ... mg [1]

Extension

4. Use textbooks or the internet to find out why some samples of water are described as 'hard' and how sodium carbonate is used to treat hard water. [4]

78

Chemistry of the environment

15.4 Fertilisers

1. Complete these sentences about fertilizers using words from the list.

   fertilisers   nitrates   nutrients   phosphates   phosphorus   proteins   salts

   For healthy growth crop plants need three major elements, nitrogen, ... and potassium.

   Plants take up these elements in the form of nitrates, ... , and potassium ....

   The .... are needed to make .... for growth. Farmers add ....

   to the soil to add back the .... which plants have absorbed for growth. [7]

2. A flow chart for making fertilisers is shown below.

   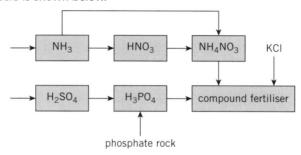

   a. Name the compounds in the diagram:

   NH_3 .... HNO_3 ....

   NH_4NO_3 .... H_2SO_4 ....

   H_3PO_4 .... KCl .... [6]

   b. Write a word equation for the reaction between NH_3 and HNO_3.

   .... [1]

   c. Name a suitable acid and base for making these fertilisers.

   i. Ammonium sulfate .... [2]

   ii. Potassium chloride .... [2]

   iii. Sodium phosphate .... [2]

   d. Name the three raw materials used to make NH_3.

   .... [3]

> **Extension**
>
> 3. Use textbooks or the internet to write about the process of eutrophication which happens as a result of nitrate and phosphate fertilisers getting into rivers. [5]

Chemistry of the environment

15.5 Air, the gas mixture we live in

1. The table shows the percentage of some of the gases in dry air in 1985 and 2015.

Gas	% by volume in 1985	% by volume in 2015
nitrogen	78.082	78.081
oxygen	20.950	20.946
carbon dioxide	0.034	0.0397
neon	0.0018	0.0018
helium	0.000524	0.000524
methane	0.00014	0.000179

   a. Which two gases have shown the largest percentage change since 1985?

   .... and .... [1]

   b. Which gas present in the air at about 1% by volume is not shown in the table?

   .... [1]

   c. What other substance is present in the air in vapour form in variable amounts?

   .... [1]

2. The apparatus shown was used to deduce the % of oxygen in the air.

   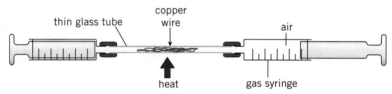

   80 cm³ of air was drawn into the gas syringe on the right. The air was then passed over the heated copper until there was no further decrease in volume. The final volume of air measured immediately in the gas syringe on the right was 62.9 cm³.

   a. What volume of oxygen had reacted? .... [1]

   b. Calculate the % of oxygen in this sample of air. Show your working.

   % O₂ in the air = ...% [1]

   c. How does this volume compare with the volume in the table? Give a reason for your answer based on your knowledge of the behaviour of gases.

   ....

   ....

   .... [3]

Extension

3. Oxygen is involved in combustion reactions. Oxides are formed as products. Write a balanced equation for the complete combustion of ethane, C_2H_6. [2]

Chemistry of the environment

15.6 Air pollution from fossil fuels

1. a. Complete these sentences about the sources of carbon monoxide and sulfur dioxide in the atmosphere using words from the list below. Not all the words are used.

    burn   carbon   excess   fossil   gaseous   limited   oxygen   sulfur

    Carbon monoxide is formed when ………………… compounds ………………… in a ………………… supply of air. Sulfur dioxide is formed when ………………… fuels containing ………………… burn in air. [5]

    b. Name a natural source of **i.** nitrogen oxides **ii.** sulfur dioxide in the atmosphere.

    i. ………………………………………………   ii. ……………………………………………… [2]

2. Give one harmful effect of

    a. an aqueous solution of sulfur dioxide on buildings made of limestone

    ……… [1]

    b. nitrogen dioxide on humans ……………………………………………………………………………… [1]

    c. carbon monoxide on humans ……………………………………………………………………………… [1]

3. Link the words **A** to **D** on the left with the phrases **1** to **4** on the right.

A methane	1 responsible for increased global warming
B particulates	2 a smoky fog
C photochemical	3 tiny particles which can cause cancer
D smog	4 reaction which involves light

    [2]

4. Explain how acid rain is formed as a result of burning fuels containing sulfur compounds.

    ………

    ……… [4]

5. a. Explain the function of a catalytic converter attached to a car exhaust.

    ………

    ……… [3]

    b. Write a balanced equation for the reaction of NO_2 with carbon monoxide in a catalytic converter.

    ……… [2]

Extension

6. Use textbooks or the internet to find out about the formation of photochemical smog. [4]

Chemistry of the environment

15.7 Two greenhouse gases

1. Complete these sentences about methane using words from the list

   absorbs   atmosphere   bacterial   digestion   vegetation

   Methane is a greenhouse gas which is formed by the .... decomposition of .... and as a waste product of .... in animals. It is present in the .... at a lower concentration than carbon dioxide but it .... much more thermal energy per mole. [5]

2. The graphs show the concentration of carbon dioxide in the atmosphere and the estimated global mean temperature over a period of 120 years.

   a. Carbon dioxide is a greenhouse gas. What is the meaning of the term *greenhouse gas*?

   ....

   .... [2]

   b. How does the information from the graphs support the idea that carbon dioxide is a greenhouse gas?

   ....

   .... [2]

   c. i. State two sources of carbon dioxide in the atmosphere apart from combustion of fossil fuels.

   ....

   .... [2]

   ii. Give two sources of methane in the atmosphere apart from animal digestion and bacterial decomposition.

   ....

   .... [2]

3. The absorption of energy by greenhouse gases leads to global warming.
   Give three effects of global warming.

   ....

   ....

   .... [2]

Chemistry of the environment

15.8 Tackling climate change

1. Link the words **A** to **D** on the left to their meanings **1** to **4** on the right.

A desulfurisation	1 farm animals
B flue gas	2 examples are solar power and wind power
C livestock	3 removal of sulfur from a fuel
D renewable energy	4 SO_2 and other gases produced by burning fuels in furnaces

   [2]

2. Explain why catalytic converters reduce pollution but do not help very much in tackling climate change.

   ....

   .... [3]

3. Explain, by referring to photosynthesis, why planting more trees can help reduce the effects of climate change.

   ....

   .... [3]

4. Complete these sentences about flue gas desulfurisation using words from the list.

         carbonate   combustion   fuels   neutralise   sulfite   sulfur   waste

   Flue gas desulfurisation is the process of removing .... dioxide from the gases

   formed during the .... of fossil .... in furnaces. The ....

   gases are passed through moist calcium .... or calcium oxide. These compounds

   .... the acidic sulfur dioxide. Solid calcium .... is formed. [7]

5. **a.** State the meaning of the term *climate change* and explain why it is important to reduce its effects.

   ....

   .... [3]

   b. State two forms of renewable energy and explain the importance of renewable energy in reducing the effects of climate change.

   ....

   .... [3]

Extension

6. One suggestion for 'capturing' the carbon dioxide given off by industry is to use the reaction:

   $$K_2CO_3(aq) + H_2O(l) + CO_2(g) \rightleftharpoons 2KHCO_3(aq)$$

   Suggest how this reaction could be used to store carbon so that it does not escape into the atmosphere. [4]

Organic chemistry

16.1 Petroleum: a fossil fuel

1. Petroleum is a fossil fuel. Name two other fossil fuels.

   .... [2]

2. The full structural displayed formulae of some organic compounds are shown below.

   A

   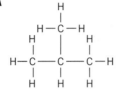

   B

   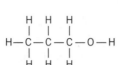

   C

   D

   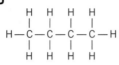

   E

   F

   a. Which of these compounds are hydrocarbons? Explain why.

      ....

      .... [2]

   b. Which of these compounds are most likely to be found in petroleum?

      .... [2]

   c. i. Which one of these compounds is a branched-chain compound? .... [1]

      ii. Which one of these compounds is a ring compound? .... [1]

   d. The molecular formula of compound **A** is C_4H_{10}.
      Deduce the molecular formulae of compounds **B** to **F**.

      B .... **C** ....

      D .... **E** ....

      F .... [5]

3. Petrol can be made from coal using the following route:

   | A coal | → | B decomposition using heat and hydrogen | → | C refining based on boiling point | → | D petrol |

   a. Which stage, **A**, **B**, **C**, or **D** involves distillation? .... [1]

   b. Which stage involves reduction? .... [1]

Extension

4. Petroleum contains a number of aromatic hydrocarbons. Use textbooks or the internet to describe the main features of aromatic hydrocarbons. Give the name of two aromatic hydrocarbons. [4]

Organic chemistry
16.2 Refining petroleum

1. Complete these sentences about the distillation of petroleum using words from the list.

   boiling   bottom   condense   further   higher   lower   temperatures   top

   There is a range of .... in the distillation column, hot at the .... and cooler at the .... Hydrocarbons with .... boiling points move .... up the column and .... when the temperature in the column falls just below the .... point of the hydrocarbons. Hydrocarbons with .... boiling points condense lower down the column. [8]

2. Link the petroleum fractions **A** to **D** on the left with their uses **1** to **4** on the right.

A bitumen		1 making chemicals
B fuel oil		2 jet fuel
C kerosene		3 fuel for home heating and ships
D naphtha		4 making road surfaces

   [2]

3. The table shows some properties of the different fractions.

Fraction	Boiling point range / °C	Size of molecules	Volatility	Viscosity	Ease of burning
1	up to 100				
2	100–150				
3	150–200				
4	200–300				

   a. In the third column draw an arrow to show how the size of the molecules varies with the boiling point range (low → high). [1]

   b. i. Some compounds are volatile. What is the meaning of the term *volatile*?

   .... [1]

   ii. In the fourth column draw an arrow to show how the volatility of the compounds varies with the boiling point range (low → high). [1]

   c. In the fifth column draw an arrow to show how the viscosity (ease of flow) of the compounds varies with the boiling point range (flows easily → flows less easily). [1]

   d. In the sixth column draw an arrow to show how the ease of burning of the compounds varies with the boiling point range (difficult → easy). [1]

> **Extension**
>
> 4. Use ideas of molecular size and intermolecular forces to explain how fractional distillation separates a mixture of compounds into different fractions. [5]

Organic chemistry

16.3 Four families of organic compounds

1. a. What is meant by the term homologous series?

   .... [2]

   b. State 3 other properties of a homologous series which you have not given in your answer to part **1.a.**

   ....

   ....

   .... [3]

2. Complete the table to show the molecular, structural and displayed formulae.

Name of compound	Molecular formula	Structural formula	Displayed formula
methane			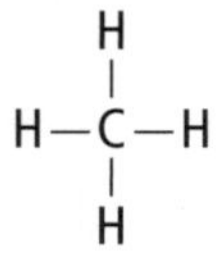 H–C–H (with H above and below)
propane	C_3H_8	$CH_3CH_2CH_3$	
propanol		$CH_3CH_2CH_2OH$	
ethanoic acid			
butene		$CH_3CH=CHCH_3$	

[10]

Extension

3. Write general formulae for the alkenes, alcohols, and a compound in the homologous series which includes $CH_3CH_2NH_2$ and $CH_3CH_2CH_2CH_2NH_2$ [3]

Organic chemistry — 16.4 The alkanes

1. Complete these sentences about alkanes.

   a. Alkanes are ………………………… because they only have hydrogen and carbon atoms in their structure. [1]

   b. All the bonds in alkanes are ………………… ………………… bonds. [2]

   c. Alkanes do not decolourise aqueous bromine. This shows that they are ………………… hydrocarbons. [1]

   d. Alkanes are generally unreactive except for ………………… and reaction with ………………… . [2]

2. Name the alkanes with unbranched chains of:

   a. five carbon atoms ………………… [1]

   b. four carbon atoms ………………… [1]

   c. eight carbon atoms ………………… [1]

3. How do the boiling points of the alkanes change with relative molecular mass?

   ………………… [1]

4. Complete these equations for the typical reactions of alkanes.

   a. C_5H_{12} + …… O_2 → …… CO_2 + …… H_2O [2]

   b. CH_4 + Cl_2 → ………… + HCl [1]

5. Which two words describe the reaction in **4.b**. Put rings around the correct answers.

   addition   cracking   neutralisation   photochemical   polymerisation   substitution

   [2]

6. a. Define the term structural isomers.

   ………………… [1]

   b. Draw two structural isomers of the hydrocarbon with the formula C_5H_{12}. [2]

Extension

   c. Draw all the structural isomers of the hydrocarbon with the formula C_6H_{14}. [3]

Organic chemistry — 16.5 Cracking alkanes

1. The bar chart shows the supply and demand for different petroleum fractions.

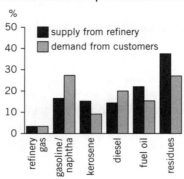

   a. Which of the fractions shown has molecules with the longest chains?

   .... [1]

   b. i. For which fractions is the demand much greater than the supply?

   .... [1]

   ii. For which fractions is the supply much greater than the demand?

   .... [1]

2. The diagram below shows the apparatus used to crack paraffin in the laboratory.

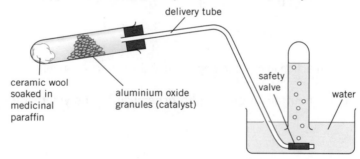

   a. Put the letter P on the diagram to show where the gaseous product is collected. [1]

   b. On the diagram, draw two arrows to show where the apparatus should be heated. [2]

   c. Suggest why the test tube placed at an angle.

   ....
   .... [2]

3. Complete these equations for cracking.

   a. $C_{10}H_{22} \rightarrow C_4H_{10} +$ .... [1]

   b. $C_{14}H_{30} \rightarrow C_3H_8 + C_4H_8 +$ .... [1]

Extension

4. Explain why it is less likely that oil companies will crack fractions containing hydrocarbons with the formulae C_8H_{18} and $C_{33}H_{68}$ than other fractions. [4]

88

Organic chemistry

16.6 The alkenes

1. a. The table gives some information about the alkenes. Complete the table in the spaces provided.

Name of alkene	Molecular formula	Boiling point / °C
ethene		−102
	C_3H_6	
		−7
pentene		30
hexene	C_6H_{12}	

[7]

   b. Which of the alkenes in the table are likely to be liquids at r.t.p.?

   .... [1]

2. The structure of compound **T** is shown below.

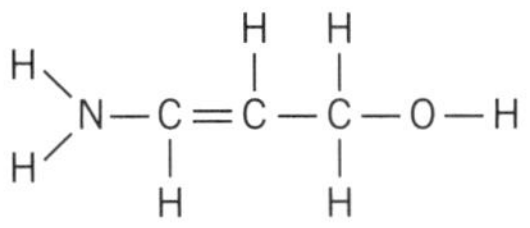

   $$\begin{array}{c} H \\ \diagdown \\ N-C=C-C-O-H \\ \diagup | | | \\ H H H \end{array}$$

   a. On the structure of **T** above draw a ring around the functional group which makes this compound unsaturated. [1]

   b. An excess of compound **A** is added to a few drops of aqueous bromine in a test tube. Predict the colour change of the mixture in the test tube.

      From .... to .... [2]

3. a. Complete the boxes in the diagram to show the structure of **A** and formula of the additional reagent **B** including the state symbol. [2]

   b. State the particular reaction conditions.

      .... [3]

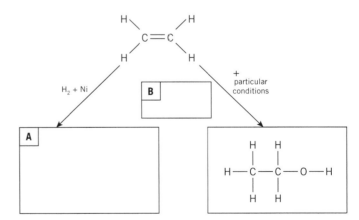

4. Draw three isomers of the compound with the molecular formula C_4H_8. [3]

Organic chemistry — 16.7 The alcohols

1. **a.** Ethanol can be manufactured by fermentation or by hydration of ethene.

   Complete the table about these reactions.

	Fermentation	Hydration of ethene
Reagents needed		
Temperature / °C		
Pressure		
Catalyst		

   [8]

   b. Give two disadvantages of producing ethanol by fermentation.

   ....

   .... [2]

   c. Give two advantages of producing ethanol by fermentation.

   ....

   .... [2]

   d. Give two advantages of producing ethanol by hydration of ethene.

   ....

   .... [2]

2. **a.** Complete the equation for the complete combustion of butanol.

   $$C_4H_9OH \;+\; \ldots\ldots O_2 \;\rightarrow\; \ldots\ldots CO_2 \;+\; \ldots\ldots H_2O$$ [2]

   b. Draw and label a diagram of the apparatus you could use to compare the energy released by burning different alcohols. [5]

Extension

3. Calculate the mass of water formed when 9.2 g of ethanol burns in excess air.

   $$C_2H_5OH \;+\; 3O_2 \;\rightarrow\; 2CO_2 \;+\; 3H_2O \quad (A_r \text{ values } H = 1, C = 12, O = 16)$$ [4]

Organic chemistry   16.8 The carboxylic acids

1. Ethanoic acid dissolves in water.

$$CH_3COOH + H_2O \rightleftharpoons CH_3COO^- + H_3O^+$$

   a. How does this equation show that ethanoic acid is a weak acid?

   ....

   .... [2]

   b. Explain why water is acting as a base in the forward reaction.

   .... [2]

2. Complete these equations for some reactions of ethanoic acid.

   a. ......CH_3COOH + ...Na → .... + ... [3]

   b. ......CH_3COOH + Mg → .... + ... [3]

   c. CH_3COOH + NaOH → .... + ... [2]

   d. .... + ... → CH_3COOCH_3 + ... [3]

3. Link the names of the esters **A** to **D** on the left to their formulae **1** to **4** on the right.

A butyl ethanoate	1 $HCOOCH_3$
B ethyl propanoate	2 $CH_3COOCH_2CH_2CH_3$
C methyl methanoate	3 $CH_3COOCH_2CH_2CH_2CH_3$
D propyl ethanoate	4 $CH_3CH_2COOCH_2CH_3$

[2]

4. Draw the displayed formulae of these esters. [2]

a. Ethyl butanoate	b. propyl methanoate

5. Name these esters:

   a. $HCOOC_4H_9$ ....   b. $C_2H_5COOC_3H_7$ .... [2]

Polymers

17.1 Introducing polymers

1. Complete the following sentences about polymers using words from the list.

   | addition | bonds | ethene | join | molecules | monomers | other | polymerisation |

   A polymer is a substance which has very large .... formed when lots of

   small molecules called .... join together. This process is called

   .... When poly(ethene) is formed, one of the C=C .... of

   .... is broken and the monomers .... together in a chain. A reaction

   where two or more molecules join and no .... molecule is formed is called an

   .... reaction. [8]

2. In the box below draw a section of the polymer chain formed by the addition of four units of ethene monomers.

   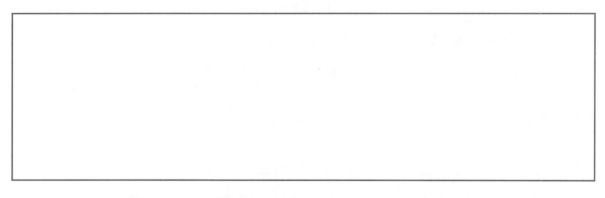

   [2]

3. The diagram below shows two types of poly(ethene). The zig-zag lines are the chains of the polymers.

   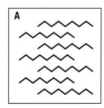 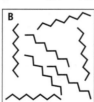

   Which polymer, **A** or **B**, has the lower density? Explain your answer.

   ....

   .... [2]

4. 56 kg of ethene was converted to poly(ethene). Each chain of poly(ethene) contains an average of 20 000 carbon atoms. Calculate the approximate number of moles of poly(ethene) formed.
   (A_r values H = 1, C = 12) [4]

Polymers

17.2 Addition polymerisation

1. The diagram shows an addition polymer.

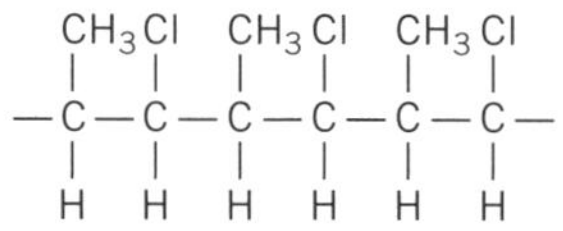

    ```
        CH₃ Cl   CH₃ Cl   CH₃ Cl
         |   |    |   |    |   |
      — C — C  — C — C  — C — C —
         |   |    |   |    |   |
         H   H    H   H    H   H
    ```

   a. Draw brackets round the repeat unit of this polymer. [1]

   b. The structure of a monomer is shown below.

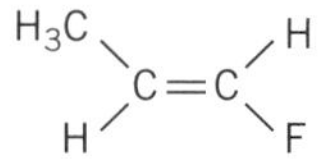

   ```
      H₃C         H
         \\     /
          C = C
         /     \\
        H       F
   ```

   Draw a section of the polymer chain formed from this monomer. Show three repeat units.

   [3]

   c. Draw the structure of the polymer formed from but-2-ene, $CH_3–CH=CH–CH_3$, as one repeat unit of this polymer with brackets and n.

   [3]

2. Draw the monomers of polymers **A** and **B**.

   ```
   A    C₆H₅ H   C₆H₅ H   C₆H₅ H   C₆H₅
         |   |    |   |    |   |    |
      — C — C  — C — C  — C — C  — C —
         |   |    |   |    |   |    |
         H   H    H   H    H   H    H
              Monomer A
   ```

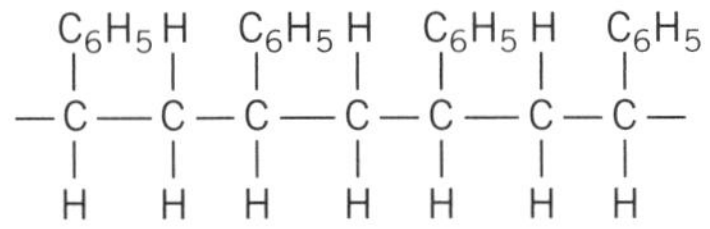

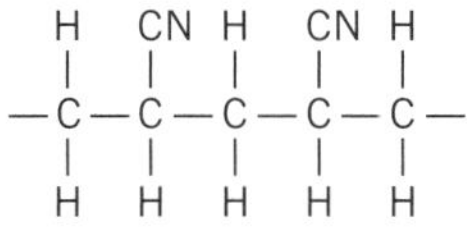

   ```
   B    H  CN   H  CN   H
        |   |   |   |   |
     — C — C — C — C — C —
        |   |   |   |   |
        H   H   H   H   H
              Monomer B
   ```

   [4]

3. Write the equation for the formation of the polymer of ethyl ethenoate, $CH_2=CH(OOCCH_3)$. Show one unit of the polymer with brackets and n.
   Hint: you first have to work out the full structure of the ethyl ethenoate. [3]

Polymers

17.3 Condensation polymerisation

1. Complete these sentences about condensation polymerisation using word from the list.

   chloride   eliminated   functional   small   water

   In condensation polymerisation, molecules with different .... groups react together. A .... molecule such as .... or hydrogen ....

   is .... [5]

2. The diagram shows two polymers **A** and **B**.

   A

   B

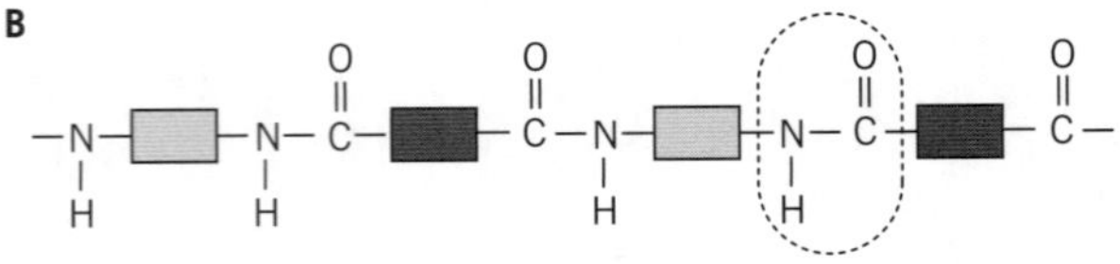

   a. On each of the diagrams above put brackets to show one repeat unit. [2]

   b. Give the name of the linking group in

      i. Polymer **A** ....   ii. Polymer **B** .... [2]

3. The structure of poly(lactic acid) is shown below.

   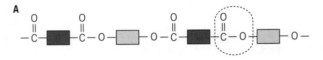

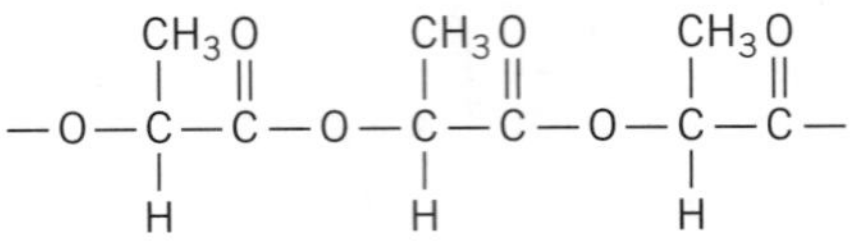

   a. Give the names of the two functional groups that react to form this polymer.

   .... and .... [2]

   b. Draw the structure of the single monomer that is used to form this polymer.

   [2]

   4. Deduce the structure of one repeat unit of the polymer formed from these two monomers:
   HOOC–(CH$_2$)$_3$–COOH and H$_2$N–(CH$_2$)$_6$–NH$_2$ [2]

Polymers

17.4 Plastics

1. **a.** Link the properties of plastics **A** to **E** on the left with the uses **1** to **5** on the right.

A Most plastics don't conduct electricity ...	**1** ... so they can be used for food containers.
B Plastics do not react with acids ...	**2** ... so they can be used as insulators.
C Plastics have a low density ...	**3** ... so they can be used to make bags.
D Plastics are flexible ...	**4** ... so they can be used to make climbing ropes.
E Many plastics are strong ...	**5** ... so they can be used to make storage boxes.

   [3]

   b. Give one use for each of these polymers.

      i. Nylon .... [1]

      ii. Poly(ethene) .... [1]

2. Suggest which properties of plastics are suitable for:

   a. a drinks bottle ....

   .... [3]

   b. a fishing line ....

   .... [3]

3. The strength of a plastic depends on the strength of the intermolecular forces between the chains and how tangled (muddled up) the chains become.

   The graph shows how the strength of a plastic depends on the length of the polymer chains.

   Suggest reasons for the shape of this graph.

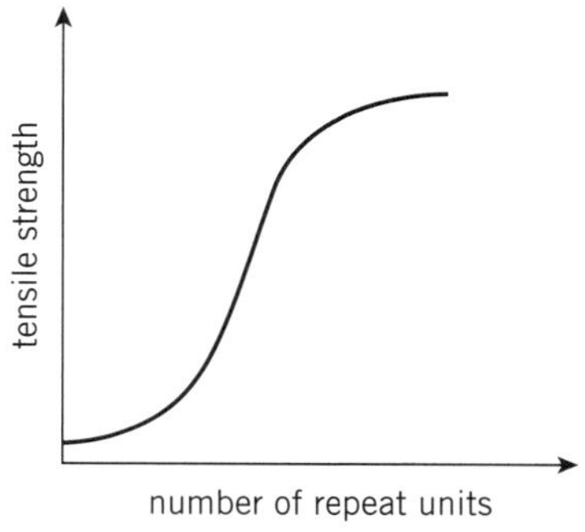

   ....

   ....

   ....

   ....

   .... [2]

   (graph: tensile strength vs number of repeat units, S-shaped curve)

4. **Extension** Use textbooks or the internet to find out the difference between thermoplastics and thermoset plastics in terms of structure and use. [6]

95

Polymers

17.5 The plastics problem

1. Many plastics are non-biodegradable.

   What is meant by the term non-biodegradable?

   .... [2]

2. We can get rid of waste plastics by recycling, through landfill sites, or by burning them.

   a. State two harmful effects of waste plastic in the environment other than problems associated with landfill sites or burning.

   ....

   .... [2]

   b. State two advantages of recycling plastics.

   ....

   .... [2]

   c. State two disadvantages of putting plastics in landfill sites.

   ....

   .... [2]

   d. State one possible advantage of burning plastics.

   ....

   .... [1]

3. a. Suggest pollution problems other than global warming that might arise when the following plastics are burned.

   i. A plastic with the structure $- CH_2 - CHCl - CH_2 - CHCl -$

   .... [1]

   ii. A synthetic rubber containing sulfur atoms.

   .... [1]

   b. i. What substances are formed when poly(ethene) is burned in excess air.

   .... and .... [1]

   ii. Polyethene usually burns with a black-edged flame. Explain why.

   .... [2]

Extension

4. Use textbooks or the internet to find out why plasticisers are added to plastics, how they work, and what problems might be associated with them. [5]

Polymers

17.6 Tackling the plastics problem

1. Complete these sentences about the disposal of plastics by burning. Use words from the list.

   air   combusted   dioxide   electricity   gas   homes   thermal   toxic   trap

   When plastics are burned in ...., they release energy. The .... energy released can be used to heat .... or to make steam to generate .... When completely ...., plastics release carbon .... which is a greenhouse .... Many plastics also release .... gases when burned. Methods are now being developed to .... these gases so they do not get into the atmosphere. [9]

2. State four other ways by which we can reduce plastic waste.

   ....
   ....
   ....
   .... [4]

3. a. The plastic, PET, can be recycled. Put these statements about the recycling of bottles made of PET into the correct order.

   A The cut-up pieces are melted
   B The pellets are melted
   C The bottles are cleaned
   D The melted pellets are moulded into more bottles or made into fibres
   E Molten PET is made into small pellets
   F The bottles are cut up

   The order is .... [2]

   b. The PET polymer can also be hydrolysed to its monomers. The monomers are then repolymerised to make food containers.

   State the meaning of the terms:

   i. polymer ....
       .... [2]

   ii. hydrolysed ....
       .... [2]

   iii. monomer ....
       .... [1]

Polymers

17.7 Proteins

1. Complete these sentences about amino acids and proteins using words from the list.

   amine   condensation   nitrogen   oxygen   sulfur   twenty

   All amino acids contain carbon, hydrogen, ..., and .... Two

   simple amino acids found in proteins contain .... as well. Proteins are

   .... polymers formed by the reaction of carboxylic acid and ....

   groups from amino acids. Most proteins are formed by the polymerisation of about ....

   amino acids. [6]

2. The diagram below shows part of a protein.

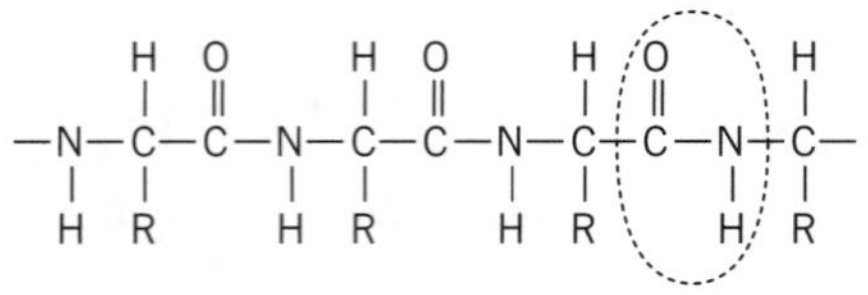

   a. On the diagram above, put brackets to show one repeat unit. [1]

   b. Give the name of the linking group. .... [1]

3. The structure of part of poly(glycine) is shown below.

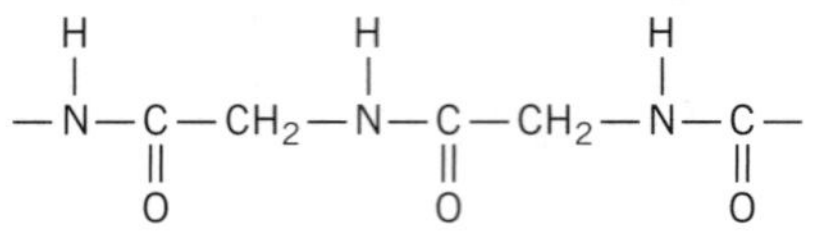

   Deduce the structure of the monomer which is used to form this polymer.

   [2]

Extension

The general structure of an amino acid is shown on the right. Draw diagrams to show the two possible compounds obtained when the amino acid cysteine reacts with the amino acid, alanine. The R– group of cysteine is –CH_2SH. The R group of alanine is –CH_3. [3]

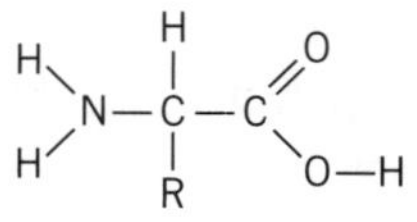

Separation and purification

18.1 Making a substance in the lab

1. The diagram shows four pieces of laboratory glassware.

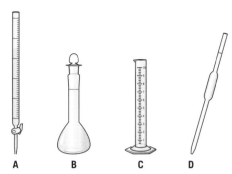

a. Name each of these pieces of glassware.

A .... B ....

C .... D .... [4]

b. Give the name of the piece of glassware you would use to do the following.

i. Make up a solution of sodium hydroxide accurately, ... [1]

ii. Deliver 25.0 cm³ of hydrochloric acid. .... [1]

2. The diagram on the right shows part of a burette.
Where should you position your eye (direction **A**,
B, **C**, or **D**) to get a precise reading?
Ring the correct answer.

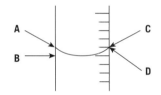

[1]

3. Describe how to prepare crystals of hydrated zinc sulfate from zinc oxide and dilute sulfuric acid.

....

....

....

....

.... [6]

Extension

4. A measuring cylinder, a burette, and a volumetric pipette are pieces of glassware. Give a use for each of these when carrying out chemical experiments. In each case explain your answer. [6]

Separation and purification

18.2 Solutions and solubility

1. a. Solid iodine dissolves in liquid carbon tetrachloride. A violet-coloured liquid is formed.

Identify the solvent, solute, and solution.

solvent .... solute ....

solution .... [3]

b. Carbon tetrachloride is a volatile liquid. What is the meaning of the term *volatile*?

.... [1]

2. a. The solubilities of some compounds are shown in the table.

Compound	Solubility g / 100 cm³ water	Compound	Solubility g / 100 cm³ water
calcium hydroxide	0.113	potassium nitrate	37.9
calcium nitrate	102.1	silver chloride	0.0002
iron(II) hydroxide	0.00003	silver nitrate	241.3

i. What type of metal compound is very soluble in water?

.... [1]

ii. Which compounds are insoluble in water?

.... [2]

iii. Which compound is sparingly soluble? .... [1]

b. The graph shows the solubility of two compounds at different temperatures.

i. Deduce the solubility of potassium nitrate at 70 °C.

.... [1]

ii. Which compound is most soluble in water at 10 °C?

.... [1]

iii. Deduce the maximum mass of potassium nitrate that dissolves in 100 cm³ of water at 60 °C.

.... [1]

iv. At what temperature is the solubility of potassium nitrate and potassium chloride the same?

.... [1]

Extension

v. A saturated solution of potassium nitrate in 200 g of water is cooled from 80 °C to 20 °C. What mass of solute crystallises? Show your working. [4]

vi. What is the minimum volume of water needed to dissolve 50 g of potassium nitrate at 90 °C? Show all your working. [2]

100

Separation and purification
18.3 Separating a solid from a liquid

1. Define these terms:

   a. filtrate .... [1]

   b. residue ....

   .... [2]

   c. saturated solution ....

   .... [2]

2. a. i. Complete the diagram by writing the correct labels on the dotted lines. [3]

   ii. On the diagram label the residue and the filtrate. [2]

   b. i. Put these statements about the crystallisation of zinc sulfate in the correct order.

   A   Filter off the crystals
   B   Heat the solution to concentrate it
   C   Dry the crystals with filter paper
   D   Wash the crystals with a small amount of distilled water
   E   Leave the solution to cool a form crystals
   F   By seeing if crystals form on a cold surface
   G   Check that a saturated solution has formed

   Order .... [2]

   ii. Why should you only use a small amount of cold distilled water to wash the crystals?

   .... [1]

3. Calcium carbonate is insoluble in water. Calcium sulfate is soluble in water.

   Describe how you could separate a mixture of powdered calcium carbonate and powdered calcium sulfate to obtain a sample of each pure solid.

   ....

   ....

   ....

   .... [4]

4. Use books or the internet to describe the process of fractional crystallisation. [5]

Separation and purification
18.4 Separating by distillation

1. a. i. Label the diagram of the distillation apparatus to show the distillation flask, the distillate, the condenser, and where cold water enters.

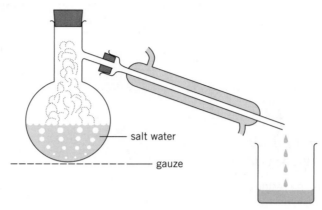

[4]

   ii. On the diagram above, draw an arrow to show where heat is applied. [1]

   b. i. Explain why this method can be used to separate salt from salty water.

   .... [1]

   ii. Explain why this method cannot be easily used to separate two liquids which have similar boiling points.

   .... [1]

2. Complete the following sentences about fractional distillation of alcohols using words from the list.

   boiling   condenser   further   higher   liquid

   lower   receiver   temperatures   vaporised   volatile

   There is a range of .... in the distillation column, ... at the top and .... at the bottom. When .... the more .... alcohols move .... up the column than the less volatile alcohols. When the alcohol reaches the .... it changes from vapour to .... The alcohols are collected one by one in the .... , those with the lower .... points condensing before those with higher ones. [10]

3. Use books or the internet to find out the following about steam distillation.

   a. Give two examples of the use of steam distillation. [2]

   b. Explain why steam distillation is used and not simple distillation. [1]

   c. Describe how steam distillation is carried out. [3]

Separation and purification

18.5 Paper chromatography (part I)

1. Complete the following sentences about chromatography using words from the list.

   attraction   filter   locating   mixture   separate   solubilities   spraying

   The method of separating a .... of coloured substances using ....

   paper is called chromatography. The colours .... if they have different

   .... in the solvent and different degrees of .... for

   the filter paper. Chromatography can also be used to separate colourless substances. These are shown

   up after chromatography by .... the paper with a ....

   agent. [7]

2. Paper chromatography can be used to separate a mixture of dyes.
   Complete the diagram below to show the apparatus set up for chromatography.
   Show the position of the baseline.
   Label your diagram.

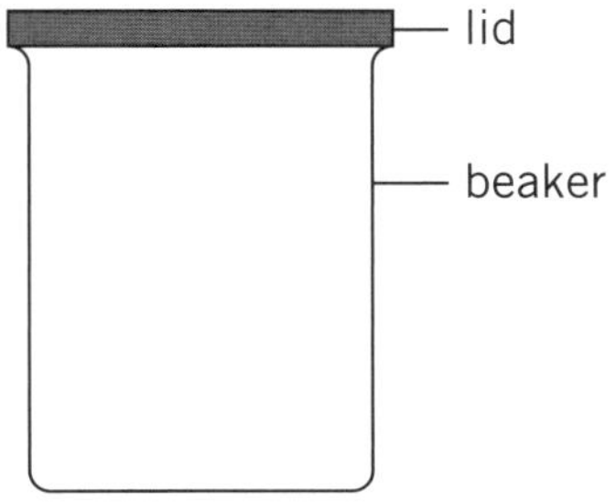

   — lid

   — beaker

   [4]

3. Give three uses of chromatography.

   ....

   ....

   .... [3]

Extension

4. a. Suggest why it is not always possible to separate different coloured substances by chromatography. [2]

   b. Use textbooks or the internet to find out about two-dimensional chromatography and its advantages. [6]

103

Separation and purification
18.6 Paper chromatography (part II)

1. A paper chromatogram of some amino acids from a mixture of amino acid is shown.

   Two pure amino acids, Ser and Gly, were also run on the same piece of paper.

   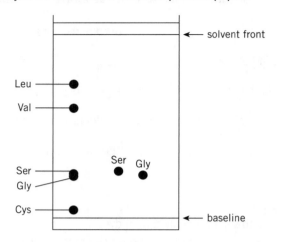

   a. Why was the base line drawn in pencil and not in ink?

      .... [1]

   b. How many amino acids have been completely separated? .... [1]

   c. Which amino acids have not been separated? .... [1]

   d. Suggest how you could you separate these amino acids.

      .... [1]

   e. Calculate the R_f value of Val. .... [1]

   f. Lysine has an R_f value of 0.14. On the diagram above, draw the approximate position of Lys. Label it Lys. [1]

2. State two factors which determine the distance an amino acid travels up the paper.

   ....

   .... [2]

3. Amino acids are colourless. How can you make the spots show up?

   ....

   .... [2]

Extension

4. Use books or the internet to answer the following.

   a. Metal ions in a coin, e.g., Ag^+, Ni^{2+}, Cu^{2+}, can be identified by paper chromatography.

      Suggest how a solution of these ions can be made from the coin. [1]

   b. Column chromatography can be used to purify medical drugs. Explain briefly how column chromatography purifies medical drugs. [6]

Separation and purification

18.7 Checking purity

1. Complete the following sentences about pure and impure substances using words from the list.

   boiling   decreased   exact   impure   increased   pure   range

   The melting and .... points of .... substances are sharp. They melt and boil at .... temperatures. The melting and boiling points of .... substances are not sharp. They melt over a .... of temperatures. The boiling point of a liquid is .... if impurities are present. The melting point of a liquid is .... if impurities are present. [7]

2. a. Which two of these substances are most likely to be pure?
   Underline the correct answers.

   air   aspirin tablets   orange juice

   oxygen gas   sodium chloride crystals   tap water   [2]

   b. Why is distilled water and *not* tap water used in chemistry experiments?

   .... [1]

   c. Seawater is a mixture.

   Suggest a value for the melting point of seawater. .... [1]

3. Sulfur melts at 119 °C and boils at 445 °C

   Draw lines between the boxes on the left and the boxes on the right to complete the sentences.

Left	Right
Pure sulfur …	… melts over a 4 °C temperature range.
Impure sulfur …	… turns to a vapour at 450 °C.
	… solidifies at 119 °C.
	… has a sharp boiling point.

   [2]

4. Solder is a mixture of tin and lead which is used to join metals.
   The melting point of tin is 232 °C. The melting point of lead is 328 °C.
   Solder melts at 183 °C.

   a. Why does solder have a lower melting point than either tin or lead?

   .... [2]

   b. Suggest an advantage of the low melting point of solder.

   .... [1]

Experiments and tests in the lab

19.1 The scientific method and you

When planning an experiment, you have to think about what things you can change (the variables) and what things you can measure.

- The variable that you choose the values for is the *independent variable*, e.g., 10 s, 20 s, 30 s, and so on.
- The variable that you measure at each of these values is the *dependent variable*, e.g., 15 cm^3 gas at 10 s, 28 cm^3 gas, at 20 s and so on.
- All the other values that have to be kept constant to make the experiment a fair test are the *control variables*.

Identify the three types of variable in each of these experiments.

1. The effect of temperature on the rate of reaction of hydrochloric acid with calcium carbonate was investigated by measuring the volume of carbon dioxide released at 10 s intervals.

   a. Independent variable: .... [1]

   b. Dependent variable: .... [1]

   c. Control variables: ....

   .... [2]

2. The energy released by burning different fuels was compared by measuring the temperature rise of the water in the copper can when 1 g of fuel was burnt.

   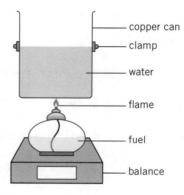

   a. Independent variable: .... [1]

   b. Dependent variable: .... [1]

   c. Control variables: ....

   .... [2]

> **Extension**
>
> 3. During the electrolysis of aqueous copper(II) sulfate using copper electrodes copper is removed from the anode. The amount removed depends on the electric current and the time.
>
>   mass removed = constant × current (amps) × time (seconds)
>
>   A student wanted to find out how the electric current affected the mass of copper removed. Identify the independent variable, the dependent variable, and the control variables. [4]

Experiments and tests in the lab

19.2 Writing up an experiment

Many salts increase in solubility as the temperature increases. Plan an experiment to see if this is true using the salt potassium chloride as an example. This exercise guides you through the stages in this experiment.

1. Planning:

    a. What apparatus do you need?

    ....

    ....

    .... [5]

    b. What are the independent and dependent variables?

    ....

    .... [2]

    c. What will you keep constant?

    ....

    .... [2]

2. Carrying out: Describe how you will carry out the experiment. Give possible volumes and masses of the substances used.

    ....

    ....

    ....

    ....

    .... [5]

3. Evaluation:

    a. Explain why it might be difficult to control the temperature.

    ....

    .... [2]

    b. Suggest improvements that you could make to the experiment.

    ....

    .... [2]

> **Extension**
>
> 4. Suggest why scientists publish their results in scientific journals. [3]
>
>   ....

107

Experiments and tests in the lab

19.3 Preparing and testing gases

1. The diagram shows four ways of collecting gases in the laboratory.

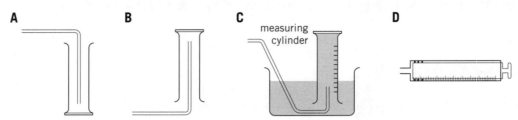

Which method of gas collection, **A**, **B**, **C**, or **D** are the following used for?

a. Measuring the volume of a gas which is sparingly soluble in water. .... [1]

b. Collecting a gas which is lighter than air. .... [1]

c. Measuring the volume of a gas accurately. .... [1]

d. Collecting a gas which is heavier than air. .... [1]

2. Give the method of gas collection, **A**, **B**, **C**, or **D** which involves:

a. Upward displacement of air. .... [1]

b. Collection in a gas syringe. .... [1]

3. Link the gases **A** to **F** on the left with the best test results **1** to **6** on the right.

A ammonia	1 relights a glowing splint
B carbon dioxide	2 turns damp red litmus paper blue
C chlorine	3 turns acidified aqueous potassium manganate(VII) colourless
D hydrogen	4 turns limewater milky
E oxygen	5 bleaches damp litmus paper
F sulfur dioxide	6 'pops' with a lighted splint

[3]

> **Extension**
>
> 4. Are these gases soluble in water, insoluble in water, or slightly soluble in water?
>
>   a. carbon dioxide   b. sulfur dioxide   c. carbon monoxide   d. oxygen
>   e. hydrogen bromide   f. hydrogen sulfide   g. hydrogen? [7]

Experiments and tests in the lab

19.4 Testing for cations

1. Complete the table showing what happens when aqueous solution of ions react with aqueous sodium hydroxide and aqueous ammonia.

Aqueous ion	Reaction with sodium hydroxide	Reaction with aqueous ammonia
$Al^{3+}(aq)$	At first .... In excess	At first .... In excess ....
$Cr^{3+}(aq)$	At first .... In excess	At first .... In excess ....
$Cu^{2+}(aq)$	At first .... In excess	At first .... In excess ....
$Fe^{3+}(aq)$	At first .... In excess	At first .... In excess ....

[16]

2. Aqueous zinc ions and calcium ions both give a white precipitate on addition of a small amount of aqueous sodium hydroxide. Describe how you could distinguish between these two ions.

....

.... [2]

3. What colour do these ions give to a non-luminous (blue) Bunsen flame?

   a. lithium .... b. potassium ....

   c. barium .... d. calcium .... [4]

Extension

4. Write the ionic equation for the reaction of iron(II) sulfate with aqueous sodium hydroxide. Include state symbols. [3]

109

Experiments and tests in the lab

19.5 Testing for anions

1. Link the anion **A** to **E** on the left with the best test results **1** to **5** on the right.

A aqueous bromide ions	**1** ammonia produced when heated with sodium hydroxide and aluminium foil
B carbonate ions	**2** white precipitate formed on addition of aqueous nitric acid and barium nitrate
C aqueous nitrate ions	**3** acidified aqueous potassium Manganate(VII) turns from purple to clear and colourless when added
D sulfite ions	**4** effervescence of carbon dioxide on the addition of an acid
E aqueous sulfate ions	**5** cream precipitate on addition of aqueous nitric acid and silver nitrate

   [3]

2. a. Write a symbol equation for the reaction of aqueous silver nitrate with aqueous sodium chloride. Include state symbols.

   .... [2]

   b. Convert this equation into an ionic equation.

   .... [2]

3. Compound **A** was warmed with aluminium and sodium hydroxide. A gas was given off which turned damp red litmus blue.

   When compound **B** was electrolysed, a gas was released at the anode which bleached damp litmus paper. **B** also gave a yellow colour in the flame test.

   When an aqueous solution of **A** was added to an aqueous solution of **B**, a white precipitate was formed.

   Identify compounds **A** and **B**. Explain your answers.

   ....

   ....

   ....

   ....

   .... [4]

Extension

4. Write ionic equations, including state symbols for these reactions.

   a. The reaction of aqueous barium chloride with aqueous potassium sulfate. [2]

   b. The reaction of sulfite ions with hydrogen ions. [3]

Mathematics for chemistry

20.1 Counting atoms and using brackets

1. - A number in front of a formula multiplies all the way through.
   - The number can refer to atoms or ions, or moles of atoms, or moles of ions.

     So 2NaCl contains 2 Na ions and 2 Cl ions and 5CO contains 5 C atoms and 5 O atoms.
   - A small subscript number after an atom or ion refers only to that atom or ion.

     So in $CaCl_2$ there is 1 Ca ion and 2 Cl ions and in Al_2O_3 there are 2 Al ions and 3 O ions.

     In $3SO_3$ there are 3×1 S atoms and $3 \times 3 = 9$ S atoms.

     How many of each atom or ion are there in the formulae shown?

   a. Na_2O .... b. Mg_3N_2 ....

   c. $5PCl_3$ .... d. $2Al_2O_3$ ....

   e. $4H_2SO_4$ ....

   f. $3Li_2CO_3$ .... [6]

2.
   - Brackets keep particular groups of atoms together, e.g., (NO_3) for nitrates, (OH) for hydroxides.
   - You must not change the numbers within the brackets.
   - A subscript after a bracket multiplies all the number of atoms inside the brackets.

   So in $Mg(NO_3)_2$ there is 1 Mg ion and 2 NO_3 ions.

   In $2NO_3$ ions there are 2 N atoms and $2 \times 3 = 6$ O atoms.

   And in $4Mg(NO_3)_2$ there are 4 Mg ions, 4×2 N atoms and 4×6 N atoms.

   How many atoms of each element are there in the formulae shown?

   a. $Sn(SO_4)_2$ ....

   b. $(NH_4)_2SO_4$ ....

   c. $Ni(ClO_4)_2$ ....

   d. $2Ba(IO_3)_2$ .... [4]

3. Water of crystallisation is added on separately.

   e.g. $CuSO_4 \cdot 5H_2O$ contains $(1Cu + 1S + 4O) + 5 \times (2H + 1O)$

   How many atoms of each element are there in $CoCl_2 \cdot 6H_2O$?

   .... [1]

4. You need to work out the number of atoms correctly in order to calculate the relative formula masses of compounds.

   Calculate the relative formula mass of $Cr_2(SO_4)_3$.

   .... [1]

Mathematics for chemistry

20.2 Rearranging expressions

Learn to rearrange expressions from first principles rather than having to rely on a 'triangle' to help you.

- The idea is that whatever you do to one side of the equation, you do to the other.

    Example: $\text{moles} = \dfrac{\text{mass}}{M_r}$

- To make mass the subject: multiply both sides by M_r (to cancel M_r on the right).

    $\text{moles} \times M_r = \dfrac{\text{mass}}{\cancel{M_r}} \times \cancel{M_r}$ So $\text{moles} \times M_r = \text{mass}$

- To make M_r the subject: multiply both sides by *mass* (to cancel mass on the right).

    $\dfrac{\text{moles}}{\text{mass}} = \dfrac{\cancel{\text{mass}}}{M_r \times \cancel{\text{mass}}}$ then turn both sides upside down: $M_r = \dfrac{\text{mass}}{\text{moles}}$

Now try rearranging these expressions:

1. % yield $= \dfrac{\text{actual yield}}{\text{theoretical yield}} \times 100$

    a. Make actual yield the subject:

    [1]

    b. Make theoretical yield the subject:

    [1]

2. concentration (in mol/dm³) $= \dfrac{\text{moles}}{\text{volume (in dm}^3)}$

    a. Make moles the subject:

    [1]

    b. Make volume (in dm³) the subject:

    [1]

3. Write the formula for density making mass the subject.

    [1]

4. Energy = mass × specific heat capacity × temperature rise

    Make mass the subject of the expression.

    [1]

112

Mathematics for chemistry

20.3 Large numbers, small numbers, and percentages

1. Sometimes, when you do calculations, the number will come out as, for example, 2.5 – 04 on your calculator. The –04 is called the index or power to the base 10. Numbers like this on your calculator are examples of standard form. We write this 2.5×10^4.

   $1 \times 10^1 = 10$

   $1 \times 10^2 = 10 \times 10 = 100$

   $1 \times 10^3 = 10 \times 10 \times 10 = 1000$

   $2.5 \times 10^3 = 2.5 \times 10 \times 10 \times 10 = 2500$

   a. Write 1 000 000 in standard form .... [1]

   b. Write 7×10^4 in non-standard form .... [1]

   c. Write 3300 in standard form .... [1]

2. Very small numbers can also be written in standard form.

   $1 \times 10^{-1} = 0.1$ or $\frac{1}{10}$

   $1 \times 10^{-2} = 0.01$ or $\frac{1}{100}$

   $1 \times 10^{-3} = 0.001$ or $\frac{1}{1000}$

   $2.5 \times 10^{-3} = 2.5 \times 0.001 = 0.025$

   a. Write 0.00001 in standard form .... [1]

   b. Write 5×10^{-3} in non-standard form .... [1]

   c. Write 0.0035 in standard form .... [1]

3. When you multiply numbers in standard form, you simply add the indices (superscripts).

   Example 1: $(2.4 \times 10^3) \times (2 \times 10^2) = 2.4 \times 2 \times 10^{3+2} = 4.8 \times 10^5$

   Example 2: $(5.0 \times 10^{-2}) \times (1.5 \times 10^4) = 5.0 \times 1.5 \times 10^{-2+4} = 7.5 \times 10^2$

   a. What is the product of $(4.0 \times 10^{-3}) \times (3.5 \times 10^2)$? .... [1]

   b. What is the product of $(2.4 \times 10^{-2}) \times (1.5 \times 10^{-3})$? .... [1]

4. When you divide numbers in standard form, you simply subtract the indices.

   Example: $\frac{2.4 \times 10^5}{1.2 \times 10^2} = \frac{2.4}{1.2} \times 10^{5-2} = 2.0 \times 10^3$

   What is the result of $(4.0 \times 10^{-3}) \div (3.5 \times 10^2)$? .... [1]

5. Percentages:

   In chemistry the result of a smaller number divided by a larger number is multiplied by 100 to get the percentage.

   What is the percentage yield if the actual yield of a product in a reaction is 4.5 g and the theoretical yield is 5.5 g?

   % yield = $\frac{\text{actual yield}}{\text{theoretical yield}} \times 100$ % yield .... [1]

113

Mathematics for chemistry

20.4 Volumes and areas

1. The diagram shows how to calculate the area of one side of a cube and the volume of a cube.

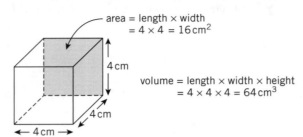

- The area of a rectangle = length × width. If the length and width are in cm, then the area is in cm^2.
- The volume of a regular figure like a cube is length × width × height. If the dimensions are in cm, then the volume is in cm^3.

Look at the diagram of the cube above.

a. i. How many sides does the cube have? .... [1]

   ii. What is the area of one side? .... [1]

   iii. What is the total surface area of the cube? .... [1]

b. i. Look at the diagram of the cube on the right.
      How many smaller cubes has it been cut up into?

      .... [1]

   ii. What is the surface area of each of the smaller cubes?

      .... [1]

   iii. What is the total surface area of all the cubes?

      .... [1]

   iv. How does this help explain why the same mass of smaller particles reacts faster with acid than larger particles?

      ....
      .... [2]

2. A decimetre (dm) is one-tenth of a metre.

   a. i. How many cm are there in 1 metre? .... [1]

      ii. How many cm are there in 1 decimetre? .... [1]

   b. Explain why there are 1000 cm^3 in 1 dm^3.

      ....
      .... [2]

Mathematics for chemistry

20.5 Working through calculations

1. When doing chemical calculations, it is important that we give the answer to the correct number of significant figures and round up figures correctly.

   Significant figures:

   236.38 has five significant figures

   32.4 has three significant figures

   0.0067 has two significant figures (zeros before a number are not significant figures)

   0.0300 has three significant figures (zeros after a number after a decimal point are significant figures).

   Rounding up:

   2.3<u>6</u>6 rounded to two significant figures is 2.4

   2.5<u>5</u>7 rounded to two significant figures is 2.6

   2.3<u>4</u>6 rounded to two significant figures is 2.3

   You can see that when rounding if the next figure along is 5 or above, then the figure to be rounded goes up by 1.

   a. Round these values to three significant figures:

   i. 4.357 .... ii. 0.08732 ....

   iii. 137.2 .... iv. 0.005498 .... [4]

   b. Round these values to two significant figures:

   i. 436 .... ii. 3.447 ....

   iii. 56.79 .... iv. 0.00545 .... [4]

2. When performing a calculation in several stages **do not round up between the steps**. You should only round up at the end. You should round up to the same number of significant figures as the data in the question.

   To see the effect of rounding in the middle of a calculation, work through this example.

   When 1 mole of pentane is burnt in excess air, 5 moles of carbon dioxide are formed. Calculate the volume of carbon dioxide when 6.67 g of pentane is burnt.

Calculation	Answer when keeping the figures in your calculator	Value when rounding
moles pentane = $\dfrac{6.67}{72.0}$	....	round to one significant figure ....
multiply by 5 (because 5 moles of carbon dioxide are formed from 1 mole of pentane)	....	round to one significant figure ....
multiply by 24 to get dm³ of carbon dioxide	answer to three significant figures	answer to three significant figures ....

   [6]

Mathematics for chemistry
20.6 Drawing graphs (1)

1. When drawing graphs remember:

   - The axes should be fully labelled and include units.
   - Use as much of the graph paper as possible.
   - Use an × to plot the points rather than + or • which cannot be so easily seen.
   - If it looks like the line will form a curve, do not use a ruler to join the points to each other.
   - Draw the line of best fit (with equal numbers of points each side of the line if necessary).
   - Ignore any points which do not fit in with the general trend of the line (anomalous points).

   What is wrong with each of these graphs?

   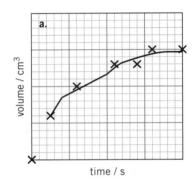 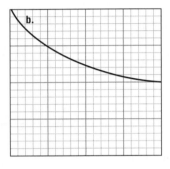 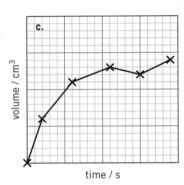

   a. ....

   ....

   .... [3]

   b. ....

   ....

   .... [3]

   c. ....

   .... [2]

2. Extrapolation and interpolation:

   The graph on the right shows how to extrapolate and interpolate values.

   Always make sure that you draw lines as shown to the values that are asked for.

   Deduce the volume of gas released in the first:

   a. 1.4 minutes .... [1]

   b. 5 minutes .... [1]

   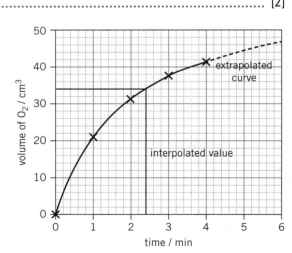

116

Mathematics for chemistry

20.7 Drawing graphs (2)

1. The table shows how the electrical conductivity of a solution changes as an acid is added to an alkali.

Volume of acid / cm^3	0	2	3	4	5	6	7	8
Conductivity / ohm s^{-1} m^{-1}	2.8	1.8	1.3	0.8	0.7	1.0	1.2	1.5

   a. On the grid below plot the points using the data in the table. [3]

   b. Draw two straight lines to connect these data points that intersect. Label this intersection point **P**. [2]

   c. Deduce the volume of acid added at point **P**. .... [1]

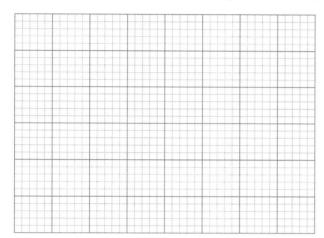

2. The table shows how the volume of gas changes when magnesium reacts with hydrochloric acid. Plot a graph of these results on the grid below. [4]

Time / s	0	10	20	30	40	50	60	70
Volume of gas / cm^3	0	24	39	47	52	54	55	56

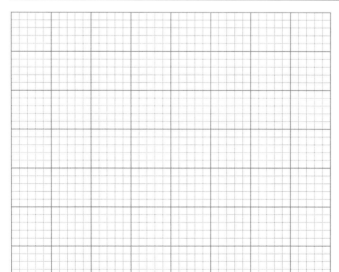

Mathematics for chemistry

20.8 Drawing graphs (3)

1. Look at the graph below.

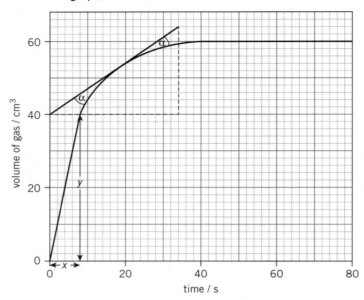

- We can find the initial rate of reaction from a graph by taking the rise, y, over the run, x, of the gradient (slope). This is 40 cm³ ÷ 8 s. So the rate is 5 cm³/s.

- We can find the rate at any other point by drawing a tangent to the curve (see the graph above). Note that the angles α should be equal.
  In this case the gradient is $\frac{66-40}{34-0}$ = 0.76 cm³/s

   a. The table shows how the mass of a product in a reaction increases with time.

Time / s	0	20	40	60	80	100	120	140
Mass / g	0	0.08	0.16	0.24	0.30	0.34	0.37	0.40

   Plot a graph using these results.

   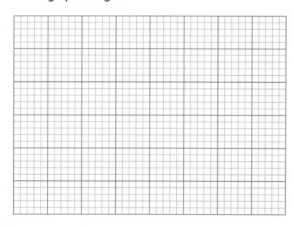

   [4]

   b. Calculate the initial rate of reaction over the first 40 seconds.

   .... [2]

   c. Why would the rate calculated over the first 100 seconds be an average rate?

   .... [1]

118

Revision

21.1 Using command words (1)

Command words tell us what sort of thing we need to write in response to a question. Here is a list of the command words used in chemistry and how to respond to them.

Calculate: You need to work out a problem using numbers.
- The problem may be in several stages.
- Look out for the number of marks: This often shows you the number of stages needed in the calculation.
- Always show your working.

Example: Calculate the mass of 11 dm^3 of carbon dioxide. The answer involves **i.** finding the moles of carbon dioxide using the relationship that 1 mol of a gas occupies 24 dm^3 then **ii.** multiplying moles by the molar mass of carbon dioxide.

Compare: You have to comment on similarities and differences.

Example: Compare the properties of the transition elements and the Group I elements.

Deduce: Conclude from available information.

Example: Sodium sulfate is Na_2SO_4. Deduce the formula of the sulfate ion. Answer: SO_4^{2-}.

Define: Give a precise meaning. You need to write down the main points about a term.
- The only way to do this is by memorising key terms.

Example: Define oxidation in terms of electron transfer. Answer: Oxidation is loss of electrons.

Describe: State the main points about something. You may have to write about a sequence of events, draw a diagram, or state what happens.
- If you are asked to describe observations, remember to state what you see, hear, smell, or feel. Do not describe the names of the substances.

Example 1: Describe how to obtain sodium chloride crystals from a solution of sodium chloride.

Answer: Warm to the crystallisation point then filter off the crystals.

Example 2: Describe what happens when you add acid to an aqueous solution of sodium carbonate.

Answer: Bubbles are seen. NOTE: The answer 'carbon dioxide is given off' is not correct.

Determine: The answer can be obtained from a graph, by calculation, or other information.

Example: Determine the value of the gas released after 20 seconds.

Evaluate: Write something about the quality, importance, or value of something. It often involves being critical.

Example: Evaluate the experiment by referring to the apparatus and the range of results.

Explain: You have to use particular ideas to describe why something happens.

Example: Explain why the volume of a gas increases with temperature.

Answer: The particles of gas move faster and get further away from each other (use of kinetic particle theory).

Revision
21.2 Using command words (2)

Identify: Name, select, or recognise something from given information.

Example: Identify the reducing agent in this reaction.

Justify: Support a case with evidence or ideas.

Example: Justify the position of silicon in the Periodic Table using its electronic configuration and the information about the physical properties of other elements in Group IV given.

Predict: You have to make connections between various items of data.

- You often have to extrapolate or interpolate data when answering these questions.

Example: Predict the melting point of potassium (when given the melting points of other Group I elements). The answer involves looking at the melting points of the elements either side of potassium and choosing a suitable value in between these.

Show (that): Give structured evidence that leads to a result.

Example: Show by calculation that calcium carbonate is the limiting reactant.

State / Give: Produce a short answer from a given source or memory.

Example: State / Give the electronic structure of sodium. Answer: 2,8,1.

Suggest: You have to use your general chemical knowledge to write about a situation which is unfamiliar to you. You may need to:

- Think of similar substances to the one which is being asked about.
- Think of general ideas of structure, bonding, electrolysis, redox, rate or equilibrium.

Example: The structure of boron nitride is similar to graphite. Suggest why boron nitride is slippery.

Answer: Think about the properties of graphite that make it slippery, then repeat these for boron nitride, for example weak forces between the layers, layers can slide over each other.

NOTE: Command words are often combined:

Example: State the meaning of the term combustion.

Describe and explain the effect of increasing the temperature on the position of this equilibrium.

1. Underline the command words in each of these questions.
    a. Use the information in the table above to suggest a value for the boiling point of propane. [1]
    b. Describe how distillation is carried out and give the name of the physical property on which it is based. [2]
    c. Use this information to deduce the formula of this oxide of tin. [1]
    d. Describe the process of diffusion and explain this process in terms of the kinetic particle theory. [2]
    e. Draw a graph of volume of carbon dioxide against time to determine the volume of carbon dioxide formed in the first 30 seconds. [2]

Revision

21.3 Helping you revise

You should find the best way of revising for yourself. There is no one correct way of revising.
- Don't just read through books or notes and hope that you will remember things.
- Don't leave revision to the last moment. It is best to revise material throughout the year.
- Revision should be active.

Here is a check list of things to help you find the best way for you to revise:

- Find the best time of day to revise. Some people revise better in the evening, others in the morning.

  When do I revise best? ....

- Find a time when you will not be disturbed.

  When is this most likely to be? ....

- Find the best conditions needed for you to revise. Some people prefer to revise in absolute silence; others find it useful to have some music in the background.

  Is music in the background really good for you when revising? ....

  ....

- Revise regularly. You may find it useful to revise a topic about a week after you have finished it, to make sure that you have really understood it.

  Do you revise only for exams or tests? ....

- Find the best length of time for each revision session. You may find that several short periods of revision, for example, 3 spells of 20 minutes with breaks in between are more productive than one longer period of revision.

  What's your best revision span? ....

- Don't imagine that you are revising usefully unless you test yourself from time to time to prove that you are remembering material.

  Do you test yourself? ....

- Make sure that you pay more attention to topics which you find difficult. Don't ignore them!

  What topics in Chemistry do you find difficult? ....

  ....

- Do you remember information better in written form or in the form of diagrams?

  ....

Revision

21.4 Active revision

Active revision involves you carrying out different sorts of activities and testing yourself to see if your revision has been successful.

- Revise with others, especially with other classmates. Asking each other questions is a useful way of helping you remember things.
- Test yourself or get someone else to test you.
- Make a list of key areas that you find difficult and concentrate on these.
- Make up mnemonics like OIL RIG for Oxidation Is Loss of electrons and Reduction Is Gain of electrons.
- Look through the syllabus and text book and list general areas which need revision, e.g. definitions and key terms to learn, e.g. element, isotopes, relative atomic mass. You can test yourself by writing the terms and definitions on a sheet like this:

Term	Definition
isotopes	Atoms with the same proton number having different numbers of neutrons.
element	A substance which contains only one type of atom.
empirical formula	A formula which shows the simplest whole number ratio of the different atoms or ions in a compound.

When you think you have learnt the definitions, cover up or fold over the definition side and see if you can remember it.

1. Give three other general topics throughout the syllabus which could be revised in this way.

   .... [3]

2. On a separate piece of paper write the two columns as shown below.

Properties of acids	Result
litmus	turns red litmus blue
metals	gives salt + hydrogen

   Complete the table to give at least four other properties of acids. [4]

3. Make a table similar to the one above to help you revise the properties of hydrocarbons. [16]

Using past papers

- It is useful to look at the wording in past papers to get a feeling for the language used.
- Look not only for the command words but also the smaller words which instruct you what to do.
- Look at the number of marks given for the question. This often gives you an indication of how many different points you need to include in your answer. For simple questions, however, you may need to write two points to get one mark.
- Underline the key words.
- Work through calculations and extended exam questions and use the mark schemes if available to see where the marks are awarded.

Revision
21.5 Mind mapping

Mind maps are simplified diagrams which show the main points of a topic in the form of a diagram. They are useful summaries because all the words which get in the way of learning the essential points are removed. They can be made as simple or as complicated as required but it is best to make them simple at the start. Mind maps can also be constructed to show links between different topic areas. An example is shown below.

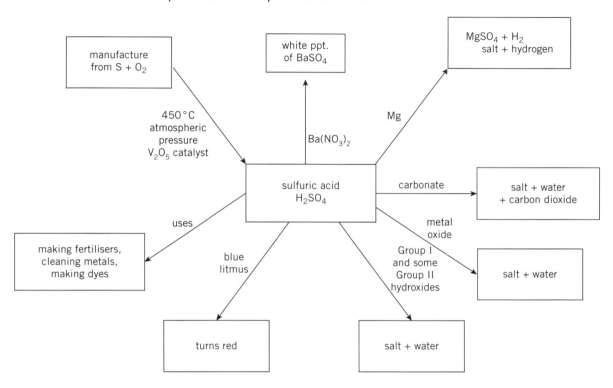

Suggested topics for mind maps which you could make:

Electrolysis; Acids and bases; Methods of purification; Hydrocarbons; Polymers; Properties of the halogens; Iron and steel (or properties of metals); Equilibrium.

In the space below draw a simple mind map (no more than 7 boxes) for a topic of your choice.

Revision
21.6 Making mind maps

1. Complete the mind map for structure by filling in the gaps **A** to **L**.

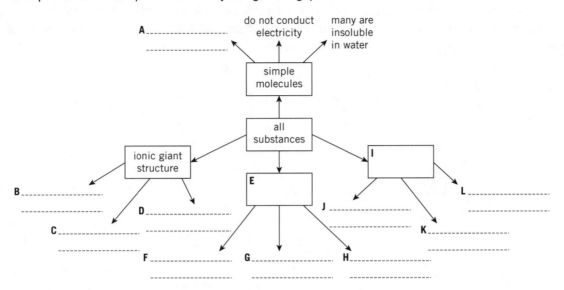

[12]

2. In the space below complete a mind map about rates of reaction.

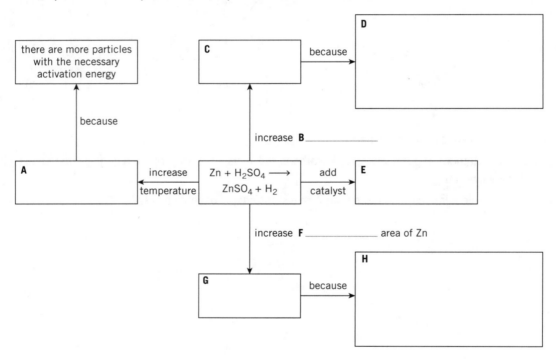

[8]

Exam-style questions

1. Phosphorus is an element in Group V of the Periodic Table.

   a. Deduce the electronic configuration of an atom of phosphorus.

   .... [1]

   b. An isotope of phosphorus has 15 protons and 31 nucleons.

   Deduce the number of neutrons in this isotope of phosphorus.

   .... [1]

   c. Phosphorus has a simple molecular structure.

   Describe two physical properties of phosphorus.

   ....
   .... [2]

   d. Phosphorus burns in excess oxygen to form an oxide with the formula P_2O_5.

   Write a balanced equation for this reaction.

   .... [2]

   e. P_2O_5 reacts with sodium hydroxide to form sodium phosphate, Na_3PO_4.

   Deduce the formula of the phosphate ion.

   .... [1]

   f. Phosphate ions are present in many fertilisers.

   Name another anion that is present in most fertilisers.

   .... [1]

   g. Explain why farmers spread fertilisers on the soil where crop plants are grown.

   ....
   .... [2]

   h. Draw the electronic configuration of phosphine, PH_3. Show only the outer shell electrons.

   [2]

   Total = 12

Exam-style questions

2. The structure of allyl alcohol is shown below.

$$CH_2=CH-CH_2-OH$$

   a. What feature of allyl alcohol shows that it is an unsaturated compound?

   .... [1]

   b. Describe a test for an unsaturated compound.

   Test ....

   Result .... [2]

   c. Allyl alcohol can be reduced by hydrogen in a similar way to ethene.

   i. Explain the term reduction in terms of electron transfer.

   .... [1]

   ii. State the conditions needed for this reduction.

   ....

   .... [3]

   iii. Give the displayed formula of the compound formed by this reduction.

   [2]

   d. Compounds with structures similar to allyl alcohol are found in green onion leaves.

   i. Suggest how you could make a solution of the green pigments from onion leaves.

   ....

   .... [2]

   ii. Several green pigments are present in onion leaves. State the name of the method you would use to separate these pigments from each other.

   .... [1]

   Total = 12

Exam-style questions

3. The structure of caesium chloride is shown below.

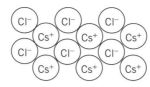

a. Deduce the simplest formula for caesium chloride.

.... [1]

b. Explain in terms of structure and bonding why caesium chloride has a high melting point.

....

.... [2]

c. Explain why aqueous caesium chloride conducts electricity.

.... [1]

d. Molten caesium chloride is electrolysed using graphite electrodes.

   i. Give two reasons why graphite electrodes are used.

   ....

   .... [2]

   ii. Write ionic half equations (ion electron equations) for the reactions at:

   the anode ....

   the cathode .... [3]

e. Caesium chloride is formed when caesium burns in chlorine.

$$2Cs + Cl_2 \rightarrow 2CsCl$$

When 5.32 g of caesium is burned in excess chlorine, 6.4 g of caesium chloride is formed. Calculate the percentage yield of caesium chloride.

[3]

Total = 12

Exam-style questions

4. A student investigated the reaction at r.t.p. between 0.05 g of magnesium ribbon and excess hydrochloric acid of concentration 2.0 mol / dm³.

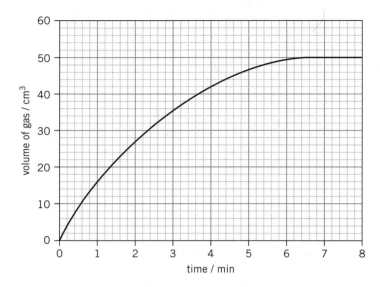

   a. At what time was the reaction just complete?

   .... [1]

   b. i. Deduce the volume of hydrogen released during the first minute of the reaction.

   .... [1]

   ii. Deduce the average rate of reaction during the first two minutes.

   .... [1]

   c. The experiment was repeated at r.t.p. using hydrochloric acid of concentration 2.5 mol / dm³.
      On the grid above draw a line to show how the volume of hydrogen released changes with time. [2]

   d. Explain, using the collision theory, why increasing the concentration of acid increases the rate of reaction.

   ....

   ....

   .... [2]

   e. The experiment was repeated using 2 mol/dm³ hydrochloric acid and 0.05 g of magnesium powder. Would the reaction be faster or slower? Explain your answer.

   ....

   .... [2]

   Total = 9

Exam-style questions

5. When 1 mole of calcium carbonate is heated, 1 mole of calcium oxide and 1 mole of carbon dioxide are formed.

   a. What type of reaction is this? Draw a circle around **two** of the words below.

   addition   catalysed   decomposition   endothermic

   exothermic   oxidation   reduction   [2]

   b. Describe a test for carbon dioxide.

   Test ....

   Result .... [2]

   c. The table shows the mass of calcium carbonate converted to products in 5 minutes at different temperatures. The same mass of calcium carbonate was used in each experiment.

Temperature / °C	500	700	800	900	950	1000
Mass converted	0.0	0.4	1.8	3.5	3.7	3.8

   i. On the grid below draw a graph of these results.

   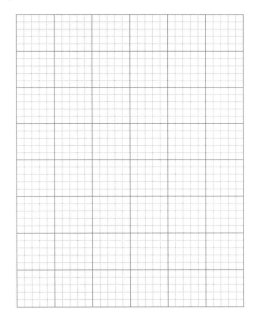

   [3]

   ii. Use your graph to help you calculate the volume of carbon dioxide formed when calcium carbonate is heated for 5 minutes at 850 °C.

   [3]

   Total = 10

Exam-style questions

6. The diagram shows the preparation of ammonia by heating ammonium sulfate with concentrated sodium hydroxide.

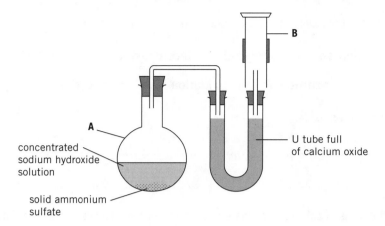

a. i. On the diagram above, show where heat is applied. [1]

   ii. State the names of the pieces of apparatus labelled **A** and **B**.

   A ....

   B .... [2]

   iii. What is the purpose of the calcium oxide?

   .... [1]

   iv. Explain how you can show when **B** is full of ammonia.

   ....

   .... [2]

b. Complete the equation for the reaction.

   $(NH_4)_2SO_4$ + ... → .... + ... + H_2O [2]

c. Hydrazine, H_2N-NH_2, like ammonia, contains hydrogen and nitrogen.

   Draw the electronic configuration of a molecule of hydrazine. Show only the electrons in the outer shells.

   [2]

   Total = 10

Exam-style questions

7. The structure of lactic acid is shown below.

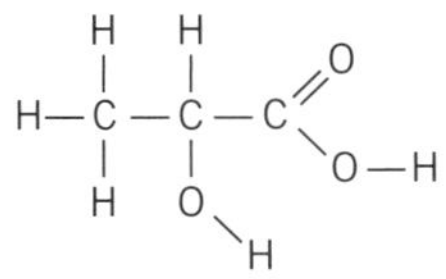

   a. On the structure above put a ring around the alcohol functional group. [1]

   b. Lactic acid can be made by fermenting the sugar lactose.

      i. State the three different types of atom present in sugars.

      .... [1]

      ii. Give the name of another compound which can be made by fermentation.

      .... [1]

   c. Calcium carbonate neutralises lactic acid. Complete the word equation for this reaction.

      lactic acid + calcium carbonate → calcium lactate + ... + ... [2]

   d. Calcium lactate is insoluble in water. Suggest how you could separate calcium lactate from a mixture of calcium lactate and aqueous salts.

      .... [1]

   e. The simplified structure of the polymer of lactic acid is shown below.

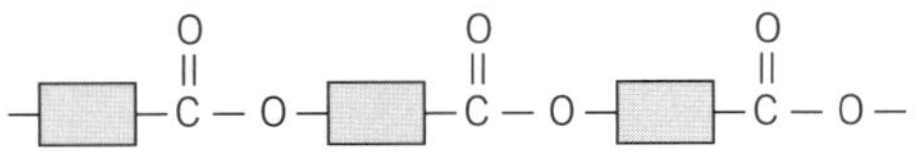

      i. State the name of the linkage group.

      .... [1]

      ii. Explain why this is not an example of addition polymerisation.

      ....

      .... [2]

   f. Lactic acid is oxidised to ethanoic acid by acidified potassium manganate(VII). What colour change would you observe when excess lactic acid is added to acidified potassium manganate(VII)?

      .... to .... [2]

      Total = 11

131

Exam-style questions

8. The table shows some physical properties of four noble gases.

Gas	Melting point / °C	Boiling point / °C	Density at r.t.p. in g / dm³	Atomic radius / nm
helium	−272	−269	0.18	0.050
neon	−248	−246	0.90	0.065
argon	−189	−186	1.78	
krypton	−157	−152	3.74	0.110

a. i. The density of air is 1.20 g/dm³. Which of these gases could be used to fill a toy balloon to float in air?

.... [1]

ii. Deduce the atomic radius of argon.

.... [1]

iii. What is the state of krypton at −118 °C? Explain your answer.

.... [2]

iv. Describe the trend in boiling point down the group.

.... [1]

b. Xenon tetrafluoride, XeF_4, reacts with potassium iodide.

$$XeF_4 + 4KI \rightarrow Xe + 2I_2 + 4KF$$

i. Potassium salts are colourless. What is the final colour of the reaction mixture?

.... [1]

ii. Explain why potassium iodide is acting as a reducing agent in this reaction.

....

.... [2]

iii. Calculate the maximum volume of xenon formed when 8.28 g of xenon tetrafluoride reacts with excess potassium iodide.

[3]

Total = 11

Exam-style questions

9. Nitrogen dioxide, NO_2, is a brown gas which pollutes the atmosphere.

  a. i. Give one source of nitrogen dioxide in the atmosphere.

  .... [1]

  ii. Describe one effect of nitrogen dioxide on the environment.

  .... [1]

  iii. Nitrogen dioxide is a gas at r.t.p. Describe the proximity (closeness) and motion of the particles in nitrogen dioxide at r.t.p.

  ....

  .... [2]

  b. The colourless gas dinitrogen tetroxide, N_2O_4, forms an equilibrium mixture with nitrogen dioxide.

  $$N_2O_4(g) \rightleftharpoons 2NO_2(g)$$

  i. Describe and explain what you would observe when the pressure on this equilibrium mixture is increased.

  ....

  ....

  .... [3]

  ii. Calculate the relative molecular mass of:

  nitrogen dioxide ....

  dinitrogen tetroxide .... [2]

  iii. At 55 °C the average relative molecular mass of the equilibrium mixture is 61.0 but at 140 °C, the average relative molecular mass is 46.0.

  Explain how this shows that the forward reaction is endothermic.

  ....

  ....

  .... [3]

  c. At temperatures above 150°C nitrogen dioxide decomposes to nitrogen(II) oxide and oxygen.
  Write a symbol equation for this reaction.

  .... [2]

  Total = 14

Exam-style questions

10. 25 cm³ of aqueous potassium hydroxide was placed in a flask. A few drops of an acid–base indicator were then added. The solution was neutralised by 12.5 cm³ of 0.2 mol / dm³ sulfuric acid added from a burette.

$$2KOH(aq) + H_2SO_4(aq) \rightarrow Na_2SO_4(aq) + 2H_2O(l)$$

a. Suggest a suitable indicator that could be used in this reaction.

.... [1]

b. Give the name of the salt formed in this reaction.

.... [1]

c. Calculate:

i. The number of moles of sulfuric acid added from the burette.

[1]

ii. The number of moles of potassium hydroxide in the flask.

.... [1]

iii. The concentration of potassium hydroxide in the flask in mol/dm³.

[1]

d. Write the simplest ionic equation for this reaction.

.... [1]

e. Sulfuric acid catalyses the reaction between butanol and ethanoic acid.

Draw the displayed formula for the ester formed in this reaction.

[2]

Total = 8

Project ideas

23.1 Comparing the hardness of different samples of water

Introduction

This could be done at home or in the school laboratory.

- Hard water does not lather well with soap.
- Soft water lathers well with soap.
- Permanent hardness in water cannot be removed by boiling.
- Temporary hardness in water can be removed by boiling.

Purpose of the experiments

To find the volume of soap solution (or washing up liquid) needed to form a permanent lather with different samples of water.

Sources of water

- Distilled water.
- Temporary hard water (bubble carbon dioxide through limewater until the white precipitate has disappeared).
- Permanent hard water (add some hydrated calcium sulfate to distilled water then filter).
- Natural sources of water, e.g. tap water, rainwater, seawater.

Carrying out the experiments

1. There are two ways in which the experiment can be carried out.
    a. Add the water sample to a flask and then see how many drops of soap solution (added from a burette or pipette) are needed to form a lather on shaking that does not disappear after leaving for a minute.
    b. Adding a certain number of drops of soap solution to a tube of water, shaking, and measuring the height of the lather formed.
2. Make a list of all the equipment that you need including safety equipment/clothing.
3. What do you need to vary and what do you need to keep constant?

Analysing the results

- Draw a table of results for the number of drops (or height of lather) with different types of water including boiled hard water (temporary and permanent).
- Repeat your experiments to get consistent results.
- Suggest how you could improve your experiments.

Conclusions

1. Which samples of water are hard and which are soft?
2. Classify tap water, rainwater, seawater, and other sources of water you have analysed as hard or soft.
3. Which samples contain temporary hardness and which contain permanent hardness?

Project ideas

23.2 Comparing the energy released when burning different foods

Introduction

This could be done at home or in the school laboratory.

- The labels on packets of food usually state the amount of energy they contain in kilojoules or kilocalories. Make a list of these values for the foods you choose.
- When dry foods are burned, they release energy. The reaction is exothermic.
- The carbohydrate, fats, and proteins burn to form carbon dioxide and water.

Purpose of the experiments

To compare the energy released by different foods.

Sources of foods

- The foods should be dry. You can dry wet foods in an oven but don't let them char (go black).
- Make a list of the energy values for the foods you choose by looking on the sides of the packets.
- Crisps, bread, nuts, and rice are good sources of foods.
- Dried meats, beans, and cheese could also be used.
- It is possible to burn cooking oils if you use a cotton or string wick.

Carrying out the experiments

1. There are two ways in which the experiment can be carried out.
   a. Burning different foods of known mass on the end of a large needle. The burning foods heat a known volume of water in a test tube or beaker.
   b. Burning the food on a tin lid beneath a beaker or tin of water. This is more useful for fats and oils.
2. Make a list of all the equipment that you need including safety equipment/clothing.
3. What do you need to vary and what do you need to keep constant?
4. You could also investigate the relationship between the mass of a particular food burnt and the temperature rise.

Analysing the results

- Draw a table of results for the temperature rise on burning a known amount of food material using a fixed volume of water.
- Repeat your experiments to get consistent results.
- Suggest how you could improve your experiments.

Conclusions

1. Calculate the energy released in kJ per gram of food by using the relationship

    energy released (Joules) = mass of water (g) × 4.18 × temperature rise (°C)

2. Which foods released the most energy per gram?
3. Compare the energy values you obtained with the energy values on the labels of the foods you used. Were they in the same order of energy as the results of your experiments? If not, suggest why not.
4. Suggest reasons why your experiment may not be a fair test.

Project ideas

23.3 The effect of temperature on solubility

Introduction
This is best done in the laboratory.

- Many compounds are much more soluble in water at higher temperatures than lower temperatures. Others do not show much difference in solubility as the temperature increases.

Purpose of the experiments
To find how the solubility of different compounds changes with temperature.

Suggested compounds to use
Potassium nitrate, sodium nitrate, potassium chloride, and sodium chloride.

Carrying out the experiments

1. a. You heat some water (4 or 5 cm³) with the solute until the solute dissolves.
   b. The solution is then cooled using the apparatus shown below until crystallisation occurs. The temperature of crystallisation is recorded.

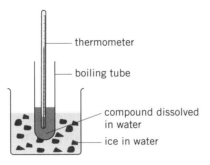

   c. Then add more water (not more than 2 cm³) to the solution in the boiling tube and heat to dissolve. The temperature when crystals appear is recorded.
   d. Repeat step **c.** several times.
2. Make a list of all the equipment that you need including safety equipment/clothing
3. What do you need to vary and what do you need to keep constant?

Analysing the results

- For each salt draw a table of results for the temperature at which crystallisation occurs.
- Repeat your experiments to get consistent results.
- Suggest how you could improve your experiments.

Conclusions

1. Which compounds show the greatest difference in crystallisation temperature?
2. Compare your results with the tables showing the solubility of each of these compounds at different temperatures.
3. Suggest reasons why your experiment may not be a fair test.

Project ideas

23.4 Finding the percentage by mass of carbon in different carbonates

Introduction
This should be done in the laboratory.

- When carbonates react with acids carbon dioxide is released.
- The mass of the reaction mixture decreases as the reaction proceeds.
- The diagram below shows some of the apparatus that can be used to follow the rate of this reaction.

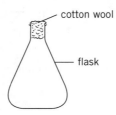

Purpose of the experiments
To find the percentage of carbon dioxide and hence the percentage by mass of carbon in different carbonates.

Suggested carbonates to use
Sodium carbonate, sodium hydrogencarbonate, calcium carbonate, copper(II) carbonate, barium carbonate.

Carrying out the experiments
1. The hydrochloric acid needs to be in excess. Why?
2. Deduce the amounts of hydrochloric acid and calcium carbonate you need.
3. Make a list of all the equipment that you need including safety equipment/clothing.
4. What do you need to vary and what do you need to keep constant?

Analysing the results
- Draw up a table of results for the volume of carbon dioxide given off for each carbonate.
- Repeat your experiments to get consistent results.
- Suggest how you could improve your experiments.
- Calculate the mass of carbon released in each experiment.
- Calculate the percentage by mass of the carbon in the carbonate.

Conclusions
1. Put the carbonates in order of their percentage composition carbon by mass.
2. The CO_3^{2-} is common to all the carbonates. So why are the percentage compositions different?
3. Suggest reasons why your experiment may not be a fair test.

Glossary

Acid: A proton donor.

Acidic oxide: An oxide that reacts with alkalis to form a salt and water.

Acid rain: Rain that has a pH below 5.6 due to the reaction of rainwater with acidic gases.

Activation energy: The minimum amount of energy particles must have to react when they collide.

Addition polymerisation: Polymerisation of monomers containing a C=C double bond to form a polymer and no other compound is formed.

Addition reaction: A reaction in which a single product is formed from two or more reactant molecules and no other product is made.

Alcohols: Organic compounds with branched or unbranched chains containing the –OH functional group.

Alkali: A base that is soluble in water.

Alkanes: Saturated hydrocarbons with the general formula C_nH_{2n+2}.

Alkenes: Hydrocarbons containing at least one C=C double bond.

Alloy: A mixture of a metal with another element.

Amphoteric oxide: An oxide that reacts with both acids and alkalis.

Anions: Negative ions.

Anode: The positive electrode.

Atom: The smallest particle that cannot be broken down by chemical means.

Atomic number: The number of protons in the nucleus of an atom.

Avogadro constant: The number of particles in a mole of defined particles (atoms, ions, or molecules).

Base: A proton acceptor.

Basic oxide: An oxide that reacts with acids to form a salt and water.

Brownian motion: The random bombardment of molecules on small suspended particles leading to a random irregular motion of the suspended particles.

Carboxylic acids: A homologous series of organic compounds with the –COOH group.

Catalyst: A substance that speeds up a chemical reaction but remains unchanged at the end of the reaction.

Catalytic converter: A part added to vehicle to reduce the emissions of carbon monoxide and nitrogen oxides from exhausts of petrol engines.

Cathode: The negative electrode.

Cations: Positive ions.

Collision theory: The theory that moving particles react when they collide with sufficient energy and in the correct orientation.

Compound: A substance made up of two or more different atoms (or ions) joined together by bonds.

Condensation polymerisation: Polymerisation occurring when two types of monomer bond together with the elimination of small molecule.

Condensing: The change of state from gas to liquid.

Conductors (electrical): Substances that have a low resistance to the passage of electricity.

Corrosion: The gradual reaction and 'eating away' of a metal inwards from its surface caused by another substance.

Covalent bond: A shared pair of electrons.

Cracking: The decomposition of larger alkane molecules into a mixture of smaller alkanes and alkenes.

Delocalised electron: Electrons that are not associated with any particular atom.

Diatomic: Molecules containing two atoms.

Diffusion: The spreading movement of one substance through another due to the random movement of the particles.

Displayed formula: Shows how the atoms and bonds in a compound are arranged.

Dot and cross diagram: A diagram showing the electronic configuration of atoms ions or molecules.

Double bond: Two covalent bonds between the same two atoms.

Ductile: Can be drawn into wires.

Electrochemical series: The order of reactivity of metals, with the most reactive at the top.

Electrodes: Rods that conduct electric current to and from an electrolyte.

Electrolysis: The decomposition of a compound when molten or in aqueous solution by an electric current.

Electrolyte: A molten ionic compound or a solution containing ions that conducts electricity.

Electron: The negatively charged particles outside the nucleus of an atom.

Electron shells: Spherical areas surrounding the nucleus, which contain one of more electrons.

Electroplating: Coating of the surface of one metal with a layer of another, usually less reactive, metal.

Element: A substance made up of only one type of atom that cannot be broken down into anything simpler by chemical reactions.

Empirical formula: Shows the simplest whole number ratio of atoms or ions in a compound.

Endothermic reaction: A reaction that absorbs energy from the surroundings.

Enthalpy change: The heat energy exchanged between a chemical reaction and its surroundings at constant pressure.

Enzymes: Biological catalysts.

Ester: A compound with the formula R–COO–R' formed by the reaction of an alcohol with a carboxylic (alkanoic) acid.

Esterification: Making an ester by the reaction of an alcohol with a carboxylic acid.

Evaporation: The change of state from liquid to vapour that takes place below the boiling point of a liquid.

Glossary

Exothermic reaction: A reaction that releases energy to the surroundings.
Fermentation: The breakdown of organic materials by microorganisms with effervescence and the release of heat energy.
Filtrate: The solution passing through a filter paper when a mixture of solid and solution are filtered.
Flue gas desulfurisation: Removal of sulfur dioxide in industry arising from burning fossil fuels containing sulfur.
Fraction: A product of petroleum distillation that is a mixture of hydrocarbons having a limited range of molar masses and boiling points.
Fractional distillation: A method used to separate two or more liquids with different boiling points from each other using a distillation column.
Freezing: The change of state from liquid to solid.
Functional group: A group that is characteristic of a given homologous series.
General formula: A formula that can be applied to all members of a given homologous series.
Giant molecular structure: A structure having a three-dimensional network of covalent bonds.
Global warming: The heating of the atmosphere caused by absorption of infra-red radiation by greenhouse gases.
Greenhouse gases: Gases that are good absorbers of infrared radiation and cause global warming.
Group: A vertical column in the Periodic Table.
Half equations: Equations showing the oxidation and reduction reactions separately.
Halogens: The elements in Group VII.
Homologous series: A group of compounds with the same general formula and the same functional group.
Hydrocarbons: Compounds containing only carbon and hydrogen atoms.
Hydrogenation: A reaction involving the addition of hydrogen to a compound.
Hydrolysis: The breakdown of a compound by water often catalysed by acids or alkalis.
Incomplete combustion: Combustion when air or oxygen is limiting.
Indicator: A compound or mixture of coloured compounds that changes colour over a specific pH.
Insulators: Non-conductors.
Ion: An atom or group of atoms with either a positive or negative charge.
Ionic bond: The strong force of attraction between oppositely charged ions.
Ionic equation: A symbol equation that shows only those ions and molecules that take part in a reaction.
Isotopes: Atoms of elements with the same number of protons but different numbers of neutrons.
Kinetic particle theory: The idea that particles are in constant motion.

Lustrous: Having a shiny surface.
Macromolecules: Very large molecules made up of repeating units.
Malleable: Can be shaped by hitting.
Mass number: The number of protons + the number of neutrons in an atom.
Melting: The change of state from solid to liquid.
Metallic bond: A bond formed by the attractive forces between the delocalised electrons and the positive ions.
Metallic conduction: The movement of mobile electrons through the metal lattice when a voltage is applied.
Mixture: This consists of two or more elements or compounds that are not chemically bonded together.
Molar concentration: The number of moles of solute dissolved in a solvent to make 1 dm^3 of a solution.
Molar gas volume: The volume of a mole of gas at r.t.p. or s.t.p.
Molar mass: The mass of a substance in moles.
Mole: The amount of substance that contains 6.02×10^{23} defined particles (atoms, ions, or molecules).
Molecular equation: A full symbol equation.
Molecular formula: Shows the number of atoms of each particular element in one molecule of a compound.
Molecule: A particle containing two or more atoms. The atoms can be the same or different.
Monomers: The small molecules that react and bond together to form a polymer.
Neutralisation: The reaction between an acid and a base to form a salt and water.
Neutral oxide: An oxide that does not react with acids or alkalis.
Neutron: The neutral particle in the nucleus of an atom.
Noble gas configuration: Atoms having a complete outer shell of electrons.
Nucleus: A tiny particle in the centre of an atom containing protons and neutrons.
Oxidation: The gain of oxygen or loss of electrons by a substance.
Oxidation number: A number given to each atom or ion in a compound to show the degree of oxidation.
Oxidising agent: A substance that accepts electrons and gets reduced.
Paper chromatography: A method used to separate a mixture of different dissolved substances depending on the solubility of the substances in the solvent and their attraction to paper.
Percentage yield: $\dfrac{\text{actual yield of product}}{\text{theoretical yield of product}} \times 100$
Periodic Table: Arrangement of elements in order of increasing atomic number so that most Groups contain elements with similar properties.
Periodicity: The regular occurrence of similar properties of the elements in the periodic table so that some groups

Glossary

have similar properties or a trend in properties.

Period: A horizontal row in the Periodic Table.

Petroleum: A thick liquid mixture of unbranched, branched, and ring hydrocarbons extracted from beneath the Earth's surface.

Photochemical reaction: A reaction that depends on the presence of light.

pH scale: A scale of numbers from 0 to 14 used to show how acidic or alkaline a solution is.

Physical properties: Properties that do not generally depend on the amount of substance present.

Pollution: Contaminating materials introduced into the natural environment (earth, air, or water).

Polyamide: Condensation polymer containing –NH-CO– linkages.

Polyester: Condensation polymer containing –COO– linkages.

Polymerisation: The conversion of monomers to polymers.

Polymers: Macromolecules made up by linking at least 50 monomers.

Precipitate: The solid obtained in a precipitation reaction.

Precipitation reaction: A reaction in which a solid is obtained when solutions of two soluble compounds are mixed.

Proton: The positively charged particles in the nucleus of an atom.

Radioactive isotopes: Isotopes with unstable nuclei, which break down.

Rate of reaction: The change in concentration of a reactant or product with time at a stated temperature.

Reaction pathway diagram: A diagram showing the enthalpy change from reactants to products for exothermic or endothermic reactions (the activation energy can also be shown).

Redox (reaction): A reaction where there is simultaneous oxidation and reduction.

Reducing agent: A substance that loses electrons and gets oxidised.

Reduction: The loss of oxygen or gain of electrons by a substance.

Relative atomic mass: The weighted average mass of naturally occurring atoms of an element on a scale where an atom of carbon-12 has a mass of exactly 12 units.

Relative formula mass: The relative average mass of one formula unit of a compound on a scale where an atom of the carbon-12 isotope has a mass of exactly 12 units.

Relative molecular mass: The relative mass of one molecule of a compound on a scale where an atom of the carbon-12 isotope has a mass of exactly 12 units.

Repeat unit: A regularly repeating part of a polymer.

Residue: The solid remaining on the filter paper when a mixture of solid and solution are filtered.

r.t.p.: Room temperature and pressure. (20 °C and 1 atmosphere pressure).

Rusting: Corrosion of iron and iron alloys caused by the presence of both water and oxygen.

Salt: A compound formed when the hydrogen in an acid is replaced by a metal or ammonium ion.

Saturated compounds: Organic compounds with only single bonds.

Separating funnel: Piece of apparatus used to separate immiscible liquids that have different densities.

Simple distillation: The separation of a liquid from a solid that involves the processes of boiling and condensation using a condenser.

Solubility: The number of grams of solute needed to form a saturated solution per 100 grams of solvent used.

Solution: A uniform mixture of two or more substances.

Solute: A substance that is dissolved in a solvent.

Solvent: A substance that dissolves a solute.

Sonorous: Rings when hit with a hard object.

Spectator ions: Ions that do not take part in a reaction.

Standard concentration: A concentration of 1 mole of substance in 1 dm^3 of solution under standard conditions.

State symbols: Letters put after a chemical formula showing whether it is a solid, liquid, gas, or aqueous solution.

Strong acid: An acid that ionises completely in solution.

Strong base: A base that ionises completely in solution.

Structural formula: Shows the way the atoms are arranged in a molecule with or without showing the bonds.

Structural isomers: Compounds with the same molecular formula but different structural formulae.

Substitution reaction: A reaction in which one atom or group of atoms replaces another.

Thermal decomposition: The breakdown of a compound when heated.

Titration: A method used to determine the amount of substance present in a given volume of solution of acid or alkali.

Titre: The final burette reading minus the initial burette reading in a titration.

Triple bond: Three covalent bonds between the same two atoms.

Unbranched hydrocarbons: Hydrocarbons with carbon atoms linked in a chain without alkyl side groups.

Unsaturated compounds: Organic compounds containing double or triple carbon–carbon bonds (in addition to single bonds).

Volatile: Easily evaporated at room temperature.

Weak acid: An acid that only partially dissociates / ionises in solution.

Weak base: A base that only partially dissociates / ionises in solution.

Answers

Unit 1.1
1. a. Put your finger over the top of tube and lower (slowly) into the water [1]
      Drop the crystal down the tube then raise the tube slowly [1]
   b. i. dissolving [1]
      ii. diffusion [1]
   c. Particles (of dye and water) move randomly / move in any direction [1]
      Dye particles spread out / diffuse [1]
      Overall movement of the dye is from area of high concentration (of the dye particles) to lower concentration (of dye particles) [1]
   d. Atom → the smallest neutral particle that can take part in a chemical change
      Ion → a particle with a positive or negative charge
      Molecule → two or more atoms joined (bonded) together
      All three have to be correct for 1 mark
2. a. Dust particles [1]
      You can see dust particles but not particles of oxygen/nitrogen/gases in the air [1]
   b. More particles in the air bombard (hit) the dust particle on one side than on another (or hit with greater force) [1]
      Dust particles move in direction of the greater number of hits [1]
      Particles in the air move randomly so the direction of the movement of the dust particles is also random [1]
   c. A: single atoms [1]
      B: ions [1]
      C: molecules [1]
      D: molecules [1]

Unit 1.2
1. Liquids i. fixed volume [1] ii. takes the shape of container only as far as it is filled [1]   Gases i. volume not fixed [1]
   ii. spreads everywhere (within a container) [1]
2. A: liquid [1]
   B: gas [1]
   C: solid [1]
   D: liquid [1]
3. A: melting / fusion [1]
   B: boiling / evaporation [1]
   C: freezing [1]
   D: condensing [1]
4. a. methane [1]
   b. naphthalene [1]
      Melting point is above room temperature [1]
   c. ethanol [1]
      Melting point is below room temperature and boiling point is above room temperature / room temperature is between melting point and boiling point [1]
5. a. The change in temperature is too rapid / goes from 114°C to 184°C too quickly [1]
      So the liquid state not noticed [1]
   b. Heat iodine in bath of suitable liquid – liquid with higher boiling point than water [1]
      The temperature of the bath is kept between the melting point and boiling point of iodine [1]

Unit 1.3
1. a. The particles in a solid are arranged in a **fixed** pattern (**lattice**). The forces of **attraction** between the particles are **strong** enough to keep them **together** and so the particles only **vibrate**. When a liquid evaporates, the particles with the **highest** energy leave the **surface** of the liquid first. (1 mark for each correct word)
   b. Box B: (solid): particles touching each other [1]
      particles arranged regularly / in more than 1 regular row [1]
      Box C: (liquid): particles touching each other [1]
      particles arranged irregularly / not in rows [1]
   c. The forces of attraction between the particles in a **liquid** are stronger than those between **gas** particles but weaker than those between the particles in a **solid**. Particles in a **solid** only vibrate.
      Particles in a **liquid** move more slowly than those in a **gas.** (1 mark for each correct word)
   d. Boiling only happens at the boiling point / in boiling bubbles of gas are seen throughout the liquid [1]
      Evaporation occurs at temperatures below the boiling point (and above the melting point) [1]
   e. i. (energy) absorbed [1]
      ii. (energy) released [1]
      iii. (energy) released [1]
      iv. (energy) absorbed [1]
   f. Arrangement goes from regular to irregular [1]
      Separation goes from touching / close together to far apart [1]
      Motion goes from vibrating to moving freely / moving fast [1]
   g. Silicon has strong forces of attraction between the particles [1]
      A lot of energy is needed to overcome these forces / a high temperature is needed to overcome these forces [1]
      Phosphorus has weak forces of attraction between the particles [1]
      Only a little energy is needed to overcomes these forces / a lower temperature is needed to overcome these forces [1]

Unit 1.4
1. When a liquid above room temperature cools, the **kinetic** energy of the particles **decreases**. The **temperature** of the liquid falls. At the melting point, the temperature stays **constant** for a time. The is because thermal energy (heat) is being **released** when a liquid **freezes**. (1 mark for each correct word)
2. A: solid and liquid [1]
   B: liquid [1]
   C: liquid and vapour / liquid and gas [1]
   D: vapour / gas [1]
3. Temperature increases because the kinetic energy of the particles increases [1]
   Temperature remains constant when solid changes to liquid [1]
   Because heat energy / thermal energy is being absorbed [1]
   To overcome the attractive forces between the particles in the solid [1]
4. Correct shape (from 120 °C to −10 °C) [2]
   If these two marks not scored allow 1 mark for a vertical section followed by a horizontal section
   100 °C at correct place [1]
   0 °C at correct place [1]

Unit 1.5
1. a. Diagram showing plunger pushed down so volume smaller and the same number of particles randomly arranged [1]
   b. More particles hit the wall [1]
      Every second [1]
      So the force on the wall is greater [1]
   c. Pressure decreases [1]
2. a. As pressure doubles the volume halves [2]
      If 2 marks not scored: 1 mark for increase in pressure decreases the volume
   b. As temperature increases, volume increases.
3. a. White solid forms where hydrogen chloride reacts with ammonia [1]
      Hydrogen chloride has a higher relative molecular mass than ammonia [1]
      So rate of diffusion of hydrogen chloride less than that of ammonia [1]
   b. Any two of hydrogen fluoride/ hydrogen bromide / hydrogen iodide (1 mark each)

142

Answers

    c. White ring forms about half way along the tube [1]
       Because hydrogen chloride has a similar relative molecular mass to methylamine [1]
       So rate of diffusion of both gases are approximately equal [1]

Unit 2.1
1. (1 mark for each correct word)
   Atoms are the **smallest** particles of matter which can take part in a **chemical** change. Atoms cannot be **broken** **down** by chemical means. An **element** contains only one type of atom.
2. a. carbon / tin [1]
   b. rubidium/ tin [1]
   c. iron/ cobalt/ nickel / copper [1]
   d. magnesium / Mg [1]
   e. H, B, C, N, O all shaded [2]
      4 correctly shaded [1]
   f. VII / halogens [1]
      VIII / 0 / noble gases [1]
3. a. single compound [1]
   b. single element [1]
   c. single element [1]
   d. mixture [1]
   e. single compound [1]
   f. mixture [1]
4. In a compound, iron and sulfur cannot be separated by physical means / in a mixture the iron and sulfur can be separated by physical means [1]
   In a compound the properties are different from those of the elements which went to make it / in a mixture the properties are those of iron and sulfur [1]
   In a compound iron and sulfur are combined in a definite proportion by mass / in a mixture iron and sulfur can be present in any proportion by mass [1]
   ALLOW: (for one mark) there is an energy change when iron combines with sulfur / there is no energy change when iron is mixed with sulfur

Unit 2.2
1. Atoms are the **smallest** particles of matter which can take part in a **chemical** change. Each atom consists of a **nucleus** made up of protons and **neutrons**. Outside the nucleus are the **electrons**. These are **arranged** in electron **shells** or energy **levels**.
   (1 mark for each correct word)
2. a. i. − / negative [1]
      ii. 0 / no charge (do not accept −) [1]
      iii. + / positive [1]
   b. i. The mass is using a particular mass as a comparison / relative to a twelfth mass of a carbon-12 atom [1]
      ii. 1/1700 to 1/2000 or 0.00054 or 0.0005 [1]
3. a. The number of protons / positive charges in the nucleus of an atom [1]
   b. atomic number [1]
   c. Proton number increases by one across a period [1]
4. a. 26 electrons [1] 26 protons [1] 32 neutrons [1]
   b. 1 electron [1] 1 proton [1] 0 neutrons [1]
   c. 35 electrons [1] 35 protons [1] 46 neutrons [1]
   d. 36 electrons [1] 36 protons [1] 48 neutrons [1]
5. Nucleus containing 3 protons and 4 neutrons [1]
   Protons labelled [1]
   Neutrons labelled [1]
   Nucleus labelled [1]
   Electrons outside nucleus (do not have to be in shells as not yet done) [1]
   Electrons labelled [1]
6. 149 [1]

Unit 2.3
1. The arrangement of the electrons in shells is called the electron **configuration**. An atom of fluorine has nine electrons, **two** in the first shell and **seven** in the second shell. Atoms of elements in the same **group** have the same number of electrons in their **outer** shell. As we move across a **period**, each atom has **one** more **electron** in its outer shell than the element before it.
   1 mark for each word in the correct place
2.

Element	Number of electrons in an atom	Electron configuration
nitrogen	7	2,5
oxygen	8	2,6
fluorine	9	2,7
neon	10	2,8
sodium	11	2,8,1
argon	18	2,8,8
calcium	20	2,8,8,2

1 mark for correct number of electrons in each atom, 1 mark for each correct electron configuration

3. 1 mark each correct structure. Electrons should be drawn in shells but do not have to be paired (although this is preferable)

2,8,3	2,4	2,8,7	2
aluminium	carbon	chlorine	helium
2,8,2	2,8	2,8,5	2,8,8,1
magnesium	neon	phosphorus	potassium

4. Complete outer shell of electrons in its atom / has eight electrons in its outer shell [1]
   This is a stable electronic configuration [1]
   The atom cannot gain, lose or share electrons [1]

Unit 2.4
1. Isotopes are **atoms** of the same **element** with the same number of **protons** but different numbers of **neutrons**.
   1 mark for each word in the correct place
2. a. 1 [1]
   b. It has no neutrons [1]
3.

Atom / ion of	Protons	Neutrons	Electrons
chlorine	17	18	17
cerium	58	78	58
sodium ion	11	12	10
phosphide ion	15	16	18

[12]

4. $^{139}_{57}$La [1]
5. (185 × 37.1) + (187 × 62.9) [1]
   18625.8 / 100 ALLOW: answer to first step divided by 100 [1]
   186.3 [1]
6. The average mass of the isotopes of an element [1]
   Idea of comparison with one-twelfth of the mass [1]
   Idea of comparison with isotope carbon-12 [1]

Unit 3.1
1. Separating iron from sulfur using a magnet [1]
   Melting zinc [1]
   Distilling plant oils from a mixture of plant oils and water [1]
2. 12 correct = 6, 10, or 11 correct = 5, 8, or 9 correct = 4, 6 or 7 correct = 3, 4, or 5 correct = 2, 2, or 3 correct = 1.

	Compound	Mixture
	The **elements** cannot be **separated** by **physical** means.	The substances in it can be **separated** by **physical** means.
	The properties are **different** from those of the **elements** which went to make it.	The properties are the **average** of the substances in it.
	The elements are **combined** in a **definite** proportion by mass.	The substances can be **present** in **any** proportion by mass.

3. a. Temperature of reaction mixture rises / test tube feels warmer / surroundings get warmer [1]

143

Answers

    b. Temperature of reaction mixture falls / test tube feels colder / surroundings get colder [1]
    c. melting / boiling [1]
    d. freezing / condensing [1]
4. a. CH_4 [1] b. C_2H_6 [1] c. H_2S [1] d. NH_3 [1]
5. a. tin(II) oxide + hydrochloric acid → tin(II) chloride + water [1]
    b. calcium carbonate → calcium oxide + carbon dioxide [1]
    c. copper + sulfuric acid → copper(II) sulfate + water + sulfur dioxide [1]

Unit 3.2
1. Any three (1 mark each) of:
   Colour of sodium chloride is different to the colour of a either chlorine or sodium [1]
   Sodium chloride is not acidic whereas chlorine is slightly acidic [1]
   Sodium chloride dissolves in water but sodium reacts with water [1]
   Heat is given out when the sodium chloride forms [1]
2. a. An ion is a **charged** particle [1]
   b. Ions have unequal numbers of **protons** and **electrons** / Ions have unequal numbers of **electrons** and **protons**
      (1mark for each gap correctly filled)
3. 2,8 [1] 2,8,8 [1] 2 [1] 2,8,18,8 [1]
4. a. K $^+$ b. F $^-$ c. O $^{2-}$ d. P $^{3-}$ e. Al $^{3+}$ f. Mg $^{2+}$
   (1 mark for each correct structure)
5. a. V^{2+} and V^{3+} Fe^{2+} and Fe^{3+} Co^{2+} and Co^{3+} Cu^+ and Cu^{2+}
      (2 marks for all correct, 1 mark for 6 correct or with 1 ion which are incorrect e.g. Fe^+)
   b. Most form ions with charges of 2+ and 3+ / [1]
      apart from Cu+ [1]
      (if no marks scored allow 1 mark for all form ions with several different charges)

Unit 3.3
1. A sodium chloride **lattice** is a **regular** arrangement of **positive** sodium ions and **negative** chloride ions which **alternate** with each other. The ions are held together by **strong** ionic **bonds**. This structure is called a **giant** ionic structure. (1 mark for each correct word)
2. Ionic compounds are formed ... by the reaction of metals with non metals.
   Ionic compounds have no ... overall charge.
   When a metal atom forms an ion ... it loses one or more electrons.
   When a non-metal atom forms an ion .... it gains one or more electrons.
   (4 correct = 2 marks, 2 correct = 1 mark)
3. a. 8 electrons in outer shell of Mg [1]
      8 electrons in outer shell of S [1]
      2– charge on S [1]
   b. Lithium chloride:
      2 electrons in one shell around Li [1]
      2,8,8 electrons for chlorine [1]
      + charge for Li and – charge for Cl at top right of each [1]
      Magnesium fluoride:
      2,8 electronic structure for Mg [1]
      2,8 electronic structure for each F [1]
      Each F has single negative (–) charge at top right [1]
      Mg has 2+ charge at top right [1]
   c. Calcium nitride:
      Three Ca ions and two nitride ions shown [1]
      Electronic structure is 2,8,8 for calcium [1]
      Electronic structure is 2,8 for nitride [1]
      2+ charge for Ca and 3– charge for nitride at top right of each [1]

Unit 3.4
1. a. A $MgBr_2$ [1] B Na_2O [1] C HCl [1]
      D $AlCl_3$ [1] E K_3N [1] F CaS [1]
      G Al_2S_3 [1] H Fe_2O_3 [1]
   b. I $Mg(NO_3)_2$ [1] J K_2SO_4 [1] K NH_4NO_3 [1]
      L $(NH_4)_2SO_4$ [1] M $Ca(OH)_2$ [1] N $NaHCO_3$ [1]
      O $Al(NO_3)_3$ [1] P Li_2CO_3 [1]
2. Q magnesium iodide [1] R strontium hydroxide [1]
   S iron(II) sulfate [1] T zinc nitrate [1]
   U ammonium carbonate [1] V calcium hydrogencarbonate [1]
3. a. $KMnO_4$ [1]
   b. Na_2O_2 [1]
   c. $Ca_3(PO_4)_2$ [1]
   d. $CaSO_3$ [1]
   e. Na_3PO_4 [1]

Unit 3.5
1. A covalent bond is formed when a **pair** of **electrons** is **shared** between two atoms leading to the **noble** gas electronic **configuration**.
   1 mark for each correct word
2. a. A group of atoms held together by covalent bonds [1]
   b. CO Cl_2 N_2 O_2 [2]
      (1 mark if 3 correct)
3. a. [dot-and-cross diagrams of H_2, Br_2, O_2, N_2]
   b. i. 2 around the hydrogen and eight around the bromine, oxygen, and nitrogen [1]
         (no mark for eight alone)
      ii. The electron shells are complete / full [1]
          This is a stable structure [1]
          Electrons cannot easily be lost or gained [1]
          Noble gas electron configuration [1]
          (note that bromine was not mentioned because electrons can still be added to the outer electron shell although the electronic structure 2,8,18,8 is stable)
4. 1 mark for each up to a maximum of 3, e.g., aluminium chloride (vapour) / beryllium chloride / tin tetrachloride / stannane, SnH_4 / plumbane, PbH_4

Unit 3.6
1. a. hydrogen bromide, water, ammonia, hydrogen sulfide, methane, phosphorus trichloride
   [dot-and-cross diagrams]

144

Answers

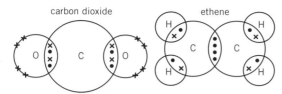

(1 mark for each correct structure)

b. hydrogen bromide, water, ammonia, hydrogen sulfide, phosphorus trichloride (all correct 2 marks, 3 or 4 correct 1 mark)

2. a. 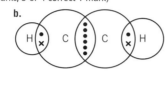 b.

c. 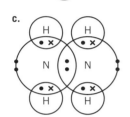 d.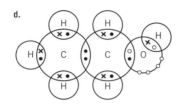

(1 mark each correct structure)

Unit 3.7

1. Magnesium oxide: ionic
   Carbon tetrachloride: covalent
   Potassium bromide; ionic
   Carbon disulfide: covalent
   Octane: covalent
   (2 marks if all correct and 1 mark if one error)
2. A with 4
   B with 7
   C with 1
   D with 2
   E with 6
   F with 3
   G with 5
   All 7 correct = 3 marks 5 or 6 correct = 2 marks, 3 or 4 correct = 1 mark
3. CS_2, I_2, S_8 [1]
4. The ions are not free to move [1]
   (do not allow 'there are no ions'/ 'the ions are free')
5. a. The molecules dissolving in water all have oxygen atoms found in OH groups [1]
   b. 1 mark for each soluble substance, e.g., ammonia / methylamine / sucrose / other alcohols / ethanoic acid / many amino acids

Unit 3.8

1. Diamond: B, C, D [1]
   Graphite: A, D, F [1]
   Silicon dioxide: B, C, D [1]
2. A with 4
   B with 1
   C with 5
   D with 2
   E with 3
   (all correct = 2 marks but 3 or 4 correct = 1 mark)
3. a. i. 4 [1]
      ii. 3 [1]
      iii. 4 [1]   2 [1]
   b. Diamond: tetrahedral [1] Graphite: hexagonally arranged / arranged in rings of 6 [1]
4. Diamond and graphite because they are the same element but the atoms are arranged differently [1]

5. a.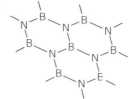

   Two or more layers drawn (two layers not shown in diagram) [1]
   (Layers of) hexagons drawn similar to graphite structure [1]
   B atoms alternate with N atoms [1]
   b. Weak force between the layers [1]
   So the layers can slide when a force is applied [1]

Unit 3.9

1. a.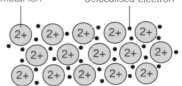

   Metal ions shown as + or 2+ [1]
   Metal ions labelled [1]
   Electrons shown as dot randomly dispersed between the metal ions [1]
   Electrons labelled free electrons / delocalised electrons / mobile electrons [1]
   b. i. Electrons are delocalised / electrons are mobile [1]
      They move between the metal ions when voltage applied [1]
      ii. When force applied the force of attraction between metal ions and mobile electrons is weakened [1]
      The layers slide over each other [1]
      (When force removed) new forces of attraction between metal ions and electrons formed [1]
      iii. strong forces of attraction between metal ions and mobile electrons [1]
      It needs a high amount of energy to weaken these forces of attraction [1]
2. a. D [1]
   It has a very high / the highest melting point [1]
   b. A, B, and C [1] Idea that metals are to the left of Group IV / to the left of covalent giant structures (in the Periodic Table) [1]
   c. E and F [1] They have low melting points / they are to the right of Group IV [1]
3. The different sized ions disrupt the regular arrangement of the metal ions [1]
   The layers cannot slide as easily (compared with pure metals) [1]

Unit 4.1

1. The formula for giant covalent and **ionic** compounds is the **ratio** of **atoms** or ions in the compound. The formula of a simple molecule shows exactly how many atoms are **bonded** together in each molecule. For example, ammonia has one **nitrogen** and three **hydrogen** atoms so its **molecular** formula is NH_3.
   (1 mark for each correct word)
2. a.

								H 1	
Li 1						B 3	C 4	N 3	O 2	F 1	Ne 0
Na 1	Mg 2					Al 3			S 2	Cl 1	
K 1	Ca 2		transition elements variable		Zn 2					Br 1	

1 mark for each column correct (= 8) 1 mark for H, 1 mark for transition elements
   b. Li, Na, K, Mg, Ca, Zn, Al [1]
   c. B, C, N, O, F, Cl, Br [1]

145

Answers

d. Any suitable e.g., C and N/ O /S / F / Cl / Br
H and O/N/ O /S / F / Cl / Br / N and O / S and O [1]
e. i. H_2S [1]
   ii. B_2O_3 [1]
   iii. CS_2 [1]
   iv. CBr_4 [1]
   v. Ca_3N_2 [1]
   vi. Al_2O_3 [1]
   vii. CH_4 [1]
3. a. (−)1 [1]
   b. 3 [1]
   c. 2 [1]
   d. 1 [1]
   e. 4 [1]
   f. (−)1 [1]

Unit 4.2
1. a. $O_2 + 2H_2 \rightarrow 2H_2O$
      Correct balance [1] correct use of + and → [1]
   b. $2C + O_2 \rightarrow 2CO$
      Correct balance [1] correct use of + and → [1]
2. a. atoms $2 \times H + 2 \times Cl$ $1 \times H$ $1 \times Cl$ [1]
      balance $H_2 + Cl_2 \rightarrow 2\,HCl$ [1]
   b. atoms $1 \times Mg + 2 \times O$ $1 \times Mg$ $1 \times O$ [1]
      balance O $1 \times Mg + 2 \times O \rightarrow 2\,MgO$ [1]
      balance Mg $2Mg + O_2 \rightarrow 2MgO$ [1]
3. a. $2K + Br_2 \rightarrow 2KBr$ [1]
   b. $4Al + 3O_2 \rightarrow 2Al_2O_3$ [1]
   c. $4Na + O_2 \rightarrow 2Na_2O$ [1]
   d. $N_2 + 3H_2 \rightarrow 2NH_3$ [1]
   e. $2Rb + 2H_2O \rightarrow 2RbOH + H_2$ [1]
   f. $I_2O_5 + 5CO \rightarrow I_2 + 5CO_2$ [1]
   g. $MgO + 2HNO_3 \rightarrow Mg(NO_3)_2 + H_2O$ [1]
   h. $Ca(OH)_2 + 2HCl \rightarrow CaCl_2 + 2H_2O$ [1]
   i. $3PbO + 2NH_3 \rightarrow 3Pb + N_2 + 3H_2O$ [1]

Unit 4.3
1. Relative atomic mass (symbol A_r) is the **average** mass of naturally occurring **isotopes** of an element compared to one-**twelfth** of the mass of an atom of **carbon-12**. The relative **molecular** mass (symbol M_r) is the **sum** of the relative atomic masses of the atoms in a molecule. For ionic substances, we use the term relative **formula** mass. (1 mark for each correct word)
2. a. 2 marks for each correct M_r (If 2 not scored, 1 mark for correct number of atoms)

Compound	Number of each atom	A_r of atom	M_r calculation
phosphorus trichloride PCl_3	P = 1 Cl = 3	P = 31 Cl = 35.5	1×31 $+ 3 \times \underline{35.5}$ $M_r = 137.5$
magnesium hydroxide $Mg(OH)_2$	Mg = 1 O = 2 H = 2	Mg = 24 O = 16 H = 1	1×24 2×16 $+ \underline{2 \times 1}$ $M_r = 58$
ethanol C_2H_5OH	C = 2 H = 6 O = 1	C = 12 H = 1 O = 16	2×12 6×1 $+ \underline{1 \times 16}$ $M_r = 46$
ammonium sulfate $(NH_4)_2SO_4$	N = 2 H = 8 S = 1 O = 4	N = 14 H = 1 S = 32 O = 16	2×14 8×1 1×32 $+ \underline{4 \times 16}$ $M_r = 132$
glucose $C_6H_{12}O_6$	C = 6 H = 12 O = 6	C = 12 H = 1 O = 16	6×12 12×1 $+ \underline{6 \times 16}$ $M_r = 180$

b. i. 342 [1] ii. 183 [1] iii. 220 [1]
c. i. 284 [1] ii. 363 [1] iii. 393 [1] iv. 287 [1]

Unit 4.4
1. a. i. $2H_2 + O_2 \rightarrow 2H_2O$
         $2 \times 2 + 1 \times 32 \rightarrow 2 \times 18$ [1]
         $4\,g + 32\,g \rightarrow 36\,g$ [1]
      ii. $2Al + 3Cl_2 \rightarrow 2AlCl_3$
          $2 \times 27 + 3 \times 71 \rightarrow 2 \times 133.5$ [1]
          $54\,g + 213\,g \rightarrow 267\,g$ [1]
   b. i. $\frac{12}{48} \times 80 = 20\,g$
         (1 mark) (1 mark)
      ii. 4.8 g [1]
      iii. 280 g [1]
2. a. $\frac{2 \times 12}{(2 \times 12) + (6 \times 1)} \times 100 = 80\%$
      2 marks for correct answer (1 mark if answer wrong but M_r incorrect)
   b. $\frac{14}{17} \times 100 = 82.4\%$ (2 marks if correct, 1 mark if answer wrong but M_r incorrect)
   c. $\frac{3 \times 23}{164} \times 100 = 42\%$ (2 marks if correct, 1 mark if answer wrong but M_r incorrect)
3. $\frac{29.25}{30.00} \times 100 = 97.5\%$ [1]

Unit 5.1
1. A: 2, B: 3, C: 4, D: 1 (all 4 correct = 2 marks, 2 or 3 correct = 1 mark)
2.

Element or compound	Formula mass, M_r	Mass taken / g	Number of moles
O_2	32	4	0.125 [1]
NaCl	58.5 [1]	11.7	0.2 [1]
$CaSO_4$	136 [1]	27.2	0.2 [1]
P_2O_5	142 [1]	56.8 [1]	0.4
CO_2	44 [1]	4.4 [1]	0.1
P_4	124 [1]	86.8	0.7 [1]
CH_4	16 [1]	384 [1]	24.0

3. a. 28 [1]
   b. 20 [1]
   c. 1.204×10^{25} [1]
4. A_r = mass/ moles [1] 27 [1]

Unit 5.2
1. a. i. $2 \times 24 + 1 \times 32 \rightarrow 2 \times 40$ [1]
         $48\,g + 32\,g \rightarrow 80\,g$ [1]
      ii. $4 \times 34 \rightarrow 4 \times 31 + 6 \times 2$ [1]
          $136\,g \rightarrow 124\,g + 12\,g$ [1]
      iii. $1 \times 76 + 3 \times 71 \rightarrow 1 \times 154 + 1 \times 135$ [1]
           $76\,g + 213\,g \rightarrow 154\,g + 135\,g$ [1]
   b. i. 5 [1]
      ii. 1 [1]
      iii. 2 [1]
      iv. mol $I_2O_5 = 24.84/334 = 0.07$ [1]
          So $5 \times 0.07 = 0.35$ mol CO_2
          mass = $M_r CO_2 \times$ moles $CO_2 = 44 \times 0.30 = 13.2\,g$ [1]
      v. mol CO = 21/28 = 0.75 [1] So 0.75 / 5 = 0.15 mol I_2
         mass = $M_r \times$ l2 moles $I_2 = 254 \times 0.15 = 38.1\,g$ [1]
2. a. 232 − 168 = 64 g [1]
   b. 64/16 = 4 mol [1]
   c. 168/56 = 3 mol [1]
   d. 3Fe:4O [1] Fe_3O_4 [1]
3. 2 moles Cl_2 produces 2/3 mole CCl_4 [1]
   = 2/3 × 154 g = 102.7 g CCl_4 [1]

Answers

Unit 5.3

1. a. 1000 cm³ [1]
   b. 24 dm³ [1]
   c. (number of) moles of gas × 24 [1]
   d. $\dfrac{\text{volume of gas in dm}^3}{24}$ [1]

2.
Gas	M_r of gas	Mass of gas / g	Moles of gas / mol	Volume of gas / dm³
ammonia	17	8.5	**0.5** [1]	**12** [1]
oxygen	32	**64** [1]	**2** [1]	48
carbon dioxide	44	3.08	**0.07** [1]	**1.68** [1]
hydrogen chloride	**36.5** [1]	292	8	**192** [1]
ethane	30	**3.75** [1]	**0.125** [1]	3

3. a. 50 cm³ [1]
   b. 75 cm³ [1]
   c. 2:3
   d. $2N_2O(g) \rightarrow 2N_2(g) + O_2(g)$ [1]

4. 8.8 g propane = 8.8/44 = 0.2 mol [1]
   So 3 × 0.2 moles = 0.6 moles CO_2
   Volume of CO_2 = 0.6 × 24 = 14.4 dm³ [1]

Unit 5.4

1. a. concentration in mol/dm³ = $\dfrac{\text{amount of solute in \textbf{moles}} [1]}{\text{\textbf{volume of solution}} [1] \text{ in dm}^3}$ [1]
   b. amount of solute (moles) = concentration (mol/dm³) × volume of solution (dm³) [1]
   c. volume (dm³) = $\dfrac{\text{amount of solute in moles}}{\text{concentration (mol/dm}^3)}$ [1]

2. a. i. 200 cm³ [1]   ii. 40 cm³ [1]
      iii. 3500 cm³ [1]   iv. 8 cm³ [1]
   b. i. 0.025 dm³ [1] ii. 0.75 dm³ [1]
      iii. 4.0 dm³ [1] iv. 0.156 dm³ [1]

3.
Solute	M_r of solute	Mass of solute / g	Volume of solution / cm³ or dm³	Concentration of solution mol/dm³
sodium hydroxide	40	8	250 cm³	**0.8** [1]
silver nitrate	170	**17** [1]	200 cm³	0.5
copper(II) sulfate	160	40	**2.0 dm³** [1]	0.125
potassium sulfate	174	3.48	750 cm³	**0.027** [1]
ammonium chloride	53.5	**214** [1]	5.0 dm³	0.8
sulfuric acid	98	4.9	**25 cm³** [1]	2.0

4. Molar mass of CuF_2 = 102 [1]
   Solubility in g/dm³ = (4.54 × 10⁻³) × 102 = 0.463 g/dm³ [1]
   Mass in 200 cm³ = 0.0926 g [1]
   mass remaining = 0.15 − 0.0926 = 0.057 [4] [1]

Unit 5.5

11. a. moles of Pb = 0.1 mol   moles of Cl = 0.4 mol [1]
    Divide by   Pb $\dfrac{0.1}{0.1}$ Cl $\dfrac{0.4}{0.1}$ [1]
    lowest number of moles
    Result of division = 1   = 4
    Simplest ratio **1Pb:4Cl** [1]   So empirical formula is $\mathbf{PbCl_4}$ [1]

    b. mole % of C = $\dfrac{85.7}{12}$ = 7.14   mole % of H = $\dfrac{14.3}{1}$ mol = 14.3 [1]
    Divide by   C $\dfrac{7.14}{7.14}$ H $\dfrac{14.3}{7.14}$ [1]
    lowest number of moles
    Result of division = 1   = 2
    Simplest ratio **1C:2H** [1]   So empirical formula is $\mathbf{CH_2}$ [1]

    c. mole % of N = $\dfrac{85.7}{14}$ = 6.12   mole % of H = $\dfrac{12.5}{1}$ mol = 12.5 [1]
    Divide by   N $\dfrac{6.12}{6.12}$ H $\dfrac{12.5}{6.12}$ [1]
    lowest number of moles
    Result of division = 1   = 2
    So empirical formula is $\mathbf{NH_2}$ [1]

2. a. Weigh the tube [1]
   Weigh the aluminium powder accurately / weigh tube + aluminium powder [1]
   Pass the chlorine over the heated aluminium until reaction is complete [1]
   Weigh the tube + aluminium chloride [1]
   Find the mass of the aluminium chloride by subtraction [1]
   Deduce mass of chlorine (from mass of aluminium chloride − mass of aluminium) [1]
   Deduce moles of aluminium and moles of chlorine [1]
   Find simplest ratio in which aluminium and chlorine combine [1]
   b. Use of fume cupboard [1]
   Absorb excess chlorine in suitable chemical [1]
   Use of gloves setting up and manipulating apparatus [1]

Unit 5.6

1. The molecular formula of a **compound** shows the **actual** number of **atoms** that combine. The empirical formula shows the **simplest** ratio of atoms which combine. The formula of an **ionic** compound is the same as its **empirical** formula.
   (1 mark for each correct word)

2. a. HO   b. CH_2 c. NO_2 d. Sb_2O_3 e. C_2H_5 f. P_2O_5 g. Na_2SO_4
   (1 mark each)

3. A empirical formula mass 110 [1]   molecular formula P_4O_6 [1]
   B empirical formula mass 67.5 [1] molecular formula S_2Cl_2 [1]
   C empirical formula mass 30 [1]   molecular formula $C_2H_4O_2$ [1]
   D empirical formula mass 33 [1]   molecular formula C_4Cl_8 [1]

4. Mass of O = 360 − 168 = 192 [1]
   Dividing by atomic masses [1]
   C: 144/12 = 12, H 24/1 = 24, O = 192/16 = 12
   Dividing by 12 to get empirical formula, CH_2O [1]
   Empirical formula mass = 30 [1]
   Relative molecular mass = $C_6H_{12}O_6$ [1]

Unit 5.7

1. a. 100 g/mol [1]
   b. 3.840 dm³ [1]
   c. 3.840/24 = 0.16 mol [1]
   d. 0.16 mol [1]
   e. 0.16 × 100 = 16 g
   f. 16/18 (× 100) = 89%

2. a. 122 g/mol [1]
   b. 24.4/122 = 0.2 mol [1]
   c. 0.2 mol [1]
   d. 136 g/mol [1]
   e. 0.2 × 136 = 27.2 g
   f. 25.84/27.2 (× 100) = 95% [1]

3. Mol Al = 5.4/27 = 0.2 mol [1]
   Mol Al_2O_3 expected = 0.1 mol [1]
   Mass of Al_2O_3 expected = 0.1 × 102 = 10.2 g [1]
   % yield = 8.67/10.2 (× 100) = 85% [1]

Unit 6.1

1. Reactions which involve both oxidation and **reduction** are called **redox** reactions. Oxidation is the **gain** of oxygen and reduction is the **loss** of oxygen. Combustion involves the **oxidation** of a substance in which **heat** is given out and one or more of the **reactants** is a gas.
   (1 mark for each word)

2. a. Arrow from hydrogen to water labelled oxidation [1]
      Arrow from oxygen to water labelled reduction [1]
   b. Arrow from lead oxide to lead labelled reduction [1]
      Arrow from hydrogen to water labelled oxidation [1]

147

Answers

c. Arrow from iron oxide to iron labelled reduction [1]
   Arrow from carbon to carbon monoxide labelled oxidation [1]
d. Arrow from carbon to carbon monoxide labelled oxidation [1]
   Arrow from methane to hydrogen labelled reduction [1]
e. Arrow from zinc oxide to zinc labelled reduction [1]
   Arrow from carbon to carbon monoxide labelled oxidation [1]
f. Arrow from iron to iron oxide labelled oxidation [1]
   Arrow from water to hydrogen labelled reduction [1]

3. a. Arrows from methane to both carbon dioxide and water labelled oxidation [1]
      Arrows from oxygen to carbon dioxide and water labelled reduction [1]
   b. Arrow from carbon disulfide to carbon labelled reduction [1]
      Arrow from hydrogen to hydrogen sulfide labelled oxidation [1]

Unit 6.2

1. a. $Ca \rightarrow Ca^{2+} + 2e^-$ [1] oxidation [1]
   b. $Cl_2 + 2e^- \rightarrow 2Cl^-$ [1] reduction [1]
   c. $Al^{3+} + 3e^- \rightarrow Al$ [1] reduction [1]
   d. $Fe^{2+} \rightarrow Fe^{3+} + e^-$ [1] oxidation [1]
   e. $O_2 + 4e^- \rightarrow 2O^{2-}$ [1] reduction [1]
   f. $Pb^{4+} + 2e^- \rightarrow Pb^{2+}$ [1] reduction [1]
   g. $2Br^- \rightarrow Br_2 + 2e^-$ [1] oxidation [1]

2. a. Na^+ and OH^- [1]
   b. Mg^{2+} and Cl^- [1]
   c. Ba^{2+} and NO_3^- [1]
   d. Cu^{2+} and SO_4^{2-} [1]
   e. Al^{3+} and O^{2-} [1]
   f. Fe^{2+} and OH^- [1]

3. a. Ions $Cu^{2+} + 2Cl^-$ [1] $(2Na^+) + 2Cl^-$ [1]
      Cancel: $Cu^{2+} + 2Cl^-$ and $(2Na^+) + 2Cl^-$ [1]
      Equation: $Cu^{2+}(aq) + 2OH^-(aq) \rightarrow Cu(OH)_2(s)$ [1]
   b. Ions: $Ba^{2+} + 2Cl^-$ $Mg^{2+} + SO_4^{2-} \rightarrow Mg^{2+} + 2Cl^-$ [1]
      Cancel: $Ba^{2+} + 2Cl^-$ $Mg^{2+} + SO_4^{2-} \rightarrow Mg^{2+} + 2Cl^-$ [1]
      Equation $Ba^{2+}(aq) + SO_4^{2-}(aq) \rightarrow BaSO_4(s)$

4. a. $Pb^{2+}(aq) + 2Cl^-(aq) \rightarrow PbCl_2(s)$
      (1 mark for reactants and products, 1 mark for balance and state symbols)
   b. $Cl_2(aq) + 2I^-(aq) \rightarrow I_2(s) + 2Cl^-(aq)$
      (1 mark for reactants and products, 1 mark for balance and state symbols)

Unit 6.3

1. Oxidation number tells us how many **electrons** each atom of an element has gained, lost or **shared** when forming a **compound**. The oxidation state of **atoms** of an uncombined element is **zero**.
   (1 mark for each correct word)

2. a. +2 b. +4 c. −2 d. +3 e. −1 f. +4 g. +3
   h. +1 i. +6
   (1 mark each)

3. a. 0 to +3 [1] oxidation [1]
   b. 0 to +4 [1] oxidation [1]
   c. +2 to 0 [1] reduction [1]
   d. 0 to −1 [1] reduction [1]
   e. 0 to +3 [1] oxidation [1]

4. a. +7 b. +6 c. +3 d. +4 e. +5 (1 mark each) [5]

Unit 6.4

1. A with 3, B with 4, C with 2, D with 1
   (2 marks if all 4 correct, 1 mark if 2 correct)

2. Acidified potassium manganate(VII) is ... an oxidising agent ... which turns from purple ... to colourless ... in the presence of a reducing agent.
   (2 marks if all correct, 1 mark if 1 error)
   Acidified potassium iodide is ... a reducing agent ... which turns from colourless ... to red-brown ... in the presence of an oxidising agent.
   (2 marks if all correct, 1 mark if 1 error)

3. a. Oxidising agent is O_2, reducing agent is Mg [1]
   b. Oxidising agent is PbO, reducing agent is H_2 [1]
   c. Oxidising agent is Cl_2, reducing agent is I^- [1]
   d. Oxidising agent is H_2O_2, reducing agent is I^- [1]
   e. Oxidising agent is CuO, reducing agent is NH_3 [1]
   f. Oxidising agent is Cu^{2+}, reducing agent is Zn [1]

Unit 7.1

1. a. i. (indicator) bulb/ lamp labelled [1]
         cells / battery / power source labelled [1]
      ii. Arrow in clockwise direction, from − of battery through the bulb and solid to the + of the battery [1]

2. Electrolyte: liquid that conducts electricity [1]
   Electrolysis: breakdown of ionic substance when molten or in solution [1]
   by passage of electricity [1]
   Insulator: substance that does not conduct electricity / substance that is a poor conductor of electricity [1]

3. A with 3, B with 1, C with 4, D with 2 (2 marks if 4 correct, 1 mark if 2 or 3 correct)

4. a. Good electrical conductor [1]
      Low density / lightweight [1]
   b. (Fairly good) electrical conductor [1]
      Strong [1]

5. Four substances having delocalised electrons. (1 mark for each two)
   e.g., graphite / metal (only 1 allowed) / aromatic hydrocarbons e.g. benzene, phenol, graphene / nanotubes
   Some substances containing delocalised electrons are molecules [1]
   Electrons cannot flow from one molecule to another / electrons cannot flow between molecules [1]

Unit 7.2

1. A battery/ cell(s) / power supply [1]
   B anode [1]
   C cathode [1]
   D electrolyte [1]

2. More reactive elements such as **sodium** are **more** likely to form ions than **less** reactive elements such as **silver**. If a metal is more reactive than **hydrogen**, its **ions** stay in solution and hydrogen arising from hydrogen ions in **water** bubbles off.
   (1 mark for each correct word)

3. 1 mark for each 'cell' correct

Electrolyte	Cathode (−) product	Anode (+) product	Observations at the anode
Concentrated KCl(aq)	hydrogen	chlorine	bubbles of gas, green when collected
ZnBr(l)	zinc	bromine	red-brown vapour
Dilute H_2SO_4(aq)	hydrogen	oxygen	colourless bubbles
Dilute NaCl(aq)	hydrogen	oxygen	colourless bubbles
Concentrated HCl(aq)	hydrogen	chlorine	bubbles of gas, green when collected
Dilute $AgNO_3$(aq)	silver	oxygen	colourless bubbles

4. a. Hydrogen formed at the cathode because sodium is too high in the reactivity series to be discharged [1][1]
      Bromine formed at the anode [1] because halogens are discharged more readily than hydrogen and the concentration of bromine is high [1]
   b. Hydrogen formed at the cathode [1] because sodium is too high in the reactivity series to be discharged [1]
      Mixture of chlorine and oxygen formed at the cathode [1]
      Neither concentrated enough, where chlorine would be largely discharged, or dilute enough, where oxygen would be largely discharged [1]

Answers

Unit 7.3
1. a. molten zinc bromide
   b. dilute sulfuric acid

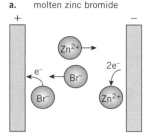
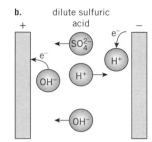

   c. concentrated hydrochloric acid
   d. aqueous copper(II) sulfate

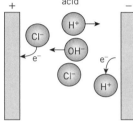
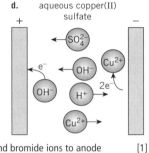

   a. Zinc ions moving to cathode and bromide ions to anode [1]
      Bromide ions donating electrons to anode and zinc ions taking electrons from cathode [1]
   b. Hydrogen ions moving to cathode and hydroxide and sulfate ions to anode [1]
      Hydroxide ions donating electrons to anode and hydrogen ions taking electrons from cathode [1]
   c. Hydrogen ions moving to cathode and chloride and hydroxide ions to anode [1]
      Chloride ions donating electrons to anode and hydrogen ions taking electrons from cathode [1]
   d. Hydrogen ions and copper ions moving to cathode and hydroxide and sulfate ions to anode [1]
      Hydroxide ions donating electrons to anode and copper ions taking electrons from cathode [1]

2. a. i. positive [1]
         gain [1]
      ii. negative [1]
         lose [1]
      iii. cathode, anode [1]
   b. i. $Zn^{2+} + \underline{2e^-} \rightarrow \underline{Zn}$ [1]
      ii. $\underline{2}Cl^- \rightarrow \underline{Cl_2} + \underline{2e^-}$. (1 mark for 2 and Cl_2, 1 mark for balance with electrons)
      iii. $\underline{2}H^+ + \underline{2e^-} \rightarrow \underline{H_2}$ (1 mark for 2 and H_2, 1 mark for balance with electrons)
      iv. $Al^{3+} + \underline{3e^-} \rightarrow \underline{Al}$ [1]

3. a. $4OH^- \rightarrow O_2 + 2H_2O + 4e^-$
      (1 mark for correct formulae including electrons, 1 mark for balance)
   b. $2O^{2-} \rightarrow O_2 + 4e^-$
      (1 mark for correct formulae including electrons, 1 mark for balance)

Unit 7.4
1.

Mass of the electrodes	anode: no change [1] cathode: increases slightly [1]	anode: decreases [1] cathode: large increase [1]
Appearance	anode: none / bubbles given off [1] cathode: goes pink / brown [1]	anode: gets thinner [1] cathode: gets thicker with lighter colour pink deposit [1]
Electrolyte	remains same depth of colour [1]	gets a lighter blue / fades [1]

2. a. A = rod, C = jug, E = liquid / solution in which the anode and cathode dip [1]
      (3 correct = 2 marks, 1 or 2 correct = 1 mark)

   b. Gains mass (slightly) [1]
      Becomes silvery [1]
3. a. $4OH^- \rightarrow O_2 + 2H_2O + 4e^-$
      (1 mark for correct formulae including electrons, 1 mark for balance)
   b. $Ni^{2+} + 2e^- \rightarrow Ni$ (2 marks if completely correct but if not, 1 mark for Ni^{2+})

Unit 8.1
1. a. endothermic [1] b. exothermic [1] c. endothermic [1]
   d. exothermic [1]
2. a. Energy on the vertical axis of both L and M [1]
      Reactants on lines on the left of both L and M [1]
      Products on the lines on the right of both L and M [1]
      Downward arrow between the two lines in L [1]
      Upward arrow between the two lines in M [1]
   b. The energy of the reactants is greater than the energy of the products [1]
3. (1 mark for each correct word)
   An exothermic reaction transfers **thermal** energy to the **surroundings**. This leads to an **increase** in the **temperature** of the surroundings. The transfer of thermal **energy** during a reaction is called the **enthalpy** change.
4. a. 8.8 g propane = 8.8/44 = 0.2 mol [1]
      0.2 × −2219 = −443.8 kJ [1]
   b. 4.8 dm³ = 4.8/24 = 0.2 mol CO_2 [1]
      For every mole of CO_2 it only needs one-third of a mole of propane to be burnt
      So moles of propane = 0.2/3 = 0.067 mol [1]
      0.067 × −2219 = −147.9 kJ [1]
5. a. The minimum energy that particles must possess in order to react when they collide [1]
      E_a kJ/mol (1 mark for correct symbol, 1 mark for correct unit) [2]
   b. The transfer of thermal energy to or from the surroundings during a chemical process [1]
      ΔH kJ/mol (1 mark for correct symbol, 1 mark for correct unit) [2]

Unit 8.2
1. A: 4, B:1, C:2; D: 3 (all 4 correct = 2 marks, 2 or 3 correct = 1 mark)
2.

Axes correctly labelled [1]
Reactants and products correct, with products above reactants in terms of energy [1]
Arrow for enthalpy change correct and pointing upwards [1]
Arrow for activation energy correct and pointing upwards [1]
Arrows correctly labelled [1]
3. In exothermic reaction, the arrow for enthalpy change points down [1]
   and the products have a lower energy than the reactants [1]
4. Endothermic [1]
   because the enthalpy change is positive [1]
   bond breaking is endothermic / thermal decomposition reactions are endothermic [1]

Unit 8.3
1. In an exothermic reaction ... the energy released ... in forming new bonds ... in the products ... is greater than ... the energy absorbed ... in breaking the bonds ... in the reactants. [1]
   In an endothermic reaction ... the energy released ... in forming new bonds ... in the products ... is less than ... the energy absorbed ... in breaking the bonds ... in the reactants. [1]

Answers

2.

Bonds broken (endothermic +) / kJ		Bonds formed (exothermic −) / kJ	
4 × (C–H) = 4 × 413 = **1652**	[1]	2 × (C=O) = 2 × 805 = 1610	[1]
2 × (O=O) = **2** × 498 = **996**	[1]	4 × (O–H) = 4 × 464 = 1856	[1]
Total = +2648		Total = −3466	

Overall energy change = (+ 2648) + (−3466) = −818 kJ [1]

3.

Bonds broken (endothermic +) / kJ		Bonds formed (exothermic −) / kJ	
2 × (H–H) = 2 × 436 = 872	[1]	4 × (O–H) = 4 × 464 = 1856	[1]
1 × (O=O) = 1 × 498 = 498	[1]		
Total = +1370	[1]	Total = −1856	

Overall energy change = (+ 1370) + (−1856) = −486 kJ [1]

4. CH_3 groups in propane / no CH_3 groups in CO_2 [1]
   groups next to C=O affect the bond energy of the C=O bond [1]

Unit 8.4

1. A fuel cell consists of two **porous** electrodes coated with **platinum**. The electrolyte is either an acid or an **alkali**. Hydrogen and **oxygen** are bubbled through the porous electrodes where the **reactions** take place. When connected to an **external** circuit, **electrons** flow from the **negative** electrode to the positive electrode.
   (1 mark for each correct word)

2. a. voltmeter [1]
   b. D [1]
   c. A [1]

3. a. $2H_2 + 4OH^- \rightarrow 4H_2O + 4e^-$ (1 mark for correct symbols, 1 mark for balance)
   b. $O_2 + 2H_2O + 4e^- \rightarrow 4OH^-$ (1 mark for correct symbols, 1 mark for balance)

4. Advantages: 1 mark each for any two of: no pollutants formed or only water formed / lighter in weight / more efficient or fewer moving parts / produces more energy per g of fuel burnt
   Disadvantages: 1 mark each for any two of: hydrogen more flammable / hydrogen is mainly made from fossil fuels (at present) / difficulties with storing gas

5. Magnesium is more reactive than copper [1]
   Magnesium forms ions more readily than copper [1]
   When in a circuit connected to copper magnesium loses electrons [1]
   The electrons flow along the wires to the copper strip [1]

Unit 9.1

1. To find the rate of reaction we can either measure how **quickly** the reactants are **used**. up or how quickly the **products** are formed. To calculate the **rate** of reaction we need to find out how some measurement changes with **time**. For example, the **volume** of gas given off per **second**, or how the mass of the reaction mixture **decreases** with time.
   (1 mark for each correct word)

1. B, C, D, A [1]

2. a. Copper reducing in size [1]
      Solution getting darker [1]
      Gas given off [1]
   b. 1 mark each for any three of
      decrease in mass of copper per minute
      increase in volume of gas per minute
      increase in depth of colour of solution / increase in copper compound per minute
      decrease in concentration of acid per minute

3. Electrical conductivity due to movement of ions [1]
   Ions on the left but none on right [1]

Unit 9.2

1. a. 66 s [1]
   b. 46 cm^3
   c. 33 cm^3 [1]
   d. 33/30 shown on graph [1]
      rate = 1.1 cm^3/s [1]

e. Points all plotted correctly [1]
   Best curve through the points [1]

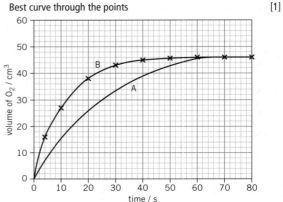

2. Any three suitable methods with (1 mark each) with reasons (1 mark each) e.g. Measure electrical conductivity [1]
   Ions have different conductivities and so the number and type of ions may be used to measure rate [1]
   Use a colorimeter [1]
   Intensity of a particular colour may change during the reaction [1]
   Sampling, quenching then titrating sample [1]
   Concentrations of acids or alkalis found by neutralisation reactions using indicator [1]

Unit 9.3

1. a.

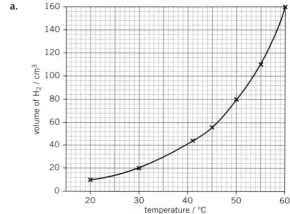

   Correct axes labelled with units [1]
   Full use of grid [1]
   7 points plotted correctly [2]
   (but 5 or 6 plotted correctly =) [1]
   Curved line of best fit [1]
   b. Increases with increase in temperature [1]
      Comment that increase gets increasingly greater / greater with each 10 °C rise [1]

2. a. A [1]
   b. 42/60 = 0.7 cm^3/s [1]
   c. At 20 s: shows correct method e.g. (60 − 10)/44 [1]
      = 1.14 cm^3/s [1]
      ALLOW: 1.0 to 1.2
      At 40 s: shows correct method e.g. (60 − 25)/53 [1]
      = 0.66 cm^3/s [1]
      Allow: 0.62 to 0.70

Unit 9.4

1. a. i. 2 × 2 × 6 = 24 cm^2 [1]
      ii. For 1 cube surface area = 1 × 1 × 6 = 6 cm^2 [1]
         For 8 cubes = 6 × 8 = 48 cm^2 [1]
      iii. B [1]
   b. Three curves levelling off [1]
      Steepest curve labelled S and shallowest curve labelled L [1]

Answers

[Graph: volume of CO₂ / cm³ vs time / s, with three curves labelled S, M, L]

2. a. The particles are more spread out / further away from each other [1]
        The concentration of the particles has decreased which leads to a lower rate of reaction
        Allow answers based on decreased collision frequency [1]
    b. The particles are less spread out / particles are closer together [1]
        The concentration of the particles has increased which leads to a lower rate of reaction
        Allow answers based on increased collision frequency [1]
3. Dust particles have very large surface area / volume ratio [1]
    Idea of many particles exposed to the air / oxygen [1]
    So reaction with air / oxygen is very fast [1]
    So fast that in the <u>presence of spark</u> there may be an explosion [1]

Unit 9.5

1. In order to react, particles must **collide** with each other. The collisions must have enough **energy** to break **bonds** to allow a reaction to happen. Increasing the concentration of a reactant **increases** the **frequency** of collisions and increases the **rate** of reaction. Increasing temperature makes particles move **faster** and increases the **kinetic** energy of the particles so that there are more **successful** collisions.
    (1 mark for each correct word) [9]

2. a. *[Diagram of particles in a container]*
        More acid particles drawn [1]
        Same number Mg particles remaining [1]
        Particles randomly spread out including water particles [1]
    b. Fewer acid particles drawn [1]
        Fewer magnesium particles drawn [1]
        Particles drawn randomly including water particles (and $MgCl_2$ particles) [1]
3. Powder has greater total surface area / ribbon has lower total surface area [1]
    More magnesium particles exposed (on the surface) for reaction in the powder / or reverse argument for ribbon [1]
    Greater frequency of collisions between the acid and magnesium for the powder / or reverse argument for ribbon [1]
4. Idea of (weak) adsorption of reactants onto catalyst surface [1]
    Idea of reactants close to each other on surface of catalyst [1]
    Idea of easier bond forming (since reactants closer to each other) [1]
    Idea of bond breaking / desorption [1]

Unit 9.6

1. a. Oxygen gas formed [1]
        Causes the detergent to bubble [1]
    b. manganese(IV)oxide [1]
    c. There was half the amount of liver than copper(II) oxide in the tube [1]
        So the number of bubbles per g would be more [1]
    d. i.   Enzyme [1]
        ii. Cut it into smaller pieces / grind it up [1]
             More enzymes would be released / more enzyme available (not increases surface area) [1]
    e. Measure volume of oxygen / gas given off [1]
        Over a particular time interval [1]
        Using gas syringe / other method of collecting gas e.g. upturned measuring cylinder or burette filled with water [1]
2. a. Reactants / substrate bonds to enzyme surface [1]
        At the active site / at a particular place on the enzyme [1]
        Enzyme changes shape to fit the reactants
        Allow lock and key hypothesis [1]
        Groups on enzyme (amino acids or metal ions) catalyse the reaction [1]
        Products diffuse away from active site [1]
    b. Room temperature / body temperature / specified values between 10 and 40 °C [1]
        pH 7 (Allow: pH between 6.5 and 8) [1]

Unit 10.1

1. a. Reversible reaction / equilibrium reaction [1]
    b. It goes pink [1]
    c. Warm / heat gently [1]
    d. i.   The water (weakly) bonded to the ions in a hydrated compound [1]
        ii   Without water / not containing water [1]
2. a. closed [1]
    b. rate, forward, rate, reverse/ backward OR rate, reverse / backward, rate, forward
        (1 mark for rate and rate, 1 mark for backward and forward in the correct positions)
3. Molecules randomly arranged in the mixture [1]
    All three types of molecule present [1]
    More molecules of hydrogen iodide than molecules of hydrogen and iodine [3]
4. a. Concentration on vertical axis and time on horizontal axis [1]
        Upward curve [1]
        Curve levelling off after time and remaining horizontal [1]
    b. Downward curve [1]
        Curve levelling off after time and remaining horizontal [1]
        Curve levels off at the same level as the one in part a. [1]

Unit 10.2

1. a. left [1]
    b. decreases [1]
    c. left [1] more [1] left [1] OR left [1] fewer [1] right [1]
        NOTE: third mark dependent on second being correct
    d. has no effect on position of equilibrium / catalysts ONLY affect rate [1]
2. a. to the right [1]
    b. to the left [1]
    c. to the right [1]
    d. no effect [1]
3. a. White precipitate disappears [1]
    b. Increase in amount of white precipitate [1]
    c. There are no gaseous reactants or products [1]
4. Temperature of 450 °C [1]
    Pressure just above atmospheric / 2 atm [1]
    The temperature is a compromise between: [1]
    A faster rate of reaction the higher the temperature [1]
    and a lower yield at higher temperature [1]
    because the reaction is exothermic [1]
    High pressure is not used because the yield is very high [1]
    So it would not be worthwhile spending extra money on expensive pressure equipment (compressors) [1]

Unit 10.3

1. The hydrogen is made by reacting <u>natural</u> gas with <u>steam</u> The nitrogen comes from the air after <u>oxygen</u> has been removed by reaction with <u>hydrogen</u>. The nitrogen and hydrogen are <u>compressed</u> and pumped into a <u>converter</u> where they react at 450 °C in the presence of a catalyst of <u>iron</u>.
    (1 mark for each correct word)

151

Answers

2. $N_2(g) + 3H_2(g) \rightleftharpoons 2NH_3(g)$
(1 mark for correct formulae, 1 mark for balance)
3. a. Increasing pressure increases % yield [1]
   b. The % yield decreases with increasing temperature [1]
   c. 52% [1]
   d. Advantage: % yield higher [1]
      Disadvantage: rate of reaction slower [1]
4. Reactant level above product level [1]
   Enthalpy change shown as negative with arrow going downwards between reactants and products [1]
   Energy curve increases from reactants to a maximum and then decreases to the products [1]
   Second energy curve of the same type but with lower maximum [1]
   Activation energy of catalysed reaction shown (upward arrow from reactants to highest point of energy curve) [1]
   Activation energy of uncatalysed reaction shown (upward arrow from reactants to highest point of energy curve for catalysed reaction) [1]

Unit 10.4

1. a. Catalyst / to speed up the rate of reaction [1]
   b. i. As temperature increases from 300 to about 450 °C there is not much difference in yield / the yield gets a little less [1]
      At temperatures higher than about 450 °C the yield decreases markedly [1]
      ii. 92–93 % [1]
      iii. For an exothermic reaction, the yield decreases as temperature increases [1]
   c. i. Increasing pressure increases shift the equilibrium to the right [1]
      There are fewer moles / smaller volume of gas on the right in the equation [1]
      ii. There is nearly 100% yield at just above atmospheric pressure [1]
2. a. $C + 2H_2SO_4 \rightarrow 2H_2O + SO_2 + CO_2$
      (1 mark for formulae, 1 mark for balance)
   b. $H_2S + H_2SO_4 \rightarrow 2H_2O + SO_2 + S$
      (1 mark for formulae, 1 mark for balance)

Unit 11.1

1. a. i. blue [1] ii. yellow [1] iii. blue [1] iv. red [1]
      v. red [1]
   b. Dip the litmus paper into the solution to be tested [1]
      If acidic blue litmus turns red [1]
      If alkaline red litmus turns blue [1]
      (If second two marks not scored; allow 1 mark for litmus is blue in alkaline solution and red / pink in acid)
2. a. (1 mark each)
      i. NH_3 ii. CH_3COOH iii. H_2CO_3 iv. H_2SO_4
      v. $Ca(OH)_2$ vi. H_3PO_4 vii. HNO_3 viii. $NaOH$
   b. OH [1]
   c. Dibasic has two H atoms (which can react with a base) [1]
      Tribasic has three H atoms (which can react with a base) [1]
3. Can 'eat away' at the surface of another substance [1]
4. Bases are **oxides** and hydroxides of metals. Most bases are **insoluble** in water. An example is **copper**(II) oxide. A soluble base is called an **alkali**. All Group 1 **hydroxides** are alkalis because they **dissolve** easily in water. Calcium hydroxide is slightly **soluble** in water and forms an alkaline solution.
   (1 mark for each correct word)
5. 1 mark each for any two of:
   Sodium hydroxide: corrosive at concentrations greater than 0.5 mol / dm³
   Irritant at concentrations 0.05–0.5 mol / dm³
   Low risk at concentrations less than 0.05 mol / dm³
   1 mark each for any two of:
   Hydrochloric acid: corrosive at concentrations greater than 6.5 mol / dm³
   Irritant at concentrations 2–6.5 mol / dm³
   Low risk at concentrations less than 2 mol / dm³
   1 mark each for any two of:
   Sulfuric acid: corrosive at concentrations greater than 1.5 mol / dm³
   Irritant at concentrations 0.5–1.5 mol / dm³
   Low risk at concentrations less than 0.5 mol / dm³
   1 mark each for any two of:
   Ammonia: corrosive at concentrations greater than 6 mol / dm³
   Irritant at concentrations 3–6 mol / dm³
   Low risk at concentrations less than 3 mol / dm³

Unit 11.2

1. a. i. pH 11 [1]   ii. pH 3 [1]   iii. pH 7 [1]
      iv. pH 11 [1]   v. pH 11 [1]
   b. Dip universal indicator paper into the solution [1]
      Observe the colour of the paper [1]
      Compare the colour with the universal indicator colour chart / compare the colour with the pH colour chart [1]
   c. A with 3, B with 5, C with 4, D with 1, E with 2
2. (3 marks if all correct, 2 marks if 3 or 4 correct, 1 mark is 1 or 2 correct)
   Aqueous solutions of acids contain **hydrogen** ions. In strong acids **all** the acid **molecules** are dissociated (**ionised**) to form hydrogen ions and **anions**. When weak acids are dissolved in **water** they become **partially** dissociated. We can write this as an **equilibrium** e.g. $CH_3COOH \rightleftharpoons CH_3COO^- + H^+$.
3. An aqueous solution of OH⁻ ions / hydroxide ions is formed [1]
4. Barium is most soluble and magnesium least soluble [1]
   pH of alkalis due to aqueous OH⁻ ions [1]
   Higher concentration of aqueous hydroxide ions in barium hydroxide than calcium hydroxide and higher concentration in calcium than in magnesium [1]
   The higher the concentration of OH⁻ ions, the higher the pH [1]

Unit 11.3

1. a. acid + metal → **salt** [1] + **hydrogen** [1]
   b. acid + metal oxide → **salt** [1] + **water** [1]
   c. acid + metal carbonate → **salt** [1] + **water** [1] + **carbon dioxide** [1]
   d. acid + metal hydroxide → **salt** [1] + **water** [1]
2. a. sodium hydroxide + nitric acid → sodium nitrate + water [1]
   b. zinc oxide + hydrochloric acid → zinc chloride + water [1]
   c. iron + sulfuric acid → iron sulfate + hydrogen [1]
   d. sulfuric acid + lead carbonate → lead sulfate + carbon dioxide + water [1]
   e. barium hydroxide + nitric acid → barium nitrate + water [1]
   f. hydrochloric acid + tin oxide → tin chloride + water [1]
3. a. $Zn + H_2SO_4 \rightarrow ZnSO_4 + H_2$ [1]
   b. $MgO + 2HNO_3 \rightarrow Mg(NO_3)_2 + H_2O$ (1 for correct formula, 1 for balance)
   c. $CuCO_3 + 2HCl \rightarrow CuCl_2 + CO_2 + H_2O$ (1 for correct formula, 1 for balance)
   d. $2NaOH + H_2SO_4 \rightarrow Na_2SO_4 + 2H_2O$ (1 for correct formula, 1 for balance)
   e. $Na_2CO_3 + 2HCl \rightarrow 2NaCl + CO_2 + H_2O$ (1 for correct formula, 1 for balance)
   f. $Ca + 2HCl \rightarrow CaCl_2 + H_2O$ (1 for correct formula, 1 for balance)
   g. $Ca(OH)_2 + 2HNO_3 \rightarrow Ca(NO_3)_2 + 2H_2O$ (1 for correct formula, 1 for balance)
4. Neutralisation [1]
5. $Ca(OH)_2 + 2NH_4Cl \rightarrow CaCl_2 + 2H_2O + 2NH_3$ (1 for correct formula, 1 for balance)
6. Hydroxide ions react with ammonium salts when water present (from soil / rain) [1]
   Ammonia is released [1]
   Which escapes into the air / ammonia is a gas [1]

Unit 11.4

1. a. base [1] salt [1] water [1]
   b. acid [1] salt [1] water [1]
2. a. A positively charge particle in the nucleus of an atom [1]
   b. The hydrogen ion has lost an electron [1]
      There are no more electrons so only the proton remains (in H⁺) [1]
   c. Proton acceptor [1]

Answers

3. a. H$^+$(aq) + ~~NO$_3^-$(aq)~~ + ~~Na$^+$(aq)~~ + OH$^-$(aq) → ~~NO$_3^-$(aq)~~ + ~~Na$^+$(aq)~~ + H$_2$O(l) [1]
    b. H$^+$(aq) + OH$^-$(aq) → H$_2$O(l) [1]
    c. Hydrogen ions have reacted completely with hydroxide ions to form water [1]
4. a. Arrow going from H of H$_2$O to N of NH$_3$ [1]
    b. Arrow going from H of H$_2$S to O of H$_2$O [1]
5. a. HClO$_2$ is acid [1] HCOOH is base [1]
    b. NH$_4^+$ is acid [1] H$_2$O is base [1]

Unit 11.5

1. Oxides of many metals on the **left** of the **Periodic** Table react with acids. These are called **basic** oxides. Some of these oxides react with **water** to form **alkaline** solutions. Oxides of many non-metals on the **right** of the Periodic Table react with **alkalis**. These oxides are called acidic oxides. Many of these oxides react with water to form **acidic** solutions.
    (1 mark for each correct word)
2. a. MgO + 2HCl → MgCl$_2$ + H$_2$O (1 for correct formula, 1 for balance)
    b. SO$_2$ + 2NaOH → Na$_2$SO$_3$ + H$_2$O (1 for correct formula, 1 for balance)
    c. CuO + H$_2$SO$_4$ → CuSO$_4$ + H$_2$O [1]
    d. CO$_2$ + 2NaOH → Na$_2$CO$_3$ + H$_2$O (1 for correct formula, 1 for balance)
    e. ZnO + 2HNO$_3$ → Zn(NO$_3$)$_2$ + H$_2$O (1 for correct formula, 1 for balance)
    f. CaO + H$_2$SO$_4$ → CaSO$_4$ + H$_2$O [1]
3. a. SO$_2$ + H$_2$O → H$_2$SO$_3$ [1]
    b. CO$_2$ + H$_2$O → H$_2$CO$_3$ [1]
    c. CaO + H$_2$O → Ca(OH)$_2$ [1]
    d. P$_4$O$_6$ + 6H$_2$O → 4H$_3$PO$_3$ [1]
    e. Na$_2$O + H$_2$O → 2NaOH [1]
4. amphoteric [1]
5. a. ZnO + 2KOH → K$_2$ZnO$_2$ + H$_2$O (1 for correct formula, 1 for balance)
    b. Al$_2$O$_3$ + 6HCl → 2AlCl$_3$ + 3H$_2$O (1 for correct formula, 1 for balance)
    c. Al$_2$O$_3$ + 2NaOH → 2NaAlO$_2$ + H$_2$O (1 for correct formula, 1 for balance)

Unit 11.6

1. a. Filter off the excess zinc [1]
    b. Filter off the crystals [1]
       Wash them in the filter paper with a minimum amount of water / alcohol [1]
       Dry the crystals between sheets of filter paper / dry in a **drying** oven / dry in the air [1]
2. DBEAFC [2]
    (1 mark if one pair reversed)
3. Record the volume of acid added when the indicator just changed colour [1]
    Repeat the titration without the indicator, using the value of acid recorded [1]
    Evaporate to the point of crystallisation and leave to form crystals [1]
4. a. Copper(II) nitrate may lose its water of crystallisation [1]
       Copper(II) nitrate may decompose [1]
    b. Zinc oxide/ zinc carbonate/ zinc hydroxide are insoluble in water [1]
       You could not tell when the reaction was complete very easily [1]

Unit 11.7

1. Salts such as **nitrates**, sodium salts and **ammonium** salts are soluble in water. Many **carbonates/ hydroxides** and **carbonates/ hydroxides** are insoluble except those from Group I. An insoluble substance formed when two **solutions** of soluble **compounds** are mixed is called a **precipitate**.
    (1 mark for each correct word)
2. BEADC [2] (1 mark if one pair in the incorrect order)
3. Hydrated salt: A salt which has water of crystallisation (weakly) bonded to its ions [1]
    Anhydrous salt: A salt without no water of crystallisation [1]
    Water of crystallisation: Water molecules (weakly) bonded to the ions of the salt [1]

4. a. i. Ag$^+$(aq) + ~~NO$_3^-$(aq)~~ + K$^+$(aq) + Br$^-$(aq) → AgBr(s) + ~~NO$_3^-$(aq)~~ + ~~K$^+$(aq)~~ [1]
       ii. Ag$^+$(aq) + Br$^-$(aq) → AgBr(s) [1]
    b. i. Ba^{2+}(aq) + SO$_4^{2-}$(aq) → BaSO$_4$(s)
          (1 mark for correct ions, 1 mark for state symbols)
       ii. Pb^{2+}(aq) + 2Cl$^-$(aq) → PbCl$_2$(s)
          (1 mark for correct ions, 1 mark for state symbols, 1 mark for balance)
       iii. Fe^{3+}(aq) + 3OH$^-$(aq) → Fe(OH)$_3$(s)
          (1 mark for correct ions, 1 mark for state symbols, 1 mark for balance)
       iv. Mg^{2+}(aq) + CO$_3^{2-}$(aq) → MgCO$_3$(s)
          (1 mark for correct ions, 1 mark for state symbols)

Unit 11.8

1. Weigh out 40 g sodium hydroxide [1]
    Into a 250 cm^3 volumetric flask [1]
    Add **distilled** water and dissolve the NaOH [1]
    Fill flask to the graduation mark and shake [1]
2. a. 2 marks if all correct, 1 mark if one error.

    | Titre / cm^3 | 32.95 | 32.10 | 32.00 | 32.85 | 32.15 |

    b. 2nd 3rd and 5th [1]
       The figures are closest together / most consistent readings [1]
3. a. moles of acid = $0.10 \times \frac{12.2}{1000}$ = 1.22×10^{-3} mol H$_2$SO$_4$ [1]
    b. i. 2 [1]
       ii. $1.22 \times 10^{-3} \times 2 = 2.44 \times 10^{-3}$ mol NaOH [1]
    c. $\frac{2.44 \times 10^{-3}}{0.025}$ = 0.098 mol / dm^3
       (2 marks for correct answer, 1 mark for 0.025 if correct answer not obtained)
4. Moles of Ba(OH)$_2$ = 0.05 × 25/1000 = 1.25 × 10^{-3} mol [1]
    1 mol of Ba(OH)$_2$ reacts with 2 mol HCl [1]
    Mol HCl = 1.25 × 10^{-3} × 2 = 2.50 × 10^{-3} mol [1]
    Concentration of HCl = $\frac{2.50 \times 10^{-3}}{15.5 / 1000}$ [1]
    = 0.16 mol / dm^3 [1]

Unit 12.1

1. a. i. Proton number / atomic number [1]
       ii. Nucleon number / mass number / number of neutrons + protons in an atom [1]
    b. i. Proton number [1]
       ii. I to VIII [1]
       iii. Electron shells [1]
       iv. Valency electrons [1]
2. They have a stable electron configuration (8 electrons in the outer shell, 2 for He) [1]
    So it is difficult for them to lose, gain, or share electrons [1]
3. Going across and Period, from left to right there is a decrease in metallic character [1]
    Going down a Group there is an increase in metallic character [1]
    Groups I and II are all metals [1]
    Groups VII and VIII are all non-metals [1]
4. One mark each for any two of:
    Hydrogen is a gas / hydrogen usually behaves like a non-metal / when hydrogen loses its electron, there are no other electron shells present
5. a. Nitrogen and phosphorus are simple molecules [1]
       Arsenic and antimony have a grey metallic form [1]
       And molecular forms, As$_4$ or Sb$_4$ as vapour [1]
       Bismuth is a metal [1]
    b. Nitrogen oxides are either neutral (N$_2$O, NO) or acidic (NO$_2$) [1]
       Phosphorus oxides are acidic [1]
       Arsenic and antimony oxides are amphoteric [1]
       Bismuth oxide is basic [1]

Unit 12.2

1. a. i. Sodium: 1 mark each for any three of:
          Moves rapidly over the surface / Fizzes rapidly / Melts and goes into a ball / Does not burst into flame
          Rubidium: 1 mark each for any three of:

153

Answers

Moves over the surface or moves faster than potassium / Fizzes extremely rapidly or fizzes more than potassium / Bursts into flame immediately / May explode

ii. Melting point of potassium; allow between 50 and 75°C (actual = 63 °C) [1]
Metallic radius of rubidium = ALLOW between 0.21 and 0.24 nm (actual = 0.235) [1]
b. Any value between 1.7 and 2.0 g / cm³ (actual = 1.88) [1]

2. Each sodium atom loses its single outer electron to become a Na^+ ion [1]
Each chlorine atom accepts one electron to become a Cl^- ion [1]

3. 1 mark each for any 4 of:
The ease of removing an electron depends on the nuclear charge and the distance from the nucleus [1]
The further away the outer electron is from the nucleus, the lower is the attractive force between nucleus and electron [1]
The greater the nuclear charge, the greater is the attractive force between nucleus and the outer electron [1]
The outer electron in potassium is further away from the nucleus than the outer electron in sodium [1]
This effect is greater than the effect of increasing nuclear charge [1]
Because there are more electrons preventing the nuclear charge being felt by the outer electron in potassium [1]

Unit 12.3

1. a. Melting point increases <u>down the group</u> [1]
   b. fluorine: gas [1] chlorine: liquid [1] bromine: solid [1] iodine: solid [1]
   c. fluorine: pale yellow [1] chlorine: pale green [1] bromine: orange [1] iodine: grey [1]
   d. Arrow going downwards from smaller to larger [1]

2. a. When aqueous **chlorine** is added to a **colourless** solution of potassium bromide, the solution turns **orange** because **bromine** has been displaced. This is because a **more** reactive **halogen** displaces a **less** reactive halogen from an aqueous solution of its **halide**.
   (1 mark for each correct word)
   b. Orange solution turns red-brown [1] because iodine is formed [1]
   Bromine is more reactive than iodine [1]
   Because a more reactive halogen displaces a less reactive halogen from its aqueous halide [1]

3. $Cl_2(aq) + 2I^-(aq) \rightarrow I_2(aq) + 2Cl^-(aq)$
   (1 mark for correct symbols, 1 mark for correct balance)
   $Br_2(aq) + 2At^-(aq) \rightarrow At_2(aq) + 2Br^-(aq)$
   (1 mark for correct symbols, 1 mark for correct balance)

Unit 12.4

1. a. 2,8,2 2,8,3 2,8,4 2,8,5 2,8,6 2,8,7 [1]
   b. Al_2O_3 [1] SiO_2 [1] P_2O_3 [1]
   c. i. They increase to a maximum at Si then decrease [2]
      (They increase then decease = 1 mark)
      ii. metallic [1]
      iii. It is a giant structure / has a lattice [1]
      All the bonds are strong / its takes a lot of energy to break all the bonds [1]
      iv. They are simple molecules [1]
      Weak forces between (the molecules) / it doesn't take much energy to break the weak intermolecular forces [1]

2. a. 5 [1]
   b. P_2O_5 [1]

3. In forming ions Al needs to lose 3 electrons, Mg needs to lose 2 electrons, and Na needs to lose 1 electron. [1]
   As more electrons are lost, the greater is the pull of the nucleus on the rest of the electrons [1]
   So it takes more energy to remove 3 electrons than 2 electrons and more energy to remove 2 electrons than 1 electron [1]

Unit 12.5

1. a. A, D, E, G   (3 marks if all correct, 2 marks if 4 correct, 1 mark if 3 correct)
   b. i. Ag^+ [1] ii. Cu^{2+} iii. Cr^{3+} [1] iv. Fe^{3+} [1]
   c. very hard / tough / very strong [1] form complex ions [1]

2. a. Much lower melting point than transition elements [1]
      Much lower density than transition elements [1]
   b. Increases steadily from K to Cu [1]
      Then decreases rapidly [1]

3. Relatively low melting point compared to transition elements [1]
   Does not form coloured compounds [1]
   Only has one oxidation state [1]
   Does not have catalytic activity [1]
   (Not: no complex ions / lower density)

Unit 13.1

1. a. conducts electricity [1] ductile [1] malleable [1] shiny [1]
   b. i. Does not conduct electricity / shatters when hit [1]
      ii. Conducts heat / very high melting point [1]
      iii. Conducts electricity / malleable [1]
      iv. Low melting point [1]
      v. Any 2 of: has low melting point / does not conduct electricity / shatters when hit / does not conduct heat [1]

2. a. Aluminium [1] has the lowest density [1]
   b. Iron [1] has highest strength [1]
   c. Copper [1] is the best electrical conductor [1]

3. Any 6 points, one of which must refer to the Periodic Table e.g.
   Position in Periodic Table: idea of the 'step line' between metals and non-metals [1]
   They have high melting points so are like many metals [1]
   They are poor electrical conductors so unlike metals [1]
   Electrical conduction increases with temperature / they are semiconductors so unlike metals [1]
   Generally shiny so like metals [1]
   Some exist in metallic and non-metallic forms [1]
   Some forms have a degree of covalent bonding [1]

Unit 13.2

1. a. i. $2Na(s) + 2H_2O(l) \rightarrow 2NaOH(aq) + H_2(g)$
      (1 mark for H_2, 1 mark for balance, 1 mark for state symbols)
      ii. $3Fe(s) + 4H_2O(g) \rightarrow Fe_3O_4(s) + 4H_2(g)$
      (1 mark for formulae, 1 mark for balance, 1 mark for state symbols)
   b. The products formed by metals which react with **cold** water, are a metal **hydroxide** and **hydrogen**. The hydroxides are alkaline and so turn **red** litmus **blue**. The products formed by metals which only react with steam are a metal **oxide** and **hydrogen**. Copper does not react with water because it is **less** reactive than **hydrogen** and cannot take the **oxygen** away from the hydrogen in the water.
      (1 mark for each correct word)

2. a. calcium, magnesium, zinc [1]
   b. Barium: gives off bubbles very rapidly with <u>cold</u> water [1]
      Barium disappears very quickly / immediately [1]
      Lead reacts slowly (when white hot) with steam / no reaction even when heated [1]

3. lead, iron, magnesium, lithium [1]

4. $Mg(s) + 2H^+(aq) \rightarrow Mg^{2+}(aq) + H_2(g)$ [1]
   $Mg(s) \rightarrow Mg^{2+}(aq) + 2e^-$ [1]
   $2H^+(aq) + 2e^- \rightarrow H_2(g)$ [1]
   $Mg(s) \rightarrow Mg^{2+}(aq) + 2e^-$ is oxidation
   $2H^+(aq) + 2e^- \rightarrow H_2(g)$ is reduction [1]

Unit 13.3

1. a. B At start: solution blue [1]
      B After 20 min: metal brown/ pink [1] solution colourless / lighter blue [1]
      C After 20 min: metal silvery-grey [1]
      D At start: metal grey [1] solution blue [1]
      D After 20 min: metal brown/ pink solution colourless / lighter blue [1]
   b. silver < copper < iron < zinc [1]
   c. Copper is lower in the reactivity series than zinc / zinc is higher than copper in the reactivity series [1]

2. a. Reducing agent is iron, oxidising agent is copper oxide [1]
   b. Reducing agent is magnesium, oxidising agent is iron oxide [1]

Answers

3. a. $Zn(s) \rightarrow Zn^{2+}(aq) + 2e^-$ [1]
        $Cu^{2+}(aq) + 2e^- \rightarrow Cu(s)$ [1]
        Zinc is the reducing agent. [1]
    b. $Mg(s) \rightarrow Mg^{2+}(aq) + 2e^-$ [1]
        $Pb^{2+}(aq) + 2e^- \rightarrow Pb(s)$ [1]
        Magnesium is the reducing agent [1]

Unit 13.4

1. A **more** reactive metal will **reduce** the oxide of a **less** reactive metal. This reaction is **exothermic**. The more reactive metal loses **electrons** and forms **positive** ions more easily. Other reducing agents such as **carbon** or hydrogen will **remove** oxygen from the oxide of a less reactive metal when **heated**.
    (1 mark for each correct word)
2. a. Sodium, magnesium, aluminium, iron, copper, gold
        (all correct = 3 marks; 4 or 5 correct = 2 marks; 2 or 3 correct = 1 mark)
    b. Potassium, sodium, calcium, magnesium, aluminium [1]
        They are above hydrogen in the reactivity series [1]
3. a. $Fe_2O_3 + 3CO \rightarrow 2Fe + 3CO_2$ [2]
        (If 2 not scored, 1 mark for $2Fe + 3CO_2$)
    b. $ZnO + CO \rightarrow Zn + CO_2$ [1]
    c. $2CuO + C \rightarrow Cu + CO_2$ [1]
4. Carbon monoxide [1]
5. There is an aluminium oxide layer on the surface of aluminium [1]
    Which is (moderately) resistant to acids / which does not flake off easily [1]

Unit 13.5

1. a. air / oxygen [1] water [1]
    b. hydrated [1] iron(III) oxide [1]
2. a. Oil forms a layer on the surface of the chain [1]
        (The layer) is a barrier which prevents oxygen and water getting to the iron [1]
    b. The movement of the chain rubs off some of the oil [1]
        Allow idea of grit rubbing off oil
        So oxygen and water can reach the surface of the iron [1]
3. Blocks of zinc can be placed on the hull of a ship to stop it **rusting**. Zinc is **more** reactive than **iron** so it loses **electrons** and forms **ions** more easily than iron. The zinc ions go into **solution** and so the zinc **corrodes** instead of the iron. This is called **sacrificial** protection.
    1 mark for each correct word
4. a. Seawater contains sodium chloride / salt [1]
        Presence of salt increases the rate of rusting [1]
        Allow: less salt in air around bridge inland [1]
        Drier air around bridge inland [1]
    b. Both air / oxygen and water needed for rusting [1]
        There is very little water / water evaporates very quickly [1]
5. Layer of zinc [1] stops air / oxygen and water reaching the iron [1]
    Zinc more reactive than iron [1] so corrodes in preference to iron [1]
6. Any four of:
    Magnesium is more reactive than iron [1]
    So it releases electrons more readily than iron [1]
    $Mg(s) + \rightarrow Mg_{2+}(aq) + 2e^-$ [1]
    The electrons are passed on to the iron and then accepted by oxygen and water to form OH^- ions / magnesium hydroxide formed [1]
    The magnesium corrodes instead of the iron [1]

Unit 14.1

1. a. Upward arrow from gold to lithium [1]
    b. Li to Al extracted by electrolysis [1]
        Zn to Cu extracted by heating with carbon [1]
    c. i. Upward arrow in fourth column [1] upward arrow in fifth column [1]
        ii. Any reasonable answer, e.g., some ores more complex than others / sulfur may have to be removed / other substances may have to be removed / some ores may require more purification than others
    d. Silver and gold / copper, silver, and gold [1]
    e. Lead and copper [1]
2. manganese oxide + aluminium → aluminium oxide + manganese [1]

3. a. $SnO_2 + 2C \rightarrow Sn + 2CO$ (1 mark for correct formulae, 1 mark for balance)
    b. $2NiO + CO + H_2 \rightarrow 2Ni + CO_2 + H_2O$
        (1 mark for correct formulae, 1 mark for balance)
    c. $PbO + CO \rightarrow Pb + CO_2$ [1]
4. a. $Cr_2O_3 + 2Al \rightarrow 2Cr + Al_2O_3$ (1 mark for correct formulae, 1 mark for balance)
    b. $Fe_2O_3 + 3CO \rightarrow 2Fe + 3CO_2$ (1 mark for correct formulae, 1 mark for balance)

Unit 14.2

1. B [1]
    E [1]
    E [1]
    A [1]
    A [1]
    D [1]
    C [1]
2. Burning coke in air to form carbon dioxide [1]
    Reaction of carbon dioxide with coke to form carbon monoxide [1]
3. 3 marks if all correct, 2 marks if two sentences correct, 1 mark if one sentence correct
    At the high temperatures in the furnace the limestone undergoes thermal decomposition to form calcium oxide.
    The calcium oxide reacts with silicon dioxide (sand) which is an impurity in the ore.
    The calcium silicate formed is a slag which runs down the furnace and floats on top of the molten iron.
4. $Fe_2O_3 + 3CO \rightarrow 2Fe + 3CO_2$ (1 mark for correct formulae, 1 mark for balance)
5. Any 3 suitable methods (1 mark each); e.g. reduction of iron(II) oxide with hydrogen / electrolysis of iron ammonium oxalate (or other suitable compound) / thermal decomposition of iron pentacarbonyl

Unit 14.3

1. E = liquid in the cell into which rods are dipping [1]
    C = layer on the inside next to liquid [1]
    A = rods dipping into the liquid [1]
    M = layer at the bottom of the cell [1]
2. 1 mark for each correct word.
    Aluminium oxide **melts** at a very high temperature. It would require too much **energy** to keep the aluminium oxide molten at this **temperature**. So the aluminium oxide is **dissolved** in molten **cryolite** and calcium fluoride. This lowers the operating temperature to about **950** °C. The temperature is kept relatively **low** by keeping the percentage of aluminium oxide in the mixture at 5%.
3. a. i. $Al^{3+} + 3e^- \rightarrow Al$ (1 mark for correct formulae, 1 mark for balance)
        ii. $2O^{2-} \rightarrow O_2 + 4e^-$ (1 mark for correct formulae, 1 mark for balance)
    b. $2Al_2O_3 \rightarrow 4Al + 3O_2$ (1 mark for correct formulae, 1 mark for balance)
4. Oxygen reacts with the graphite / carbon electrode [1]
    Carbon dioxide formed which is given off as a gas [1]
5. $Al_2O_3 \rightarrow Al^{3+} + AlO_3^{3-}$ (1 mark for correct formulae, 1 mark for balance)
    $4AlO_3^{3-} \rightarrow 2Al_2O_3 + 3O_2 + 12e^-$ (1 mark for correct formulae, 1 mark for balance)

Unit 14.4

1. A = 4; B = 3; C = 1; D = 2 (all correct = 2 marks; 2 or 3 correct = 1 mark)
2. Aluminium food containers: 1 mark each for any 2 of: non-toxic (oxide) / resistant to corrosion / low density or lightweight
    Aluminium power cables: low density [1] conducts electricity (!)

155

Answers

Copper for electrical wiring: good conductor of electricity [1] ductile [1]
Stainless steel: Use (1 mark for each correct) e.g. chemical plant / cutlery / surgical instruments
Property: resistant to corrosion / very hard [1]
Tungsten steel: (1 mark for each correct property) e.g. resistant to wear / high melting point/ hard
Brass: attractive or shiny [1] hard or strong [1]

Unit 14.5
1. A = 4; B = 1; C = 3; D = 2 (all correct = 2 marks; 2 or 3 correct = 1 mark)
2. B [1]
3. Alloys are **mixtures** of metals or mixtures of metals with non-metals. Alloys are often **harder** and stronger than pure metals. When a metal is **alloyed** with another metal, the **difference** in the size of the metal atoms makes the **arrangement** of the layers in the lattice less **regular**. This **prevents** the layers from sliding over each other as easily when a **force** is applied.
(1 mark for each correct word)
4. Aluminium alloy: 1 mark each for any 2 of: low density or lightweight / doesn't corrode / strong (for weight)
Stainless steel: 1 mark each for any two of: rusts or corrodes less / stronger / harder
5. Idea of not a pure metal [1] Impurities lower the melting point [1]

Unit 15.1
1. a. Air is a mixture of **gases**. We need air in order to survive. We need the **oxygen** in the air for **respiration** (the oxidation of food in the body). Polluted air may contain **particulates** and harmful gases. Bacteria in the **digestive** system of animals such as cows and sheep produce **methane** gas. Methane is a greenhouse gas which is responsible for increased **global** **warming**.
(1 mark for each correct word)
   b. About 50% of our **body** is made up of water. Water acts as a **solvent** for some of the **chemicals** in our body. It is also needed to transport digested **food** and waste in the bloodstream. Our **drinking** water must be free of harmful chemical **pollutants** and harmful **bacteria**.
(1 mark for each correct word)
   c. Crop plants need **minerals** from the soil for healthy growth. Farmers put fertilisers on their fields to increase crop **growth** and to replace minerals that are **lost** from the soil when the crops are **harvested**. Many fertilisers are **soluble** in water and can drain off the fields into **rivers** and lakes when the ground is very wet. An increased **concentration** of fertilisers in rivers and lakes causes a complex process called eutrophication to take place. This removes dissolved **oxygen** from the water and so aquatic life dies.
(1 mark for each correct word)
2. A = 5, B = 1, C = 2, D = 3, E = 6, F = 4 (all correct = 3 marks, 5 correct = 2 marks, 3 or 4 correct = 1 mark)

Unit 15.2
1. A = 2; B = 3; C = 1; D = 6; E = 4; F = 5 (all correct = 3; 4 or 5 correct = 2; 2 or 3 correct = 1)
2. Plastics can get into the ocean from ships, coastal towns, and by transport in **rivers** from inland. Plastic fishing nets can **trap** or kill **fish** and other sea creatures. Very small particles of plastics called **microplastics** have been found in drinking water. These particles are so **small** that they can get into our boodstream and then to organs such as the **liver** and kidneys where they may cause harm.
(1 mark for each correct word)
3. A = 4; B = 3; C = 1; D = 2 (all correct = 2 marks; 2 or 3 correct = 1 mark)

Unit 15.3
1. In a water treatment **plant**, large objects such as plant **branches** are first trapped by metal screens. Other solids particles are then left to **settle** to the bottom of the tank. The water is then passed through a **filter** made of sand or gravel. This removes small **insoluble** particles. Carbon is added to remove bad **smells**. Chlorine is added to the filtered water to kill **bacteria** which may be **harmful** to health.
(1 mark for each correct word)

2. Oxygen: respiration of aquatic organisms [1]
Mineral salts: for health / correct functioning of enzymes in aquatic organisms [1]
3. a. Ca^{2+} [1]
   b. NO_3^- [1] and SiO_3^{2-} [1] and K^+ [1] present in much higher concentration in river water / lower concentration in seawater
   c. 2.4 mg [1]
4. Any 4 of:
Hard water form scum with soap / does not form a lather easily with soap [1]
Calcium hydrogencarbonate causes temporary hardness [1]
Calcium and magnesium sulfates cause permanent hardness [1]
Adding sodium carbonate replaces calcium ions by sodium ions [1]
The calcium carbonate precipitates (so is removed from the water) [1]
Sodium sulfate is soluble in water [1]

Unit 15.4
1. For healthy growth crop plants need three major elements, nitrogen, **phosphorus**, and potassium. Plants take up these elements in the form of nitrates **phosphates** and potassium **salts**. The **nitrates** are needed to make **proteins** for growth. Farmers add **fertilisers** to the soil to add back the **nutrients** which plants have absorbed for growth.
(1 mark for each correct word)
2. a. NH_3 ammonia [1], HNO_3 nitric acid [1], NH_4NO_3 ammonium nitrate [1], H_2SO_4 sulfuric acid [1], H_3PO_4 phosphoric acid [1], KCl potassium chloride [1]
   b. ammonia + nitric acid → ammonium nitrate [1]
   c. i. ammonia [1] sulfuric acid [1]
      ii. potassium hydroxide / potassium carbonate [1] hydrochloric acid [1]
      NOT: potassium
      iii. Sodium hydroxide / sodium carbonate [1] phosphoric acid [1]
      NOT: sodium
   d. natural gas [1] water [1] air [1]
3. Any 5 of: nitrates and phosphates cause excessive growth of algae / algae cover the water surface / and block the sunlight from reaching plants beneath / this causes water plants to die / aerobic bacteria feed on dead plants and algae / using up the dissolved oxygen in the water / so water animals also die

Unit 15.5
1. a. Carbon dioxide <u>and</u> methane [1]
   b. Argon [1]
   c. Water [1]
2. a. 17.1 cm^3 [1]
   b. (17.1 /80) × 100 [1] = 21.4%
   c. Higher [1] The apparatus had not cooled [1] So the volume of gas is greater than it would have been at a lower temperature [1]
3. $2C_2H_6 + 7O_2 \rightarrow 4CO_2 + 6H_2O$ (1 mark for correct formulae, 1 mark for balance)

Unit 15.6
1. a. Carbon monoxide is formed when **carbon** compounds **burn** in a **limited** supply of air. Sulfur dioxide is formed when **fossil** fuels containing **sulfur** burn in air.
(1 mark for each correct word)
   b. i. Lightning [1] ii. volcanoes [1]
2. a. Chemical erosion / pits the limestone [1]
   b. Breathing difficulties / irritates the throat / irritates the eyes [1]
   c. Poisonous/ toxic / stops respiration [1]
3. A with 1, B with 3, C with 4, D with 2 (2 marks for all correct, 1 mark if 2 or 3 correct)
4. Sulfur dioxide forms when fossil fuels containing sulfur burn in air [1]. The sulfur is oxidised to form sulfur dioxide [1] and dissolves in rain to form sulfuric acid [1] which falls as acid rain [1]
5. a. To turn harmful carbon monoxide [1] and nitrogen oxides [1] into nitrogen and carbon dioxide which are not harmful (to health) [1]
   b. $2NO_2 + 4CO \rightarrow N_2 + 4CO_2$ (1 mark for correct formulae, 1 mark for balance)

Answers

6. Any 4 of:
   Nitrogen, hydrocarbons, and ozone involved [1]
   In the presence of sunlight [1] there is a photochemical reaction [1]
   Ozone formed by reaction of nitrogen dioxide with
   ultraviolet radiation [1]
   Ozone reacts with hydrocarbons [1] to produce organic compounds /
   aldehydes / peroxides / organic nitrates [1]

Unit 15.7

1. Methane is a greenhouse gas which is formed by the **bacterial** decomposition of **vegetation** and as a waste product of **digestion** in animals. It is present in the **atmosphere** at a lower concentration than carbon dioxide but it **absorbs** much more thermal energy per mole.
   (1 mark for each correct answer)
2. a. Gas which absorbs energy heat / infra-red radiation [1] in the atmosphere [1]
   b. The general trend is the same of increasing concentration of CO_2 and increasing temperature of the atmosphere [1]
   Reference especially to the years 1950 to 2000 [1]
   c. i. 1 mark each for any two: e.g. respiration / bacterial decay / warming oceans / thermal decomposition of carbonates
   ii. 1 mark each for any two: e.g. marshes / rice fields / melting permafrost / oceans
3. 1 mark each for any 3 of: e.g. rise in sea level / desertification / more extreme weather / melting glaciers / warming of sea causing death of corals, etc.

Unit 15.8

1. A = 3; B = 4; C = 1; D = 2 (all correct = 2 marks; 2 or 3 correct = 1 mark)
2. They reduce the amount of nitrogen oxides and carbon monoxide getting into the atmosphere [1] but carbon dioxide is still produced [1] which is a greenhouse gas / contributes to global warming [1]
3. Tree leaves absorb carbon dioxide during photosynthesis [1]
   Carbon dioxide is a greenhouse gas [1]
   which is responsible for climate change [1]
4. Flue gas desulfurisation is the process of removing **sulfur** dioxide from the gases formed during the **combustion** of fossil **fuels** in power stations. The **waste** gases are passed through moist calcium **carbonate** or calcium oxide. These compounds **neutralise** the acidic sulfur dioxide. Solid calcium **sulfite** is formed.
   (1 mark for each correct word)
5. a. Climate change is the change in the climate / weather over a number of years due to global warming [1]
   Causing more extreme weather / example of more extreme weather e.g. more storms / more heatwaves [1]
   Important to reduce its effect otherwise get e.g. desertification *causing* loss of land for agriculture / loss of homes / habitats *caused* by sea level rise [1]
   b. Any two forms of renewable energy: e.g. wind power / solar power / wave power [1]
   Using renewable energy reduces use of fossil fuels [1]
   So reduces the amount of carbon dioxide in the atmosphere [1]
6. Pass the carbon dioxide through the mixture [1] Collect the potassium hydrogen carbonate formed [1] Allow water to evaporate from the hydrogencarbonate [1] (do not heat because it will release some carbon dioxide) Store underground away from heat source / vitrify combine it with glass [1].

Unit 16.1

1. Coal [1] natural gas [1]
2. a. A, C, D, and E [1] They contain ONLY hydrogen and carbon [1]
   b. A, C, D, and E [1]
   c. i. A [1]
      ii. C [1]
   d. B C_3H_8O [1] C C_5H_{10} [1] D C_4H_{10} [1] E C_3H_6 F $C_2H_2OCl_3$ [1]
3. a. C [1]
   b. B [1]

4. They have strong aromas [1]; they are ring compounds with delocalised electrons in the ring [1]; one mark each for any two correct names e.g. benzene / naphthalene, nitrobenzene, aniline, etc. [2]

Unit 16.2

1. There is a range of **temperatures** in the distillation column, hot at the **bottom** and cooler at the **top**. Hydrocarbons with **lower** boiling points move **further** up the column and **condense** when the temperature in the column falls just below the **boiling** point of the hydrocarbons. Hydrocarbons with **higher** boiling points condense lower down the column.
   (1 mark for each correct word)
2. A = 4; B = 3; C = 2; D = 1 (all correct = 2 marks; 2 or 3 correct = 1 mark)
3. a. Downward arrow [1]
   b. i. Easily vaporised / liquid has a low boiling point [1]
      ii. Upward arrow [1]
   c. Downward arrow [1]
   d. Upward arrow [1]
4. Shorter / smaller molecules have lower intermolecular forces than larger ones [1]
   So smaller molecules vaporise more easily [1]
   Because they have lower boiling points [1]
   Smaller molecules travel further up the tower in the same time compared with larger ones [1]
   Molecules condense at a point in the tower where the temperature falls just below their boiling point [1]

Unit 16.3

1. a. A family of similar compounds with similar chemical properties [1] due to the same functional group [1]
   b. 1 mark each for any 3 of:
      Same general formula / trend in physical properties / each successive member has one more CH_2 group / can be prepared by similar methods
2. molecular formulae: methane CH_4 [1]; propanol: C_3H_8O [1]; ethanoic acid: $C_2H_4O_2$ [1]; butene: C_4H_8 [1]
   Structural formulae: methane [1]
   ethanoic acid: CH_3COOH [1]
   Displayed formulae: 1 mark each

   ```
   H   H   H                    H   H   H
   |   |   |                    |   |   |
   H—C—C—C—H                H—C—C—C—O—H
   |   |   |                    |   |   |
   H   H   H                    H   H   H
      propane                      propanol

        H                     H   H   H   H
        |  ⟋O                 |   |   |   |
   H—C—C                  H—C—C=C—C—H
        |  ⟍O—H               |           |
        H                     H           H
     ethanoic acid               butene
   ```

3. Alkenes: C_nH_{2n} [1]; alcohols $C_nH_{2n+1}OH$ [1]; amines: $C_nH_{2n+1}NH_2$ [1]

Unit 16.4

1. a. Hydrocarbons [1]
   b. Single [1] covalent [1]
   c. Saturated [1]
   d. Combustion / burning [1] chlorine [1]
2. a. Pentane [1]
   b. Butane [1]
   c. Octane [1]
3. Boiling points increase as relative molecular mass increases [1]
4. a. $C_5H_{12} + 8O_2 \rightarrow 5CO_2 + 6H_2O$
      (1 mark for balancing carbon dioxide and water, 1 mark for balancing oxygen)
   b. $CH_4 + Cl_2 \rightarrow CH_3Cl + HCl$ [1]
5. Photochemical [1] substitution [1]
6. a. Compounds with the same molecular formula but different structural formulae [1]

157

b.

[Structures shown]

1 mark each for any 2

c.

[Structures shown]

3 marks for 5 isomers, 2 for 4 isomers, 1 for 2 or 3 isomers

Unit 16.5
1. a. Residues [1]
   b. i. Gasoline/ naphtha and diesel [1]
      ii. Kerosene and fuel oil and residue [1]
2. a. P in the 'space' at the top of the collecting tube [1]
   b. Arrow to the ceramic wool [1] arrow under the aluminium oxide [1]
   c. Paraffin vaporises very quickly [1] so may run down to neck of tube and not react over the aluminium oxide [1]
3. a. $C_{10}H_{22} \rightarrow C_4H_{10} + C_6H_{12}$ [1]
   b. $C_{14}H_{30} \rightarrow C_3H_8 + C_4H_8 + C_7H_{14}$ [1]
4. C_8H_{18} used for petrol [1] need for more petrol (gasoline) / demand for petrol more than supply [1]
   $C_{33}H_{68}$ is very viscous / almost solid fraction [1] takes too much energy to vaporise it / too much energy to crack it / will block up the chemical plant [1]

Unit 16.6
1. a. Alkenes: propene [1] butene [1]
      Molecular formulae: C_2H_4 [1] C_4H_8 [1] C_5H_{10} [1]
      Boiling points: butene −60 to −40 °C (actual −48 °C) [1]
      Hexene 50 to 80 °C (actual 63 °C) [1]
   b. Pentene and hexane [1]
2. a. C=C ringed [1]
   b. orange [1] to colourless [1]
3. a. A H H   [1]   B $H_2O(g)$ (NOT $H_2O(l)$) [1]
         | |
         H–C–C–H
         | |
         H H

   b. Heat [1] high pressure [1] catalyst [1]
4. [Structures shown]

   1 mark each for any 3 (allow cis-trans isomers if clear)

Unit 16.7
1. a. Fermentation: reagents glucose [1] temperature; allow between 10 and 40 °C [1]
      Pressure atmospheric / 1 atm [1] Catalyst enzymes / yeast [1]
      Hydration: reagents ethene and steam [1] temperature 300 °C [1]
      Pressure 60 atmospheres [1] catalyst (phosphoric) acid [1]
   b. 1 mark each for any two of: takes a long time / ethanol is dilute / need to distil off the ethanol / batch process is inefficient / lot of waste
   c. 1 mark each for any two of: Uses renewable resources / relatively cheap / does not require very high temperature and pressure
   d. 1 mark each for any two of: Reaction is fast / reaction can be run continuously / Gives pure ethanol or atom economy is (nearly) 100%
2. a. $C_4H_9OH + 6O_2 \rightarrow 4CO_2 + 5H_2O$
      (1 mark for balance of carbon dioxide and water, 1 mark for balance of oxygen)
   b. Calorimeter / tin can suspended [1] over spirit burner with alcohol in it [1]
      Calorimeter / tin can about half full of water [1] Thermometer dipping into water in can [1] At least two correct labels [1]
3. Molar mass of ethanol = 46 [1]
   moles of ethanol = 9.2 / 46 = 0.2 mol [1]
   So mol $H_2O = 0.2 \times 3 = 0.6$ mol [1] $= 0.6 \times 18 = 10.8$ g [1]

Unit 16.8
1. a. The reaction is an equilibrium reaction [1] Both unionised acid molecules and (ethanoate) ions are present [1]
   b. It is accepting a proton [1] from ethanoic acid [1]
2. a. $2CH_3COOH + 2Na \rightarrow 2CH_3COO^-Na^+ + H_2$
      (1 mark for formula of each product, allow CH_3COONa, 1 mark for balance)
   b. $2CH_3COOH + Mg \rightarrow 2(CH_3COO^-)Mg^{2+} + H_2$
      (1 mark for formula of each product, allow $(CH_3COO)_2Mg$, 1 mark for balance)
   c. $CH_3COOH + NaOH \rightarrow CH_3COO^-Na^+ + H_2O$ (1 mark for formula of each product)
   d. $CH_3COOH + CH_3OH \rightarrow CH_3COOCH_3 + H_2O$
      (1 mark for each correct reactant and 1 mark for H_2O)
3. A = 3; B = 4; C = 1; D = 2 (all correct = 2 marks; 2 or 3 correct = 1 mark)
4. a. [Structure shown]   b. [Structure shown]
   a. butyl methanoate [1]
   b. propyl propanoate [1]

Unit 17.1
1. A polymer is a substance which has very large **molecules** formed when lots of small molecules called **monomers** join together. This process is called **polymerisation**. When poly(ethene) is formed, one of the C=C **bonds** of **ethene** is broken and the monomers **join** together in a chain. A reaction where two or more molecules join and no **other** molecule is formed is called an **addition** reaction.
   (1 mark for each correct word)

Answers

2. 8 carbon atoms in a chain with two hydrogen attached to each [1]
   Continuation bonds shown on the end carbon atoms [1]
3. B because for the same number of chains / same mass [1] there are more spaces between the chains [1]
4. Molar mass of ethene = 28 [1]
   moles of ethene = 56000 / 28 = 2000 mol [1]
   20000 C atoms equivalent to 10000 ethene monomers [1]
   10000 mol ethene → 1 mol polymer so 20000 mol gives 20000/1000 = 20 mol [1]

Unit 17.2
1. a. Brackets round a CH_3CH–$CHCl$ section or $CHCl$–CH_3CH section [1]
   b.
   ```
       CH₃ H   CH₃ H   CH₃ H
        |  |    |  |    |  |
      — C— C — C— C — C— C —
        |  |    |  |    |  |
        H  F    H  F    H  F
   ```
   (1 mark for correct number of C atoms, 1 mark for rest of structure, 1 mark for continuation bonds on end carbon atoms)
   c.
   ```
          ⎡ CH₃ CH₃ ⎤
          ⎢  |   |  ⎥
       ─ ─⎢ C — C ⎥─ ─
          ⎢  |   |  ⎥
          ⎣  H   H ⎦ₙ
   ```
   (1 mark for structure, 1 mark for brackets and n, 1 mark for continuation bonds on end carbon atoms)
2. A Double bond [1] Rest of structure correct [1]
   B Double bond [1] rest of structure correct [1]
   ```
   A   C₆H₅ H      B    H   CN
         |  |            |   |
         C= C            C = C
         |  |            |   |
         H  H            H   H
   ```
3. Correct structure of monomer [1] Structure of polymer (allow errors carried forward from monomer) [1] Continuation bonds, brackets and n for polymer [1]
   ```
         H  OOCCH₃           ⎡ H  OOCCH₃ ⎤
          |   |                ⎢  |    |   ⎥
      n  C = C         →      ⎢  C — C    ⎥
          |   |                ⎢  |    |   ⎥
         H   H                 ⎣ H    H   ⎦ₙ
   ```

Unit 17.3
1. In condensation polymerisation, molecules with different **functional** groups react together. A **small** molecule such as **water** or hydrogen **chloride** is **eliminated**.
   (1 mark for each correct word)
2. a.
   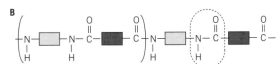

   1 mark each
   b. i. ester [1] ii. amide [1]
3. a. Alcohol [1] carboxylic acid [1]
   b.
   ```
              CH₃
               |
       HO — C — COOH
               |
               H
   ```
   COOH and OH group [1] rest of molecule correct [1]
4. –OC–(CH₂)₃–CONH–(CH₂)₆–NH–
   CONH group [1] rest of molecule correct [1]

Unit 17.4
1. a. A with 2 B with 1 C with 5 D with 3 E with 4
      (All correct = 3, 3 or 4 correct = 2, 1 or 2 correct = 1)
   b. i. Nylon: clothes / fishing lines / ropes / fishing nets / tents / curtains [1]
      ii. Poly(ethene): plastic bags / clingfilm / bowls / chairs / dustbins [1]
2. a. 1 mark each for any three of: waterproof / unreactive / can be moulded / strong / low density
   b. 1 mark each for any three of: strong / flexible / waterproof / unreactive
3. The longer the chains the more tangled they become (so stronger) [1]
   The longer the chains the greater intermolecular forces (so stronger) [1]
4. Any 6 of:
   Thermoset plastics have polymer chains which are cross-linked [1] by covalent bonds [1] This prevents the chains from moving [1] So the plastic keeps its shape / it is hard / tough [1] Thermoset plastics only char on heating / do not melt on heating [1] Thermoplastics are not cross linked [1] Weak forces between the chains [1] allows the chains to move over each other [1] so the plastic can be moulded when heated [1] Melts when heated [1]

Unit 17.5
1. They cannot be broken down / be decomposed [1] by living organisms / bacteria / fungi [1]
2. a. 1 mark each for any two of: (discarded plastics) block watercourses (or drains) / strangle animals (or animals get trapped in them) / can be ingested and harm digestive system / can get into lungs (or gills of fish) and prevent breathing / float on surface of the water and prevent light reaching water plants below
   b. 1 mark each for any two of: saves raw materials / saves energy / can be made into new objects / can be cracked to make chemical feedstock
   c. 1 mark each for any two of: can blow away / can decompose slowly to produce harmful chemicals (or harmful fillers leach out) / remain in site for a long time (or site is an eyesore)
   d. Heat can be used to generate electricity (via turbine) / saves burning fossil fuels / heat can be used directly e.g. to heat greenhouses [1]
3. a. i. Acidic gas produced / irritates eyes irritates throat [1]
      ii. Acid rain / effect of acid rain e.g. erodes limestone buildings / kills trees [1]
   b. i. Carbon dioxide [1] water [1]
      ii. Incomplete combustion [1] produces soot / carbon [1]
4. Any 5 of:
   Some plastics are brittle [1] Plasticisers make then less brittle [1] by getting in between the chains [1] So that the chains move more easily [1] Over time plasticisers may come out of the plastic [1] Some plasticisers are harmful [1]

Unit 17.6
1. When plastics are burned in **air**, they release energy. The **thermal** energy released can be used to heat **homes** or to make steam to generate **electricity**. When completely **combusted**, plastics release carbon **dioxide** which is a greenhouse **gas**. Many plastics also release **toxic** gases when burned. Methods are now being developed to **trap** these gases so they do not get into the atmosphere.
   (1 mark for each correct word)
2. Reduce production of single use plastics [1] Recycle plastics [1] Reuse plastic objects (or use plastic for other purposes) [1] Make more biodegradable plastics (which do not produce microplastic particles) [1]
3. a. The order is C, F, A, E, 3, D (2 marks if in correct order, 1 mark if one pair in wrong position)
   b. i. (synthetic) very long chain molecule / synthetic macromolecule [1] made of repeating units / made of monomers [1]
      ii. broken down / decomposed [1] by water / by dilute acid / by dilute alkali [1]
      iii. a simple molecule which when polymerised makes a polymer [1]
         Allow: the simplest unit which makes up a polymer

Answers

Unit 17.7

1. All amino acids contain carbon, hydrogen, **nitrogen (or oxygen)**, and **oxygen (or nitrogen)**. Two simple amino acids found in proteins contain **sulfur** as well. Proteins are **condensation** polymers formed by the reaction of carboxylic acid and **amine** groups from amino acids. Most proteins are formed by the polymerisation of about **twenty** amino acids.
   (1 mark for each word correct)
2. a. Correct repeat unit e.g. first bracket between the first N and CHR from the left, second bracket between the next N and CHR to the right [1]
   b. Amide / peptide [1]
3.
   H₂N—C(H)(H)—C(=O)OH

   COOH and NH₂ groups [1] rest of structure correct [1]
4.
   H₂N—C(H)(CH₃)—C(=O)—N(H)—C(H)(CH₂SH)—C(=O)—O—H
   cysteinyl alanine

   H₂N—C(H)(CH₂SH)—C(=O)—N(H)—C(H)(CH₃)—C(=O)—O—H
   alanyl cysteine

   NH–C=O group shown in both [1] Cystyl-alanine shown [1] alanyl cysteine shown [1]
   Allow: reaction of SH group with COOH group to form an ester

Unit 18.1

1. a. **A** = burette [1] **B** = **volumetric** flask [1] **C** = measuring cylinder [1]
      D = **volumetric** pipette [1]
   b. i. B [1]
      ii. A [1] Allow: D
2. B [1]
3. Add **excess** zinc oxide[1] to dilute sulfuric acid.
   Warm until no further reaction [1]
   Filter off solution (of zinc sulfate) [1]
   Heat the filtrate to point of crystallisation / heat filtrate to form a saturated solution [1]
   Allow solution to cool and deposit crystals [1]
   Filter off crystals / pick out crystals **and** dry between filter paper [1]
   ALLOW: Filter off crystals / pick out crystals **and** dry in a warming oven (for last marking point)
4. 1 mark for each experiment / procedure and 1 mark for each explanation e.g.,
   Measuring cylinder: measuring out excess acid in rate of reaction experiment [1] High accuracy not required because the acid is in excess [1]
   Burette: titration (for measuring titre) [1] High accuracy required / accuracy to 0.05 cm³ needed [1]
   Volumetric pipette: adding 25 cm³ to titration flask [1] Number of moles needs to be calculated exactly [1]

Unit 18.2

1. a. Solvent: carbon tetrachloride [1]
      Solute: iodine [1]
      Solution: iodine in carbon tetrachloride / violet-coloured liquid [1]
   b. Easily vaporised / liquid with low boiling point [1]
2. a. i. Nitrates [1]
      ii. Iron(II) hydroxide [1] silver chloride [1]
      iii. calcium hydroxide [1]
   b. i. 135 g / 100 cm³ [1]
      ii. Potassium chloride [1]
      iii. 110 g / 100 cm³ [1]
      iv. 20 °C [1]
      v. At 80 °C there is 165 g per 100 cm³ [1]
         At 20 °C there is 30 g per 100 cm³ [1]
         Difference = 165 – 30 = 135 g [1]
         For 200 cm³ water = 135 × 2 = 270 g [1]
      vi. Solubility at 90 °C = 200 g per 100 cm³ [1]
          For 50 g = $\frac{50}{200} \times 100 = 25$ cm³ [1]

Unit 18.3

1. a. A liquid or solution that has gas passed through a filter [1]
   b. A solid that remains after evaporation, distillation, filtration (or similar process) [2]
      (if 2 marks not scored, 1 mark for: A solid that remains after filtration)
   c. A solution containing the maximum concentration of a solute dissolved in a solvent [1] at a specified temperature [1]
2. a. i. In order down:
         Filter paper [1]
         Filter funnel [1]
         Flask [1]
         ii. residue on filter paper [1]
             filtrate is liquid in flask [1]
   b. i. BGFEADC (2 marks) (1 mark if 1 pair reversed)
      ii. Too much water may dissolve the crystals [1]
3. Add water to the mixture and stir. The calcium sulfate dissolves. [1]
   Filter the mixture. Calcium carbonate is the residue. [1]
   Rinse the calcium carbonate with water and dry in an oven. [1]
   Evaporate the water from the calcium sulfate solution / filtrate [1]
4. Add the mixture of crystals to the water and heat until all the mixture just dissolves (adding more water if needed). [1]
   Cool the solution in a beaker of cold water. [1]
   When crystals have formed filter the mixture. [1]
   The crystals formed are of the substance with the lower solubility. [1]
   Repeat the process with the crystals which have been collected [1]

Unit 18.4

1. a. i. Distillation flask on left [1]
         Distillate in beaker on right [1]
         Slanting tube labelled as condenser [1]
         Cold water enters the bottom of the condenser [1]
      ii. Arrow under the gauze [1]
   b. i. Salt and water have very different boiling points / salt has a high boiling point and water has a low boiling point [1]
      ii. The vapours would condense together / at the same time [1]
2. There is a range of **temperatures** in the distillation column, **lower** at the top and **higher** at the bottom. When **vaporised** the more **volatile** alcohols move **further** up the column than the less volatile alcohols. When the alcohol reaches the **condenser** it changes from vapour to **liquid**. The alcohols are collected one by one in the **receiver**, those with the lower **boiling** points condensing before those with higher ones.
   (1 mark for each correct word)
3. a. Any two examples (1 mark each): e.g. extracting lavender oil, extracting rose oil, preparation of phenylamine.
   b. Simple distillation may char / decompose substances [1]
   c. Bubble steam through mixture to be distilled [1]
      Condense the mixture of steam and oil [1]
      Use a separating funnel to separate the oily layer from the water [1]

Unit 18.5

1. The method of separating a **mixture** of coloured substances using **filter** paper is called chromatography. The colours **separate** if they have different **solubilities** in the solvent and different degrees of **attraction** for the filter paper. Chromatography can also be used to separate colourless substances. These are shown up after chromatography by **spraying** the paper with a **locating** agent.
   (1 mark for each correct word)

Answers

2.
   - beaker, lid, filter paper, baseline, solvent

   Chromatography paper dipping in solvent [1]
   Chromatography paper labelled [1]
   Solvent labelled [1]
   Baseline labelled AND above the level of the solvent [1]
3. Identification of substances [1]
   Separating mixtures of substances [1]
   Purifying substances [1]
4. a. They move up the chromatography at similar rates. [1]
      because they may have similar chemical structures / because they are weakly absorbed to the paper by similar strength forces [1]
   b. It can be used to separate different substances with the same R_f value / it can be used to separate substances which run the same distance in one-dimensional chromatography [1]
      Run the chromatography in one direct using a particular solvent and note the position of the solvent front [1]
      Remove the chromatography paper from the solvent [1]
      Evaporate the solvent from the chromatography paper [1]
      Turn the paper round 90° [1]
      Run the chromatography again using a different solvent and note the position of the solvent front [1]

Unit 18.6

1. a. So that the ink doesn't spread up the paper / graphite / pencil 'lead' doesn't dissolve in solvent [1]
   b. 3 [1]
   c. Ser and Gly [1]
   d. Use a different solvent (that separates them) [1]
   e. $\frac{\text{distance from centre of spot to baseline}}{\text{distance from solvent front to baseline}} = \frac{3}{5} = 0.6$ [1]
   f. About half way between Cys and Ser/Gly [1]
2. Affinity of compound for the paper/ how well the compound forms weak bonds with the paper [1]
   Solubility of compound in the solvent [1]
3. Spray with locating agent / named locating agent [1]
   develop spots by heating [1]
   Allow: look under ultra-violet light [1]
   Spots appear as bright / fluorescent dots [1]
4. a. dissolve the coin in concentrated hydrochloric acid / aqua regia (concentrated hydrochloric and nitric acids) [1]
   b. Any 6 points of:
      - Place resin in column (with solvent)
      - Place mixture to be separated on top of column and let it soak in
      - Add solvent to top of column and let mixture run through
      - Different substances have different affinities for the resin / some substances are better absorbed onto the resin than others
      - Substances less attracted to resin / more soluble in solvent move down column faster
      - Substances collected one by one in separate tubes at the bottom of the column
      - Substances analysed by ultraviolet / infrared spectroscopy / mass spectrometry

Unit 18.7

1. The melting and **boiling** points of **pure** substances are sharp. They melt and boil at **exact** temperatures. The melting and boiling points of **impure** substances are not sharp. They melt over a **range** of temperatures. The boiling point of a liquid is **increased** if impurities are present. The melting point of a liquid is **decreased** if impurities are present.
   (1 mark for each correct word)
2. a. Oxygen gas [1] sodium chloride crystals [1]
   b. Small amounts of impurities may react with chemicals [1]
   c. Any values from −15 °C to −1 °C

3. Pure sulfur: solidifies at 119 °C
   Pure sulfur has a sharp boiling point
   Impure sulfur: melts over 4 °C temperature range
   Impure sulfur: turns to a vapour at 450 °C
   (2 marks if all 4 correct; 1 mark if 2 correct)
4. a. In solder the tin is impure/ the lead is impure [1]
      Impurities lower the melting point [1]
   b. Less energy is used in melting the solder (than using tin or lead alone) [1]

Unit 19.1

1. a. Temperature [1]
   b. Volume of carbon dioxide [1]
   c. 1 mark each for any two of: time interval / mass of calcium carbonate / surface area of calcium carbonate / concentration of acid
2. a. Type of fuel [1]
   b. Temperature rise [1]
   c. 1 mark each for any two of volume of distance of burner from can / same copper can / same volume of water in can / same height of flame or same wick used in burner / same amount of fuel / mass of fuel burnt
3. Independent variable: current [1]
   Dependent variable: mass of copper removed [1]
   Control variable: 1 mark each for any 2 of time / concentration of copper(II) sulfate / volume of copper(II) sulfate / depth at which electrode is immersed

Unit 19.2

1. a. Thermometer [1] beaker [1] top pan balance and weighing boat [1] Water bath with temperature control; allow: Bunsen burner and tripod and gauze [1] stirring rod [1]
   b. Independent variable: temperature of the water [1]
      Dependent variable: mass of solid added that fully dissolves [1]
   c. 1 mark each for any two of: Volume of the water / rate at which heat is applied e.g. from water bath or Bunsen / rate of stirring [1]
2. Place 50 cm^3 / 100 cm^3 water in beaker [1]
   Heat water to fixed temperature [1]
   Add small weighed amounts of solid potassium chloride to the water and stir [1]
   Keep adding small weighed amounts until no more dissolves [1]
   Repeat at different temperatures [1]
3. a. 1 mark each for any two of: If using Bunsen, the water will cool while the substance is being added / if using water bath, temperature control depends on sensitivity of thermostat / heat may be given out or absorbed when substance dissolves in water.
   b. 1 mark each for any two of: Use a temperature-controlled water bath OR more sensitive temperature control / use larger volume of water so that inaccuracies due to adding small amounts of solid are reduced / use insulated container so heat losses reduced / add solid to the water until saturated solution formed, then allow to cool and take temperature when crystals first appear
4. 1 mark each for any three of: So that they get the credit for their work / to allow other scientists to check their experiments or results / to allow other scientists to develop the work further / to add to the amount of knowledge

Unit 19.3

1. a. C [1] b. B [1] c. D [1] d. A [1]
2. a. A [1] b. D [1]
3. A with 2, B with 4, C with 5, D with 6, E with 1, F with 3
   (3 marks if all correct, 2 marks if 4 or 5 correct, 1 mark if 2 or 3 correct)
4. a. slightly soluble [1] b. soluble [1] c. insoluble [1]
   d. slightly soluble [1] e. soluble [1]
   f. slightly soluble [1] g. insoluble [1]

Unit 19.4

1. Al^{3+}(aq) with sodium hydroxide: white precipitate [1] which dissolves in excess [1] with ammonia: white precipitate [1] insoluble in excess [1]
   Cr^{3+}(aq) with sodium hydroxide: green precipitate [1] which dissolves in excess [1] with ammonia: grey-green precipitate [1] insoluble in excess [1]

Answers

Cu^{2+}(aq) with sodium hydroxide: light blue precipitate [1]
insoluble in excess [1]
with ammonia: light blue precipitate [1] dissolves in excess to form a dark blue solution [1]
Fe^{3+}(aq) with sodium hydroxide: red-brown precipitate [1] which is insoluble in excess [1] with ammonia: red-brown precipitate [1] insoluble in excess [1]

2. Add excess sodium hydroxide [1] only the precipitate containing zinc dissolves [1]
OR
Add ammonia [1] only aluminium ions form a(an obvious) precipitate [1]
3. **a.** red [1] **b.** lilac [1] **c.** pale green [1] **d.** orange [1]
4. Fe^{2+}(aq) + 2OH$^-$(aq) → Fe(OH)$_2$(s)
(1 mark for correct formulae, 1 for balance, 1 for state symbols)

Unit 19.5
1. A with 5, B with 4, C with 1, D with 3, E with 2
(3 marks if all correct, 2 marks if 3 or 4 correct, 1 mark if 1 or 2 correct)
2. **a.** AgNO$_3$(aq) + NaCl(aq) → AgCl(s) + NaNO$_3$(aq)
(1 mark for correct formulae, 1 for state symbols)
   b. Ag$^+$(aq) + Cl$^-$(aq) → AgCl(s)
(1 mark for correct formulae, 1 for state symbols)
3. A must be a nitrate because ammonia given off / turns red litmus blue [1]
B is a chloride because formed chlorine at the anode when electrolysed / bleaches litmus [1]
B sodium as yellow flame in flame test [1]
B sodium chloride [1]
A silver or lead nitrate since white precipitate when added to chloride / B [1]
4. **a.** Ba^{2+}(aq) + SO$_4^{2-}$(aq) → BaSO$_4$(s)
(1 mark for correct formulae, 1 for state symbols)
   b. SO$_3^{2-}$(aq) + 2H$^+$(aq) → SO$_2$(g) + H$_2$O(l)
(1 mark for correct formulae, 1 for balance, 1 for state symbols)

Unit 20.1
1. **a.** 2 Na and 1 O [1] **b.** 3 Mg and 2 N [1]
   c. 5 P and 15 Cl [1] **d.** 4 Al and 6 O [1]
   e. 8 H, 4 S, and 16 O [1] **f.** 6 Li, 3 C, and 9 O [1]
2. **a.** 1 Sn, 2 S, and 8 O [1] **b.** 2 N, 8 H, 1 S, and 4 O [1]
   c. 1 Ni, 2 Cl, and 8 O [1] **d.** 2 Ba, 4 I, and 12 O [1]
3. 1 Co, 2 Cl, 12 H, and 6 O [1]
4. 104 + 288 = 392 [1]

Unit 20.2
1. **a.** actual yield = $\frac{\% \text{ yield}}{100}$ × theoretical yield [1]
   b. theoretical yield = $\frac{\text{actual yield}}{\% \text{ yield}}$ × 100 [1]
2. **a.** moles = concentration (in mol / dm^3) × volume (in dm^3) [1]
   b. volume (in dm^3) = $\frac{\text{moles}}{\text{concentration (in mol / dm}_3)}$ [1]
3. mass = density × volume [1]
4. mass = $\frac{\text{energy}}{\text{specific heat capacity × temperature rise}}$ [1]

Unit 20.3
1. **a.** 1 × 10^6 [1] **b.** 70000 [1] **c.** 3.3 × 10^3 [1]
2. **a.** 1 × 10^{-5} [1] **b.** 0.005 [1] **c.** 3.5 × 10^{-3} [1]
3. **a.** 1.4 [1] **b.** 3.6 × 10^{-5} [1]
4. 1.14 × 10^{-5} [1]
5. 82 % [1]

Unit 20.4
1. **a.** i. 6 [1]
      ii. 16 cm^2 [1]
      iii. 96 cm^2 [1]
   b. i. 8 [1]
      ii. 6 × 2 × 2 = 24 cm^2 [1]
      iii. 8 × 24 = 192 cm^2 [1]
      iv. The surface area is much greater / the surface area to volume ratio is larger [1]
      More particles are exposed for reaction [1]
2. **a.** i. 100 [1]
      ii. 10 [1]
   b. Volume of 1 dm^3 is 10 × 10 × 10 cm^3 [1] = 1000 cm^3 [1]

Unit 20.5
1. **a.** i. 4.36 [1] ii. 0.0873 [1] iii. 137 [1] iv. 0.00550 [1]
   b. i. 440 [1] ii. 3.4 [1] iii. 57 [1] iv. 0.0055 [1]
2. mol pentane 0.0926388 [1] rounded 0.09 [1]
   × 5   0.4631944 [1] rounded 0.45 [1]
   × 24 11.1 [1] 10.8 [1]

Unit 20.6
1. **a.** Line not continued to 0–0 point [1] Line not a continuous curve [1]
   Line has more points above it than below it [1]
   b. Points not clear [1] No units on y or x axis [1] Full grid not used / lot of grid is space [1]
   c. Anomalous point included in the line [1] Straight lines between points / not a smooth curve [1]
2. **a.** 26 cm^3 [1] **b.** 44 cm^3 [1]

Unit 20.7
1.
   a. Axes correctly labelled [1]
   Points all correct (1 mark if one point incorrect or missing) [2]
   b. Lines correct (two straight intersecting lines) [1]
   Lines intersect between 4 and 5 cm^3 and **P** labelled [1]
   c. P is 4.4 cm^3 [1]
2. Axes correctly labelled and full grid used [1]
   Points all correct (1 mark if one point incorrect or missing) [2]
   Smooth curve between the points [1]

Answers

Unit 20.8

1.
   a. Axes correctly labelled and full grid used [1]
   Points all correct (1 mark if one point incorrect or missing) [2]
   Smooth curve between the points [1]
   b. 0.16 / 40 [1] 4×10^{-3} g / s [1]
   c. The line starts to curve / the rate is not constant [1]

Unit 21.2

1.
   a. Suggest [1]
   b. Describe [1] Give [1]
   c. Deduce [1]
   d. Describe [1] Explain [1]
   e. Draw [1] Determine [1]

Unit 21.4

1. Any three suitable (1 mark each) e.g. uses of particular chemicals / properties of selected elements / chemical tests e.g. water, ions, unsaturation / types of chemical reaction e.g. neutralisation, condensation, addition, photochemical [3]
2. Any four suitable with result (1 mark each) e.g.
   Metal hydroxides → salt + water
   Metal oxide → salt + water
   Carbonate → salt + carbon dioxide + water
   Methyl orange → turns red / pink
   Ammonia → ammonium salt formed
   Taste → sour (although this is not recommended!)
   What makes them acid? → hydrogen ions [4]
3. (1 mark for each reaction or property and 1 mark for each correct result e.g.) [16]
   alkane + chlorine in presence of light → chloroalkane + HCl
   alkane + (excess) oxygen / air → carbon dioxide + water
   alkane + limited oxygen → carbon monoxide + water
   alkane (heat with Al_2O_3) → mixture of alkanes and alkenes
   alkene + bromine water → bromine water decoloursed
   alkene + hydrogen (in presence of Ni catalyst) → Alkane
   alkene + steam (in presence of catalyst) → alcohol
   alkene + (excess) oxygen / air → carbon dioxide + water

Unit 21.6

1. A low melting point [1]
   B/ C/ D High melting point [1] Conduct electricity when molten [1]
   Soluble in water [1]
   E or I metal [1] covalent giant structure [1]
   For the metal (E or I) (1 mark each for any 3 of:) Conduct electricity or conduct heat / ductile / malleable / lustrous (shiny) Ignore: high melting point / sonorous [3]
   For the covalent giant structure (E or I) (1 mark each for any 3 of:) High melting point / generally do not conduct electricity / insoluble in water [3]
2. A increase in rate [1] B concentration [1] C increase rate [1]
   D The particles collide with greater frequency [1]
   E Increases rate [1] F surface area [1] G increase rate [1]
   H Increased number of particles exposed for collisions / increased collision frequency [1]

Unit 22

Exam-style questions

1.
   a. 2,8,5 [1]
   b. 16 [1]
   c. Does not conduct electricity / does not conduct heat [1]
   Low melting point / low boiling point [1]
   d. P_4 (or 4P) + $5O_2$ → $2P_2O_5$
   (1 mark for correct formulae, 1 mark for balance) [2]
   e. PO_4^{3-} [1]
   f. Nitrate [1]
   g. Fertilisers needed for plant growth / for plant proteins [1]
   Sources of nitrogen / phosphorus / potassium in soil used up by growing plants [1]
   h.
   One pair of electrons shared between each of the 3 H atoms and the central P atom [1]
   Lone pair on the P atom [1]
2.
   a. Double C=C bond [1]
   b. Bromine water / bromine; allow acidified potassium manganate(VII) [1]
   Decolourised [1]
   c. i. Reduction is gain of electrons [1]
   ii. High temperature [1] High pressure [1] Catalyst [1]
   iii.
   ```
        H   H   H
        |   |   |
    H — C — C — C — O — H
        |   |   |
        H   H   H
   ```
   (2 marks for full structure, 1 mark if OH drawn instead of O–H) [2]
   d. i. Grind up the onion leaves in a solvent / water / alcohol [1] filter [1]
   ii. chromatography [1]
3.
   a. CsCl / Cs^+Cl^- [1]
   b. Giant structure / ionic structure [1]
   All the bonds are strong / strong electrostatic forces between all ions [1]
   (Mention of atoms / intermolecular forces = maximum 1 for question)
   c. The ions are free to move (from place to place) [1]
   d. i. Conduct electricity [1] unreactive / inert [1]
   ii. Anode: $2Cl^-$ → Cl_2 + $2e^-$ [2]
   (1 mark for formulae, 1 mark for balance)
   Cathode: $Cs^+ + e^-$ → Cs [1]
   e. Mol Cs = 5.32 / 133 = 0.04 mol [1]
   Actual yield of CsCl = 6.4 / 168.5 = 0.038 [1]
   % yield = 0.038 / 0.04 = 95 % [1]
   (or calculation based on masses)
4.
   a. 6.5 min [1]
   b. i. 16 cm^3 [1]
   ii. 26 / 2 = 13 cm^3/min [1]
   c. Initial gradient steeper [1] Ends up at the same volume of gas [1]
   d. Increasing concentration increases the number of particles per unit volume / particles closer together [1]
   Frequency of collisions increases / number of collisions per second increases [1]
   e. Faster because greater surface area of powder [1]
   More particles of magnesium exposed to hydrochloric acid [1]

163

Answers

5. a. Decomposition [1] Endothermic [1]
    b. Bubble through limewater [1] limewater turns milky / cloudy [1]
    c. i. [Graph: mass of CO_2 / g vs temperature / °C, S-curve from ~500°C to ~1000°C reaching ~3.8 g]

        Axes correctly labelled [1] Points plotted correctly [1]
        Curve of best fit drawn [1]
        ii. Mass of CO_2 from graph = 3.0 g [1]
        Moles CO_2 = 3 / 44 = 0.068 mol [1]
        Volume = 0.068 × 24 = 1.64 dm^3 [1]
6. a. i.   Arrow under the flask [1]
        ii. A flask [1] B gas jar [1]
        iii. To dry the ammonia / To remove water [1]
        iv. Put damp red litmus beneath gas jar [1]
             Full when (litmus) turns blue [1]
    b. $(NH_4)_2SO_4 + 2NaOH \rightarrow 2NH_3 + Na_2SO_4 + 2H_2O$
        (1 mark for correct formulae, 1 mark for balance) [2]
    c. [Dot-and-cross diagram of N_2H_4 showing two N atoms bonded with H atoms]
        (1 mark for bonding pairs of electrons, 1 mark for the lone pairs on each nitrogen atom) [2]
7. a. Circle around the O–H group [1]
    b. i. Carbon, hydrogen, and oxygen [1]
        ii. Alcohols [1]
    c. Carbon dioxide [1] Water [1]
    d. Filtration [1]
    e. i. Ester [1]
        ii. No continuous carbon chain [1]
            Idea of the COO groups being formed by
            condensation reactions [1]
    f. purple [1] to colourless [1]
8. a. i.   Helium **and** neon [1]
        ii. ALLOW: values between 0.08 and 0.1 [1]
        iii. Gas [1] –118 °C is above the boiling point [1]
        iv. Increases down the group [1]
    b. i.   brown [1] ALLOW: grey / black
        ii. iodide is being converted to iodine [1] / oxidation number of
             iodine increases / oxidation number of Xe decreases [1]
        iii. mol XeF_4 = 8.28 / 207 = 0.04 mol [1]
             0.04 mol Xe [1]
             0.04 × 24 = 0.96 dm^3 Xe [1]
9. a. i.   Car exhausts / High temperature furnaces / Lightning [1]
        ii. Acid rain / Kills trees / Acidifies lakes / Erodes limestone /
             Corrodes metal structures, etc [1]
        iii. Proximity: Far apart [1] Motion: fast / random [1]
    b. i.   Colour gets lighter [1] Position of equilibrium moves to
             the left [1]
             In direction of fewer gas molecules / fewer moles in the
             equation [1]
        ii. NO_2 46 [1] N_2O_4 = 92 [1]
        iii. Entirely NO_2 at 140 °C / more NO_2 at higher temperature [1]
             The higher the temperature the more the equilibrium goes
             to the right [1]
             For an endothermic reaction the position of equilibrium
             moves to the right with increase in temperature / increase
             in temperature favours the endothermic reaction [1]
    c. $2NO_2 \rightarrow 2NO + O_2$
        (1 mark for correct formulae, 1 mark for balance) [2]
10. a. Any suitable indicator, e.g. methyl orange / litmus /
        thymolphthalein [1]
    b. Sodium sulfate [1]
    c. i.   (12.5 / 1000) × 0.2 = 2.5 × 10^{-3} mol [1]
        ii. 5.0 × 10^{-3} mol [1]
        iii. 5.0 × 10^{-3} × 1000 / 25 = 0.2 mol/dm^3 [1]
    d. $H^+ + OH^- \rightarrow H_2O$ [1]
    e. [Structural formula of ester: $H-C(H)(H)-C(=O)-O-C(H)(H)-C(H)(H)-C(H)(H)-C(H)(H)-H$]
        (2 marks if all correct, 1 mark if ester group shown as COO) [2]